Clothes : their choosing, making and care

CLOTHES
their choosing, making and care

Margaret G Butler

B T Batsford Limited   London

I dedicate this book to Marie Moore Stevenson
from whom I have learnt so much about Needlecrafts
and who has given me such valuable help and encouragement
during the preparation of the text

First published 1958
Second edition 1962
Third edition 1965
Fourth edition 1975
Reprinted 1978

ISBN 0 7134 2700 0 (cased)
ISBN 0 7134 3035 4 (limp)

Printed in Great Britain by
Billing & Sons Ltd
Guildford, London & Worcester
for the publishers B T Batsford Limited
4 Fitzhardinge Street London W1H 0AH

Contents

Dedication

Preface 7

1 Necessities for dressmaking 9

2 Hand and machine stitching 12

3 Pressing 26

4 Measuring and the use of fitting lines 30

5 Straight grain lines and the alteration of patterns 36

6 Laying patterns for cutting out 49

7 Cutting out and preparing for fitting 59

8 Fitting 65

9 The treatment of fullness 75

10 Seams 104

11 The preparation and use of crossway strips 116

12 Shaped facings 126

13 Interfacings 140

14 Openings 154

15 Fastenings 167

16 Collars 199

17 Pockets 227

18 Sleeves and cuffs 248

19 Waist bands 274

20 Belts and belt carriers 281

21 Hems 291

22 The choosing and care of clothes 306

For reasons of economy it has become necessary for the publishers to present the work with smaller diagrams than in the original editions. It was felt wiser to do this than to omit a large number of drawings, which would mean losing the comprehensiveness and therefore much of the usefulness and purpose of the book. However, the necessary details are there in the diagrams, and will be seen with careful study.

Preface

The revision of *Clothes — Their Choosing, Making and Care*, has presented interesting evidence of the change and development both in the craft of dressmaking and in the approach to the teaching of the craft, during the years since the book was first prepared.

The wide range of fabrics now available, the trend of present day fashion and the advance in design of the modern domestic sewing machine, have made it seem necessary to concentrate almost exclusively on the making of clothes. Consequently the study of fabrics has been omitted, and the sections on the choosing and care of clothes have been much reduced, to make way for extra information on practical dressmaking.

It has been my aim to prepare a book which will give help and guidance to girls taking public examinations in dressmaking, and to provide a useful reference for them when working at home, or in a busy class-room, where the frequent attention of the teacher is not possible. In this way, too, I hope to make the work of the teacher a little easier, and it will be a lasting pleasure to me if I can, in some small way, relieve the heavy demands on teachers of dressmaking.

While writing and illustrating the book, I tried to envisage the problems of the inexperienced dressmaker, and to give reminders about tacking, pressing and other points which are sometimes overlooked by the young enthusiast. Above all, in this craft, we have to learn that it is forethought, care and accuracy that bring pleasing results and produce garments which we can be proud to wear. I should like, here, to recommend that the instructions for the process in hand are read from beginning to end, before embarking on that particular section of the garment.

The book has been arranged so that each section deals with an aspect of dressmaking, and endeavours to give a comprehensive coverage for most general work. This has been done to give the student of dressmaking an opportunity to understand each topic as a whole, but she will be able to pick out the specific information required for individual garments.

I hope the home dressmaker, too, will find the book useful for reference, and that the information given will provide her with helpful background knowledge. I have tried to arrange the text in such a way that the woman at home, working alone, can learn as she reads and follows the diagrams, and thus gain confidence in her work.

I should like to take this opportunity of expressing my sincere thanks and appreciation to Margaret Davies who has prepared my drawings for the press. Her interest, suggestions and encouragement have been a very great support to me.

Clacton-on-Sea   M G B

1 Necessities for dressmaking

The first necessity of an amateur dressmaker is a willingness to acquire skill in her hands. This can only be achieved by practice and patience. Practice loses any tediousness and patience turns into pleasure if there is interest in the task and a real desire to create. We all have a desire to create, but in some of us it may be hidden by early difficulties, or by lack of opportunity to indulge it. If, however, there is a real desire to make clothes, interest in needlework is awakened and with careful study of the craft, and some practice, there is no reason why we should not all be able to make wearable garments of improving quality as our experience increases.

Needlework requires the use of some special tools and equipment. These must be chosen with care and understanding, and used correctly. They must be cared for properly so that they give the maximum use and do not need frequent replacement, which is an unnecessary expense.

1 Tapemeasure
Choose a firm, good quality tapemeasure which is marked on both sides. Cheap tapemeasures become ragged at the edges and are liable to stretch. Tapemeasures with one stiffened end are very useful for measuring turning and hem widths, etc.

2 Pins
Buy dressmaker's steel pins. These are more expensive, but are sharp and fine and slip in and out of the fabric easily. Make sure the pins are stored in a dry place. Use pins to hold the fabric in position for tacking, and for fitting, but always use as few as possible in case the fabric is apt to pin-mark. Cheap pins will nearly always mark fabric as they are often blunt, thick and made from poorly finished metal. Fine needles are useful for pinning fine and white fabric as they are small and sharp. They do not leave marks in the fabric.

3 Scissors
(a) Cutting-out scissors. These should be the most expensive which can be afforded, as cheap scissors are made from inferior metal and soon become blunt and difficult to use. These scissors should be at least 152 mm. long. One blade should be narrow and pointed for slipping easily under the fabric, and the other should be wider and heavier for weighting down the cutting. *Cutting-out scissors should never be used for any other purpose whatsoever* in order to keep them sharp and well balanced.
(b) Scissors for trimming and snipping fabric during garment construction. These scissors should be 127 to 152 mm. in length and should be kept for cutting fabric. They should not be used for cutting cotton or paper.
(c) Small scissors for cutting cotton and paper. Cutting sewing cotton blunts scissors easily. That is why a special pair should be kept for the purpose.
(d) Embroidery scissors are useful additions to the work-basket and are

9

essential for some finer types of embroidery. They should have short, thin, finely pointed blades.

(e) Buttonhole scissors. These are useful for cutting horizontal button-holes. The blades are adjustable and may be set to make a cut the length required. Small, sharp pointed scissors are equally good for cutting buttonholes, and have to be used, in any case, for cutting vertical ones.

4 Sewing threads

Great care must be taken to balance the fabric as nearly as possible in thickness, colour and type, when selecting the sewing thread.

(a) Mercerised sewing cotton is available in different thicknesses and a wide variety of colours. It is suitable for use on mercerised cottons, linen, and rayons and can be used satisfactorily on light-weight woollens. When used for hand sewing, short lengths only must be threaded in the needle as this thread has a habit of fraying and breaking if it is subjected to much friction. It is more satisfactory for machining as the same length of thread is not continuously pulled through the fabric.

(b) Sewing cotton is not much used nowadays, but is suitable for use on unmercerised cottons and for household needlework. It has a dull appearance and, therefore, does not blend into fabrics which have a lustrous finish. It is stronger than mercerised sewing cotton and is easier to use for hand sewing as it does not untwist and fray as easily as mercerised thread.

(c) Sewing silk. This is made from real silk and is not to be confused with mercerised sewing cotton. It is a strong, elastic thread giving good results in machine work. It is also good for handwork as it does not twist in use. It is available in a very good colour range. It should always be used for silk fabrics, and is the best choice for wool as it is the only animal sewing thread obtainable. It can be used on rayons, and fine sewing silk often gives a good result on man-made and synthetic fabrics.

(d) Synthetic sewing threads are available in an excellent colour range and in sizes 40 and 60. These threads give a very good result on synthetic and man-made fibres. The finer thread must be used on light-weight fabric to prevent some retraction in seams.

(e) Embroidery threads. These are all too frequently wrongly termed 'silks'. The embroidery threads most generally sold in shops are made from cotton and should be referred to as embroidery cottons. Of these, stranded cottons are the most popular, but other kinds are available in varying thicknesses. An embroidery thread should be chosen to suit the thickness, texture and type of the background fabric.

5 Needles

Too little attention is usually given to the choosing of the right needle. Here is a list of some types of needles with their uses:

(a) Betweens. These are tailoring and quilting needles. As they are short they are also generally useful for people with small hands.

(b) Sharps. These are the needles used for most hand sewing. They are longer than betweens. Both betweens and sharps have round eyes specially shaped to hold sewing cotton which, being tightly twisted, forms a hard, round thread.

(c) Crewel. These needles are intended for embroidery. They are the same length as sharps, but the eyes are oval in shape to take the soft thickness of embroidery cottons and wools. Embroidery threads are more loosely twisted than sewing threads and, therefore, form softer, flatter threads which fit into

the long, oval eye of a crewel needle

(d) *Darning needles.* These are always long needles, but specially long darning needles called 'double long darners' may be bought to reach across very large holes. The eyes are long and narrow.

These four types of needles are adequate for the making and repair of clothing, but for every type of needlecraft, eg gloving, canvas embroidery, etc, there are special needles. Only the best results are achieved if the right needle is used for each particular type of work.

Sewing needles are numbered in the opposite way from English sewing machine needles.

The smaller the number of a sewing needle, the coarser it is. A fine needle should be used on fine fabrics and a coarse needle on heavy fabrics. A No. 8 is an average size and is used for most general work.

6 Thimble

This is an essential for every good needlewoman as it is impossible to get the correct rhythm of stitching without the use of a thimble. Cheap thimbles are often rough and break easily or become misshapen. Buy the best quality thimble possible. Steel lined silver ones are the most efficient as they are very smooth and strong.

The thimble is worn on the middle finger of the working hand. This finger should be flexed back so that the thimble drives the needle through the fabric after it has been guided into position by the thumb and forefinger. A great many people attempt to sew without using a thimble, but the needle is then held in a grasp which tightens the muscles at the base of the thumb. This causes fatigue and often pain. The correct use of a thimble allows an easy grasp of the needle, with the middle finger doing the pushing. The muscles used in this case are not tightly flexed, and there is no fatigue. This allows the sewing to be done quickly and rhythmically after a little practice. Use either the top or the side of the thimble, whichever is the more comfortable. Short-fingered people often prefer to use the side, as the backward stretch required is not so great.

7 Tailor's chalk

This is useful for marking temporary lines and positions on fabric. White tailor's chalk is perfectly safe to use on any fabric; coloured tailor's chalk is apt to leave an indelible mark on some light fabrics and should be tested before use.

As well as these essential items, haberdashery departments sell many gadgets as aids to dressmaking, from needle threaders to dressmaking dummies. These have a varied appeal to individual people, and are only worth buying if you feel they will be useful.

Protection of work

The work should be adequately wrapped for storage. It is best to keep it in a box lined with clean paper. Failing this, use a polythene bag or a large, washable wrapper.

2 *Hand and machine stitching*

A minimum amount of hand sewing is used in present-day dressmaking. Modern machines are constructed for use on a wide range of fabrics, and it is sensible to make full use of them. However, there are certain occasions when hand sewing is required, and a book of this type would be incomplete without some guidance on the sewing stitches still in use.

Hand sewing must be even in spacing, and as fine as the thickness of the fabric will allow, in order to be attractive in appearance and strong in use. The tension of the stitching needs to be adapted according to the coarseness of the fabric, so that the line of stitching blends into the cloth without puckering it.

Continual practice in hand sewing, with the use of a thimble, will result in the correct and rhythmical use of the hand and arm muscles, which are necessary to produce neat, regular stitching without tiring the working hand. A thimble must be used to drive the needle through the fabric, if the needle is to be held and used correctly.

Stitches may be divided into two groups, ie temporary stitches and permanent stitches.

Temporary stitches

These are varieties of tacking stitches which are used to mark important balance points to hold fabric in place ready for final stitching, or to form a line as a guide for final stitching.

A knot should never be used to begin tacking, as a machine needle can be blunted if it stitches into a hard knot. Neither are knots reliably strong. Begin and finish tacking with a double back stitch. To begin and finish tacking when preparing a garment for fitting, see page 62.

The length of the stitches should vary to suit the fabric, eg loosely woven, slippery fabric needs short tacking stitches to hold it firmly in place.

1a *Stitches and spaces approximately of equal length are used for most tacking*

1b *Alternate long and short stitches provide a stronger line of tacking, and are used on long lengths of slippery fabric*

Upright tacking (2a and 2b)
This is used to hold a flat edge over a full edge as it allows a better hanging of the fullness from the full edge. The placing and slant of the needle form upright stitches on the upper side, and slanting stitches on the underside of the work. This stitch formation gives a flexible line of tacking which allows for any slight adjustment of the gathers which may be necessary while stitching.

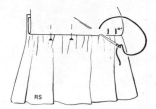

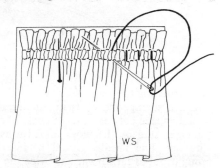

2a *Upright tacking being worked on a lapped seam for right side setting*

2b *Upright tacking being worked in preparation for joining a gathered and a straight edge with a wrong side setting*

Cross tacking (3)

This is a useful tacking stitch when two or more layers of fabric need to be held firmly together, eg a collar should be cross-tacked before setting it to a neckline. This will hold the two layers together (or the three layers if the collar is interfaced) and prevent the collar from slipping out of alignment while it is being attached.

To work cross tacking, take a straight stitch of about 5-10 mm and move forward to give a sloping stitch of 20-50 mm or more, according to the depth of fabric to be held together.

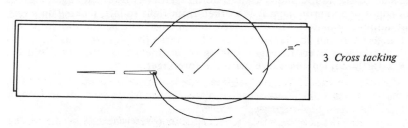

3 *Cross tacking*

Permanent stitches

These stitches are either placed to hold fabric firmly in a required position when they should be as strong, and usually, as inconspicuous as possible, or else they are decorative stitches which may be placed purely for ornamentation, or they may combine final fixing and ornamentation.

The following permanent stitches are used in dressmaking:

1 Joining stitches

Running (4)

The stitches and spaces are equal in length and should be as small as the thickness of the fabric will allow. It is not wise to take more than two or three stitches at a time on the needle if they are to be kept even and regular. Running stitches should be worked from right to left, and either on the right side or on the wrong side of the work as required. The stitches should keep parallel to the edges they are joining. The stitches appear finer on the underside, and should be placed so that this side is the one to show finally.

13

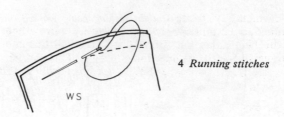

4 *Running stitches*

Back stitching (5)
This is a stronger stitch than running and must be worked evenly and finely, with no space between the stitches. The stitch is worked from right to left, on the right side of the work, and forms a right and wrong side to the line of stitching. The needle should be inserted at the end of the last stitch and brought out as far forward as twice the length of a stitch.

5 *The formation of back stitch on the right side of the work*

A back stitch is often introduced into running stitches, at regular intervals, eg 10 mm - 15 mm, to strengthen the line of stitching.

Oversewing (6)
This stitch has a limited use in modern sewing. When used it is worked on the right side of the fabric and is used to hold together two folded edges, e.g. the open edges of an apron hem. It is worked from right to left, picking up a very slight amount of material through each folded edge. The needle should pass at right angles through the fabric and point towards the worker, thus forming a stitch that slopes over the edges, joining them finely and strongly. Hold the work with the folded edges level with the forefinger.

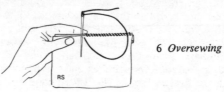

6 *Oversewing*

Faggoting
The strength and formation of this stitch make it useful as an insertion, so that it may be used for decorative seams, for joining bands or ribbon together or for joining lace etc to the edges of garments. Faggoting has waves of popularity and, when in fashion, it is used to ornament outer and under clothes for children and older people.

(a) Preparing the fabric edge
(i) For fabric which does not fray badly
Trim the turning allowance to 7 mm. Fold a turning 3 mm wide to the wrong side and machine it in place (7a)

Turn a second turning to the wrong side to bring the fitting line along the edge. Tack this turning in place (7b)

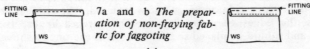

7a and b *The preparation of non-fraying fabric for faggoting*

14

(ii) For fabric which frays badly

Trim the turning to 12 mm. Turn and tack a very narrow hem to the right side, setting the hem along the fitting line (8a). Fold this hem back to the wrong side, bringing the fitting line along the edge. There are now two folded edges together along the top edge (8b). These edges will be joined together when the faggoting stitch is worked.

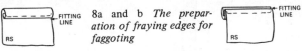

8a and b *The prepar-ation of fraying edges for faggoting*

(b) Preparing for working

The two edges to be joined must be tacked to a strip of paper before the faggoting is worked. Keep the edges parallel and about 4 mm apart (9)

9 *The edges tacked to paper ready for faggoting*

(c) Working faggoting

Use a crewel needle threaded with either fine single embroidery thread or stranded cotton or silk buttonhole twist.

(i) Working plain, crossed faggoting (10)

Hold the work so that the stitch progresses downwards from the top. The needle goes in behind the thread and over it. It should slant parallel to the last completely formed stitch. Each stitch should face the centre of the space between two stitches on the opposite side. The spacing of the stitches depends on the thickness of the fabric; they are usually 3 mm apart on thin fabrics. For a good appearance the stitches must slope evenly, and the needle should pass through the fabric close to the folded edge.

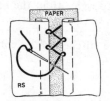

10 *Plain crossed faggot-ing*

(ii) Working knotted faggoting (11)

This is an enriched and strengthened form of plain crossed faggoting. Prepare the fabric as previously described.

Keeping the plain crossed faggoting-stitch taut, make a loop stitch over the twisted thread close to the edge of the fabric. The thread loops round to the right and to the left alternately as the knots are formed on the right-hand and left-hand edges respectively.

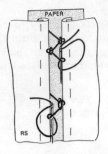

11 *Knotted faggoting*

2 Neatening stitches

Overcasting

This stitch is used to neaten raw edges on the wrong side of a garment. It may be worked from left to right or from right to left as required. For information about overcasting, refer to page 108 in the seam section.

Loop stitching: blanket stitching: buttonhole stitching

These three stitches are so often confused, that it is best to deal with them together so that the differences between them may be clearly shown.

12a *Loop stitch*

12b *Blanket stitch*

12c *Buttonhole stitch*

(a) Loop stitch

This stitch is still used occasionally, although machine zig zag stitch is fast making it obsolete as a main neatening stitch. It remains useful for neatening small areas which are difficult to reach by machine.

Loop stitch is worked from left to right. Hold the edge downwards and let the thread loop under the needle as the stitch is formed.

Loop stitch sometimes has to be worked round a corner. The best way to make a strong corner is to work three stitches which converge to a point on the diagonal of the corner (13).

13 *A loop-stitched corner*

(b) Blanket stitch

Blanket-stitch is rarely used except for neatening the edges of blankets, hence its name. It is one of the few stitches that requires a double thread for its formation. The needle passes between the double thread. Work from left to

16

right on the wrong side of the fabric. A triangular stitch is formed on the wrong side and a double upright stitch on the right side (12b).

This stitch is not used at all in dressmaking, and is shown here merely to distinguish it from loop stitch.

(c) Buttonhole stitch

Buttonhole-stitch is an upright stitch. The twist of the thread from the eye of the needle under the point from left to right forms a knot on the raw edges of the fabric as the needle is pulled upwards and away from the worker (14a).

Buttonhole stitch is used mainly for making buttonholes (see page 185), but it has other limited uses (see pages 195 and 196).

Work from left to right on the right side of the fabric. Hold the work upright, with the edge to be covered away from the worker. Work the stitches as close together as possible so that the knots touch along the raw edge (14a and 14b).

To make a join, run the new thread in between the double fabric and bring it out through the last knot. Work over the end of the old thread for three or four stitches before cutting it off (14c).

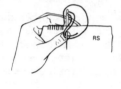

14a *Working buttonhole stitch*

14b *Showing the knot formation to enlarged size to illustrate the way in which the stitch differs in structure from loop stitch and blanket stitch*

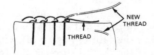

14c *Joining a new thread*

3 Stitches used to hold edge finishes

Plain hemming

This stitch is rarely used for sewing hems nowadays, as the stitch shows through to the right side of the fabric. When this is acceptable, a line of machine stitching is usually used instead. It is still used for the wrong side fixing of binding, and for catching folded edges on the wrong side of a garment, eg attaching a shaped facing across a seam, etc, (15). In this case the hemming stitches penetrate the seam turnings only. Hemming is also useful for some repair work.

The stitch is worked from right to left with the turning edge held towards the worker. It is important that the stitches are spaced and sloped evenly (15).

They should be as short and close as the thickness of the folded fabric will allow. The short length of the stitches should lie above the fold. The needle must slope in a V-shape to the last stitch and must be placed as far to its left as the previous stitch is to its right. The correct position of the needle is at 45° to the edge about to be hemmed. Unless the needle is accurately placed, the stitches will be uneven and irregular.

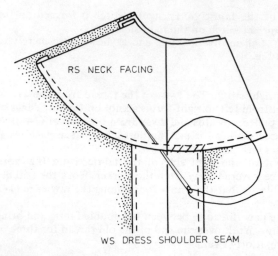

15 *Hemming being worked to hold a neck facing to the shoulder seam turnings of a dress*

RS NECK FACING

WS DRESS SHOULDER SEAM

Slip hemming

When a very neat and almost invisible hem-fixing is required, slip hemming gives a satisfactory finish. The distance between the stitches may vary according to the strength of fixing required. The farther apart they are, the less visible the hem-fixing will be, but the closer they are, the stronger the finish. A 6 mm spacing gives a finish of satisfactory strength for most general use.

Work from right to left. Fasten on with a double stitch under the fold of the hem. Pick up a very small amount of the single fabric close to the hem edge (16a). On thick fabric this stitch should not penetrate through to the right side. Pull the needle through and insert it through the fold of the hem for the required distance (16b). The thread must not be drawn tightly, or the stitches are too visible and tend to pucker the fabric. Fasten off with a double stitch on the edge of the fold, and run off the thread through the fold.

On thick fabric the stitches should not show on the right side. On thin fabric they should appear as spot stitches.

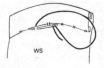

16a and b *Slip hemming. The two steps in the stitch formation are shown*

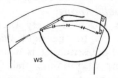

Whipping (17)

This is a stitch used to neaten raw edges on fine fabrics. The fraying edge is trimmed and rolled tightly as the whipping is worked. The roll may be turned to the right side or the wrong side, according to the effect desired. The edge must be rolled towards the worker, using the left thumb and forefinger.

The needle passes through the single fabric only. If there is fullness in the edge it may be reduced by drawing up the fabric on the whipping thread. A rope-like effect is achieved. If the whipping thread is very slightly tightened while working, a similar finish is produced without actually drawing up the fabric.

17 *Whipping*

RS or WS

Herringbone stitch

This is used to hold the raw edge of a single turning of non-fraying fabric, eg stockinet. It is also useful for holding turnings on thick, light-weight fabrics such as quilted nylon, brushed courtelle, etc. In dressmaking the stitch is always worked on the wrong side, and the needle should penetrate only the back of the fabric so that the stitches do not show through to the right side. The stitch is worked from left to right. See figure 18 for working directions.

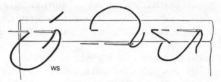

WS

18 *(i) Begin with a double stitch about 2 mm above the raw edge of the turning*

(ii) Pick up two or three threads of single fabric close to the raw edge. The needle must emerge underneath the beginning of the upper stitch

(iii) The stitches alternate on the under and upper line in regular formation, the needle always emerging in line with the beginning of the previous stitch

To fasten off an old thread and join on a new one, see figures 19a, b and c which show the stitching plan.

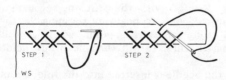

STEP 1   STEP 2

WS

19a *By following the needle movements shown in step 1 and step 2, a back stitch is formed at the top of the last complete herring bone stitch on the upper line*

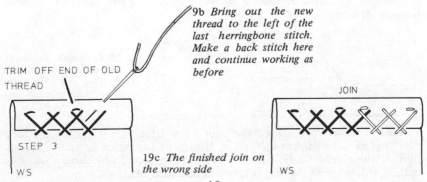

TRIM OFF END OF OLD THREAD

STEP 3

WS

9b Bring out the new thread to the left of the last herringbone stitch. Make a back stitch here and continue working as before

19c *The finished join on the wrong side*

JOIN

WS

4 Beginning, joining and ending stitches

It is best to consider this as one problem covering all varieties of stitches, so that a suitable method can be chosen for the particular stitch being worked, basing the choice on a knowledge of the different methods used for the various types of stitches.

Strong, neat methods must be used or the stitching will come undone and the appearance will be spoilt.

It is not advisable to use a very long length of thread in the needle as it is apt to fray and break, or tangle into knots. It is, therefore, necessary to develop a technique of ending an old thread and joining a new one in an inconspicuous manner. It is wise to give careful thought to these points and devise the best means of beginning, joining and ending to suit the stitch being worked, and the position of the line of stitching on the garment. Never make a series of overcasting stitches which makes a bumpy, ugly and conspicuous place in the stitching; never use a knot as it tends to dirty the thread, to come undone or to pull through the fabric with use. A knot is the sign of an unskilled and slovenly worker.

The following suggestions should be a guide to choosing suitable methods:
1 Two back stitches (20) worked over each other may be used for stitches which are to be worked in a straight line or parallel to an edge of fabric, eg tacking, running, etc.

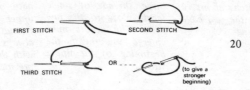

FIRST STITCH   SECOND STITCH

20

THIRD STITCH   OR   (to give a stronger beginning)

Repeat the process for the ending of a thread and for the joining of a new thread.
2 When a folded edge is to be covered with the stitching, eg hemming, oversewing, faggoting, etc, it is usually best to begin by trapping the thread inside the fold, about 25 mm from the starting-point, where it will be anchored with subsequent sewing stitches. It will then be firmly held but invisible (21, 22, 23).

These diagrams illustrate that the needle is inserted into the fold, about 25 mm within the edge, slipped along through the fold and brought out through the fold at the starting-point. A short end of thread should be left showing to ensure that the thread is really lying along inside the fold. This end must be snipped off later.

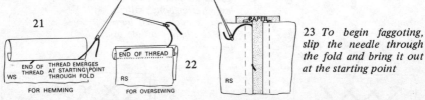

21

END OF THREAD   THREAD EMERGES
WS   AT STARTING POINT
                 THROUGH FOLD
FOR HEMMING

END OF THREAD
RS
FOR OVERSEWING

22

PAPER
RS

23 *To begin faggoting, slip the needle through the fold and bring it out at the starting point*

3 Some stitches which are worked over a raw edge, eg overcasting and loop stitching, need a different method of treatment for fastening on the thread. Run in the thread finely, back to the starting place, and cover these fine running stitches with the first few sewing stitches (24).

24a and b *Fastening on for loop stitching*

LOOP STITCH

For ending an old thread, joining a new one, and for the final fastening off, the same method may be used with slight adjustments where necessary. 4 To make a join in hemming, cut off the old thread leaving about 20 mm. Slip the eye of the needle under the fold of the hem and pull down the 20 mm end so that it comes out between the garment and the hem turning (25a). Stitching through the hem only, bring out the new thread in position for the next stitch. Twist the two thread ends together and tuck them under the hem (25b). Continue with the stitching.

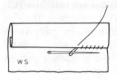

25a *Releasing the old thread*

25b *Setting the new thread*

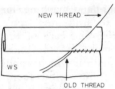

5 Some stitches join folded edges of fabric. In this case a new thread can be joined as illustrated in figure 26, which uses oversewing as an example.

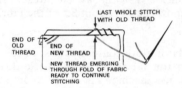

26 *The ends of the old and new threads lie side by side as the stitching is continued*

To join on a new thread in faggoting, the threads are arranged as in figure 27. The old thread is slipped through the fold and brought out 25 mm lower down. The new thread is brought out through the hole of the last stitch and the needle passes under the last stitch to complete the twist.

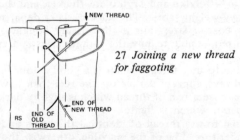

27 *Joining a new thread for faggoting*

6 Fastening off is often done in a similar way to the beginning and joining of the threads or, if this is not suitable, a double stitch may be worked in an inconspicuous position, eg faggoting is usually fastened off finally by making a double stitch on the wrong side of the edge turning. Some stitches, however, need a special arrangement to make a neat, strong ending, eg hemming (28a and 28b).

21

28a *Stitch back to the end of the last stitch to form a 'V' shape*

 28b *Stitch back into the same place again, but this time pass the needle between the layers of the hem and bring it out through the outer fold*

For ending oversewing, stitch back over the last four stitches, forming neat crosses over the folded edges. Cut off the thread.

Machine stitching

There is a wide range of sewing machines on sale nowadays. Each machine sold is accompanied by a well illustrated instruction manual. When buying a second-hand machine, make sure that the instruction manual is available. It is wise to study the book carefully and follow the directions given for the working and care of the particular machine in use. These points vary from one make of machine to another, so it is impossible to give general information which applies to all machines. However, some guidance can be given about various factors which relate to machine stitching.

A strong magnifying glass, or a linen prover, is useful for studying the fabric and the machine stitching, and comparing the balance of the two.

The fabric
Study this carefully and notice the thickness of the woven threads, and the density of the weave. It is helpful to know the fibre content of the fabric.

The thread
Choose a type of thread which is similar in fibre content to that of the fabric, ie use cotton thread, eg Sylko on cotton fabric: use a synthetic thread, eg Trylko or Drima on synthetic fabrics: use machine silk or Sylko on wool. As both silk and cotton are natural fibres, they are more compatible with wool which is also a natural fibre.

Thread can be bought in different thicknesses. Choose a thread which will not distort the density of the weave as it stitches into the fabric. For most general work, No. 50 Sylko or No. 60 Trylko are examples of suitable thread thicknesses. No. 40 Sylko and Trylko are thicker, and should be used only on thick and heavy-weight fabric. The haberdashery departments in many stores sell only the coarser sizes, but if threads are bought at a sewing machine centre, it will be possible to buy the thinner sizes and ensure good results in stitching.

Take trouble to buy thread which is a good colour match with the fabric. The colour always appears darker on the reel than it will look on a line of stitching, so choose a reel of thread which is slightly darker than the fabric in preference to one which is lighter.

It is essential to use thread of identical thickness and colour for both the upper and under threading of the machine, otherwise the line of stitching will be irregular.

The needle
Fine, medium and coarse needles should be kept in the machine box, so that a needle of suitable thickness can be used. The needle must be chosen to link with the thickness of the thread and the density of the fabric weave. Too fine a needle will be very difficult to thread and will not be able to draw the

machine thread correctly into the fabric. Too coarse a needle will make too big a hole in the fabric, thus splitting it instead of penetrating between the weave. Needle sizes are numbered in the following way:

	Fine	Medium	Coarse
Singer size	9	14	16
Continental size	70	80	90

The formation of the stitch
A machine forms what is known as a lock-stitch, i.e. the upper and under cotton lock together in the middle of the thickness of fabric being stitched — hence the stitch having the same appearance on both sides of the work(63). On fine fabric this locking is visible, on heavy fabric it is not, as it sinks into the thickness of the cloth.

 UPPER
UNDER

29 *Upper and under threads locking together in the centre of their depth*

The upper tension
Information about this can be found in the machine manual. Most modern machines have a self-adjustable upper tension and rarely require alteration.

It is most important to thread the upper tension correctly. The working principle of an upper tension is the same for all machines, although they may differ in threading method and in appearance from one make to another. Within the upper tension, pressure is exerted on the top thread when the presser foot is lowered. While the machine is stitching, the top thread passes continuously through this pressure area of the upper tension. The lower tension balances the upper tension, and together they produce regular, even stitching.

The lower tension
The lower tension is formed when the spool is correctly threaded into the spool case. Most machines have a round spool and spool case; others have a long bobbin and a boat-shaped bobbin case or shuttle. Whatever the type of machine, the principle of the working of the lower tension is similar. A flat metal spring is screwed on to the outside of the spool case or shuttle. When threading the lower cotton, it is passed between this spring and the spool case or shuttle, and so is subjected to some pressure as the machine stitches.

It is seldom necessary to alter the lower tension as it is very carefully adjusted in manufacture. The formation of this tension is such that it can usually adapt itself to varying thicknesses of cotton. The tension on the upper thread should pull equally with the tension on the under thread.

The lower tension usually needs tightening for use with very thin slippery threads, eg Terylene threads. It needs loosening if a coarse thread, eg coton à broder, is used for decorative cable stitching. These examples are exceptional cases.

NB Whenever the lower tension is altered it must be returned to a normal setting when the special work is finished.

Using the machine
Some space round the machine is most desirable so that the garment is not bunched up while it is being stitched and so that the worker may concentrate on her machining. Without concentration it is impossible to stitch evenly and accurately. Careless machining gives a very poor finished effect to a garment.

1 Inserting work in the machine

Arrange the work in the machine so that it is as flat as possible. See that the greater amount of fabric rests on the table and the smaller amount is between the needle and the balance wheel.

Place the work in position and turn the balance wheel towards you, so that the needle is lowered to enter the fabric exactly where the stitching should begin. Lower the presser foot and proceed with the machining.

2 Running the machine

The movement of the machine must be even. This will only come with practice. The pressure of the foot must be steady when using an electrically driven machine.

The fabric must be allowed to pass naturally through the feed. The left hand should be used lightly to guide it from the front. It should never be pulled through the machine as this drags on the needle and makes the stitching very uneven in length.

3 Withdrawing work from the machine

(a) Turn the balance wheel until the thread take-up lever is at its highest point and the needle is right out of the garment.
(b) Lift the presser foot.
(c) Draw the work out at the back of the presser foot in the direction in which the fabric has passed during stitching.
(d) Cut off the cotton, leaving about 102 mm from the work and 102 mm from the needle.

4 Testing the stitch

Never begin to stitch a garment without testing the stitch first. Use a piece of the garment fabric folded double, or treble, according to the number of layers of fabric to be joined together on the garment, eg two layers for most seams, three layers for a lapped seam.

Use the thread and needle that will be used for stitching the garment.

Work several inches and inspect the stitch. The stitching should look the same on both sides of the fabric. If it does not, check the threading. If this is in order, some adjustment to the stitching must be necessary. It is helpful to examine the stitching through a magnifying glass. In any case, notice the following points:

1 The appearance of the thread in relation to the fabric threads. Is it too thick or too thin? If necessary, try a different thread.

2 The stitch tension. Are the upper and under threads locking together in the centre of the thickness of fabric? (See figure 29). If they are, the tension is suitable: if they are not, notice the irregularity and consult the machine manual for guidance in correction.

3 The stitch length. The length of the stitch is the distance between the locking points of the two threads (see figure 29). The stitch should be short for fine fabrics, of medium length for average work, and long for heavy fabric. Consult the machine manual and adjust the stitch length as necessary.

4 Puckering of the line of stitching. This is caused by too long a stitch on fine fabric, or by retraction of the machine thread. The former cause is easily rectified. The latter cause is often found when using synthetic thread. Try shortening the stitch length so that a longer length of thread is machined into the seam, thus giving greater flexibility. Stretch the machined line tautly by

pinning it at each end onto an ironing board. Press with a warm iron, leave the fabric to become cold and remove the pins. Repeat if necessary. If these suggestions do not work, try another make of synthetic thread which may pair more readily with the fabric.

5 The feel of the line of machining. When drawn between the thumb and first finger, a good line of machining should feel smooth and well 'bedded' into the fabric.

Machining corners and shaped edges
(a) Corners
Every corner has a fitting point. This comes where the fitting lines of the two sides making the angle meet (30). Machine along the fitting line until the fitting point is reached. Stop when the needle is passing right down through the fabric. Lift the presser foot. Turn the fabric on the needle in position for machining the second side of the angle. Lower the pressure foot. Continue machining.

FITTING POINT

TURNING
ALLOWANCE

30

(b) Shaped edges
All curves should be tacked very accurately to give a guide line for the stitching, unless the stitching comes close to an edge which, in itself, may form the guide. It is important that a curved line should be perfectly flat if it is to set well on the finished garment.

If the curve is much shaped it is sometimes necessary to stop with the needle down through the fabric and lift the presser foot slightly. This eases the fabric round the curve. The presser foot must always be lowered before continuing the stitching.

(c) Scallops (31)   To machine scallops accurately and successfully, combine the suggestions made under the last two headings.

Small machine stitches give the best result when sewing sharp, deep scallops, as they fit more smoothly round the curves.

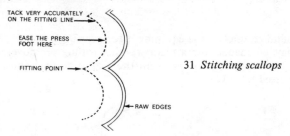

TACK VERY ACCURATELY
ON THE FITTING LINE

EASE THE PRESS
FOOT HERE

FITTING POINT

RAW EDGES

31 *Stitching scallops*

Cable stitching
Wind the bobbin very evenly by hand with coton à broder. Loosen the lower tension until the embroidery cotton runs fairly easily when threaded. Use a matching sewing cotton for the upper threading with an average tension.

Stitch the decorative lines or design with the fabric right side down, so that the embroidery cotton gives a bold effect to the design on the right side when finished.

Fasten off by pulling the embroidery thread through to the wrong side. Sew it in to the back of the stitching, or knot it firmly.

3 Pressing

Careful frequent pressing is essential throughout the making of any article or garment if it is to have a fresh and smart appearance when it is finished. Each process should be pressed as it is finished and before it is crossed by another process, eg sleeve, shoulder and underarm seams must be pressed before the sleeve is set into the armhole.

Pressing equipment
This should always be available when dressmaking is being done as it is very frequently required.

1 Iron
An electric iron with a clear, easily operated thermostat is the most convenient type of iron.

A steam iron is useful for pressing some fabrics which require dampness.

2 Ironing board
A table with an unpolished surface, if available, is useful for pressing uncut fabric, but most people manage with an ironing board. It is best to choose a wide board on a firm stand. A sleeve board provides the easiest base for pressing sleeves and small parts of a garment. These should all be fitted with blanket and have detachable white sheeting covers which can be removed easily for washing. The blanket and the covers should be smooth with no patches or seams.

3 Roller
This is a useful adjunct to the equipment for pressing seams in woollen fabric. A roller may be made from a plain wooden rolling pin covered firmly with blanket. The turnings fall away from the seam line over the roller, and can easily be pressed flat (32).

32

4 Pressing cloths
These should be made from fine white cotton fabric and should be free from hems, patches or seams. Butter muslin is the best choice for most general use as it dampens very easily but does not hold sufficient moisture, if well wrung out, to cause shrinking and water-marking of the fabric.

5 *A bowl of water* will be needed for damping the muslin if there is no tap in the room.

6 *A pad* is useful for pressing shaped areas, eg darts, sleeve crowns, etc. Pressing pads are available from dressmaking supply stores, but can be made at home. Make a paper pattern of an oval shape 20 cm x 15 cm. Use strong white or unbleached calico for the pad, and cut out two shapes from the oval pattern, allowing a 10 mm turning. Join the two pieces together, leaving a gap of about 10 cm. Crease back the turnings on either edge of the gap and tack. Trim and notch the turnings all round. Turn the pad case right side out and stuff it with kapoc, packing it very firmly to make a solid pad. Oversew the gap.

Important points to remember when pressing

1 Remove tacking threads whenever possible, otherwise they leave marks on the fabric. Make sure that there are no pins left where the pressing is to be done. If it is necessary to press over tacking stitches, eg when setting the edge of a collar or a facing, press very lightly to begin the setting of the edge. Then remove the tacking before finishing the pressing.

2 Test the heat of the iron on a spare piece of the actual fabric before touching the garment with the iron, so that a suitable heat may be found, as some fabrics scorch, melt, harden or shrivel if subjected to too great a heat. The following table is a guide to the degree of heat to choose:

Synthetic fabrics Lace	Cool iron	Little, usually no moisture.
Silks Woollens	Moderately hot iron	Moisture rarely used for silk, but usually required for woollens.
Linen Cotton	Hot iron	Moisture probably required, especially for linen.

3 Place the garment carefully on the pressing board so that the grain of the fabric is not pulled out of line, and so that the garment is not unnecessarily creased. Keep each seam in a straight line. Draw the hem edge of a skirt first over the skirt board so that the waist edge comes to the outer point of the board. Use a sleeve-board for pressing sleeves and some small parts. Press first the bodice, then the skirt of a frock.

4 Press on the wrong side of a garment to avoid shining or iron-marking the right side. If necessary slip a strip of paper underneath seam turnings to prevent their marking the right side of the fabric.

5 Use the iron with a lifting movement. Never smooth it over the fabric as in ironing. Press very carefully on the bias or crossway line of fabric to avoid stretching it. The pressure on the iron should be varied according to the type of fabric, fine fabric needing less pressure than heavy fabric. Any fabric which shines or iron-marks easily, e.g. some rayons; should be subjected to light pressure, and are probably better pressed through a dry cloth.

6 The point, or toe, of an iron is useful for pressing into points, angles and the setting line of gathers. In this case, use the iron with the heel slightly raised, so that it does not flatten or overpress the area around.

7 The side edge of the iron provides a long edge which is helpful when a turning has to be flattened as far as a fitting line, eg when a gathered edge is

prepared ready for setting. The gathered fabric on the garment side of the fitting line must be kept soft and uncrushed, but a better seam results if the gathered turning is flattened. Use the iron flat, but run the side edge along the fitting line so that the turning only is pressed.

General rules for pressing

Press each process during construction as well as when it is finished, ie press each line of stitching as it is finished with the fabric in the stitching position so that the stitching itself is flattened, eg press the fitting-line stitching of a plain open seam, and the first line of stitching of a french seam, before doing any further work on each seam.

Darts must not be pressed beyond the point to prevent creasing the fabric outside the dart. Press the stitching and the fold first, and then press the dart flat in a suitable direction, viz towards the centre front or centre back for darts at neck, shoulder and waist-lines, as this gives a softer appearance on the right side. Press them towards the waist for underarm darts and towards the wrist for elbow darts so that the fold of the dart follows the direction in which the garment will hang in wear.

Tucks must be pressed along the stitching and fold line of each tuck, covering the tuck length only and pressing on the underside' of the tuck. Stand the iron on its heel and draw the wrong side of the tucked part to and fro across the iron. This flattens the fabric on which the tucks will lie. This is adequate pressing for very narrow tucks, eg pin tucks, but wider tucks need pressing flat on to the background fabric. They should be pressed so that they all face the same way unless the block of tucks is very wide. In this case the finished appearance is usually more attractive if the block is separated in the centre, one half pressed to the left and one half to the right, but this may only be arranged if there are an even number of tucks in the block.

Pleats need very careful pressing if they are to look straight and crisp when finished. Remove as much of the tacking as possible before and during the pressing. If it is essential to press over a tacked section, use the iron very lightly at first and remove the tacking before giving the final press. In many cases a damp cloth is required to obtain a crisp finish to the pleats, but always give the final press through a dry cloth.

Armhole seams should be pressed flat first and then finally pressed away from the bodice on to the sleeve.

The final press

Work on the wrong side and press the small parts of the garment first, ie sleeves, cuffs and collar, as pressing these is bound to crush the main part of the garment a little. Then press the bodice and lastly the skirt. When pressing a large garment, eg a dressing gown, cover the floor around the skirt board with paper to prevent the garment from sweeping the floor.

If careful pressing has been done during the making of the garment, the final pressing should not be an arduous task. Be careful not to over-press at this stage, or the finished result will be disappointing and the fresh appearance spoilt.

The use of moisture in pressing

Although some fabrics press satisfactorily when they are dry, moisture is often necessary to obtain a smooth, flat finish after pressing, especially for woollen and crease-resisting fabrics.

Moisture is usually applied indirectly through a damp cotton cloth. The cloth should always be tightly wrung out so that it is only damp, not wet. Place the cloth over the wrong side of the garment and press lightly or firmly, according to the thickness of the fabric. Remove the damp cloth and finish pressing through a *dry* cloth to prevent shrinkage or a rough, dry effect. Lift the garment slightly off the pressing-board while doing this to allow the steam to escape. It is important that the fabric is *quite dry* before the pressing is finished.

A steam iron provides a quick, satisfactory method of damp pressing some fabrics, but test first on a spare piece of garment fabric to see the effect. Some fabrics, eg Crimplene, respond well to being pressed with a steam iron through a dry pressing cloth.

Removing shiny marks and lines pressed into fabric from tacking stitches and seam turnings

Such marks as these should not often occur if the initial pressing is done carefully, but occasionally they are unavoidable or come by accident. The following method of removal is usually successful. Place the offending part right side up on the pressing-board and cover it with a damp cloth. Hold a hot iron about 10 mm *above* the muslin until it steams. *The iron must not touch the muslin.* Remove the muslin and brush lightly over the right side surface with a clothes brush on woollen fabric and with soft, dry muslin on rayons, etc. Repeat the process if necessary.

Shrinking fullness from woollen fabric

This treatment is sometimes required at sleeve crowns and at hem-lines, but should only be given to fabric which does not tend to shine or water-mark with pressing, and which can stand the heat of a hot iron.

Cover the too-full part with a damp muslin on the wrong side. The muslin may need re-damping several times until the shrinkage is complete. Press very lightly at first to steam the moisture into the fabric, and increase the pressure as the shrinkage occurs. Press finally through a *dry* muslin.

When shrinking a hem-line it is essential to place a protective strip under the hem turning to protect the skirt from the imprint of the raw edge of the turning, and also from shrinking the actual garment. See page 297. A piece of old, clean blanket, or a double strip of either old sheeting or smooth clean paper can be used.

Some modern fabrics can be permanently creased by pressing with a hot iron. Therefore it is wise to test for this on spare scraps of the garment fabric before doing any final pressing, so that a safe temperature can be gauged. It can be useful, in some cases, to ensure a permanent crease, but it must be remembered that a crease set into the wrong position on such fabric cannot be removed.

Special points about pressing individual processes will be found in appropriate places throughout the text. This seemed the better placing of the information to save cross reference as, for good results, pressing must be done throughout the construction of any garment.

4 Measuring and the use of fitting lines

Positions for measuring

1 Shoulder length
2 Chest width
3 Back width
4 Back length
5 Bust
6 Waist
7 Hips
8 Skirt length
9 Inner sleeve length
10 Top arm
11 Wrist

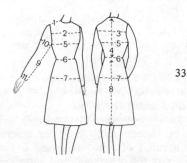

33

Preparing the body for taking measurements

Remove any bulky outer clothing, and wear, for example, a thin, plain skirt and pullover.

Pin a length of tape round the waist and the hips to act as guides for length measurements. Use the lower edge of each tape as a boundary line.

Taking measurements

It is difficult to take measurements accurately for oneself, so get someone to take them for you.

Care and thought must be given to the placing of the tapemeasure when taking measurements, as accurate measuring is essential if a well-fitting garment is to be achieved. Think about the actual position of the measurement, and relate it to the part of the garment which will cover that area of the body.

The shoulder length comes between a plain high neck line and the sleeve setting. Consider these two positions and take care to place the tapemeasure accurately when measuring along the shoulder, so that the neck and armhole lines are suitably placed.

The chest and back width lines guide the sleeve setting, so relate these measurements to the position of the arms, and think where the sleeve will need to be set. The chest width line is taken across the body about 65 mm below the front neck hollow, and the back width line about 100 mm below the nape bone.

The back length falls between the plain high neck and the waist, passing down the spine.

The bust, waist and hips are circular measurements taken round the body. In each case, place two fingers inside the tapemeasure to prevent the

30

measurement from being taken too tightly, as this always leads to a strained fitting. Take the bust measurement over the fullest point of the bust, keeping the tapemeasure straight at the back.

It is sometimes difficult to find the exact position for taking the hip measurement. If in any doubt about this, sit down and set a pin in the clothing about 25 mm above the chair seat. Stand up and take the hip measurement round the body at this level.

The skirt measurement is the one measurement which is controlled by fashion. It is taken at the back from the waist downwards, for the length required.

The inner sleeve length is difficult to measure accurately. Begin measuring from the wrist, which is easy to determine, and measure straight up the inside of the arm to the armpit area, and decide where it is necessary to stop the measurement. This point comes at the top of the sleeve seam and will be joined finally to the bodice underarm seam. The inner sleeve length measurement must end, therefore, at a point near the armpit which will be comfortable for the underarm sleeve setting.

The top arm is measured round the arm, high up near the armpit level. It corresponds, in a sleeve pattern, to a line drawn across the sleeve between the underarm points, cutting off the crown of the sleeve from the lower part. This top arm measurement must be taken loosely or the sleeve will be too tight for comfort in wear, and will be strained round the arm in this position.

The wrist measurement is only required for testing either a tight fitting sleeve with a wrist opening or a tight fitting cuff. A long sleeve, without a wrist opening, which is styled to slip over the hand, should have its wrist edge line tested against the measurement round the hand. Measure the hand at the lower thumb joint level, with the thumb turned inwards onto the palm.

Adding ease
Ease must be added to all round body measurements to allow for comfort in wear and freedom of movement. Add approximately:

    75-100 mm to bust and hip
    25-50 mm to waist

When testing a bought pattern, the ease allowance must be taken into consideration, eg when testing for a 91.5 cm bust size, the pattern measurements across the bust should add up to approximately 99-101.5 cm.

Buying a pattern
Buy skirt, shorts and trouser patterns by the hip measurement. Buy blouse, dress and nightwear patterns by the bust size. If the exact size is unobtainable, either order the pattern in the size you need, or take the next largest size.

Fitting lines
The fitting line comes where the turning allowance ends. Bought patterns usually allow a 15 mm turning allowance. Therefore the fitting line comes 15 mm inside the edge of the pattern, on all edges where a turning is needed.

Garment patterns have fitting lines and fitting points wherever joins occur. All final stitching should be done along a fitting line. At certain places the fitting lines cross. These are the fitting points, eg where armhole and bodice side seam lines meet at an angle. The point of this angle is the underarm

31

fitting point. The centre back or the centre front line of a bodice is often placed to a fold of fabric to avoid a seam. In this case there is no turning allowance along this edge of the pattern.

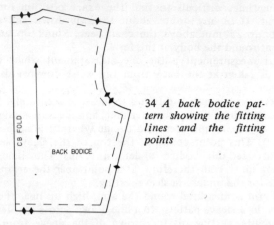

34 *A back bodice pattern showing the fitting lines and the fitting points*

On bought patterns the fitting lines are indicated by printed lines. As a guide for the final stitching, these lines may be tailor tacked or marked with chalk. Failing this, the fitting line must be followed by continuous measurement of the turning allowance width inwards from the raw edge. All tacking prior to fitting must be done on the fitting lines, otherwise the fitting cannot be tested accurately.

Testing a pattern for size

Open out all parts of the pattern which are going to be used. Have ready the list of personal measures. Test measurements with a tapemeasure, not a ruler. A tapemeasure can be used upright on curved lines, eg neck and armhole, to ensure accurate measurement.

All body measurements must be tested on the pattern and any differences accurately noted for alteration.

1 Testing a skirt pattern

(a) Length
Measure down the centre back line between the waist and hem fitting lines. Compare this with your own skirt length measurement and note any difference.

(b) Waist measurement   Measure along waist fitting line using tapemeasure upright as it is a curved line. Measure from CB line to dart, omit dart width and continue measuring from other side of dart to seam.

Measure the front waist line in the same way, omitting any darts or pleats.

Add together the back and front waist measurements and multiply by 2. This gives the whole waist measurement. The pattern measurement for a frock waist should be 50 mm bigger than your own to allow ease in wear. A skirt waist should be 25 mm bigger than your own to allow for easing into the waistband.

(c) Hip measurement   Measuring downwards from waist fitting line, mark in hip line as far below waist fitting line as your own hip measurement comes.

Do this on back and front skirt patterns. Measure these two lines from centre lines to side-seam fitting lines. Omit from measures any pleat widths. Add together back and front hip measurements and multiply by 2.

The final measurement should be at least 75-100 mm bigger than your own measurement, to allow ease for comfortable wear.

If the skirt style is very full the skirt hip measurement will be considerably larger than your own.

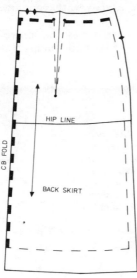

35 *The side seam and hem fitting lines are shown by dotted lines. The measuring positions are shown by heavy dotted lines at waist and centre back, and by a solid line at the hip*

2 Testing a sleeve pattern

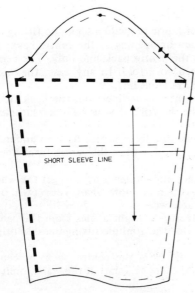

36 *The crown, seam and wrist edge fitting lines are shown in dotted lines. The measuring positions are shown in heavy dotted lines*

To test the inner length of a long sleeve, measure down the front seam line from the underarm fitting point to the wrist fitting point. It is necessary to measure the front seam line as some patterns provide an elbow allowance, eg a dart, in the back seam line.

To make a short sleeve pattern measure from crown fitting point down side seam fitting lines for the length required plus turning allowance. Rule across sleeve joining these two points.

Sleeve seam lengths should compare exactly with your own. No ease is allowed on length measurements.

To test the width of a sleeve, measure across the sleeve between the armhole points. This line should measure at least 50 mm more than your own loosely taken measurement.

3 Testing a bodice pattern

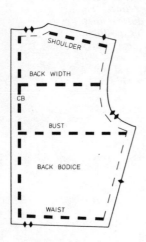

37a and b *The neck, shoulder, armhole, side seam and waist fitting lines are marked in fine dotted lines. The measuring positions are shown by heavy dotted lines*

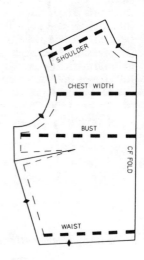

If the centre back is placed to a fold of fabric to avoid a seam, no fitting line is required. If, however, there is a seam or opening at the centre back, the measurements must be taken as far as the centre back line only. The centre front line may, or may not, be placed to a fold. In any case, the width measurements are all taken from the centre front line.

(a) back length   Measure down the centre back line from the neck fitting line to the waist fitting line. It should be the same as your own measurement. Note any difference.

(b) Bust. Back.   Measure across the bust-line from centre back to underarm fitting point. *Front.* Measure across the bust-line from the centre front line to the underarm fitting point.

Add these two measurements together and multiply by 2 to get the whole bust measurement. It should be 75-100 mm more than your own bust measurement to allow ease for comfortable wear.

(c) Back width and chest width   Measure at right angles from the centre front or centre back lines to the centre of the armhole fitting lines. Multiply each measurement by 2.

(d) Waist   Measure across the waist-line from the centre back, or centre front to the side-seam fitting line. Should there be a dart at the waist, omit its width from the measurement.

Add together the front and back waist measures and multiply by 2. This should be 50-75 mm more than your own waist measurement to allow ease in wear.

A gathered waist line may be easily adjusted to size during fitting.

The bodice waist line and the skirt waist line of a frock should balance in size;

(e) Shoulder   Test the size of the front shoulder line. Measure along the shoulder fitting line from the neck fitting point to the armhole fitting point. It should be the same as your own measurement. Should there be a dart at the front shoulder, omit its width from the measurement.

The back shoulder should be a little longer than your own measurement, so that it is eased slightly to fit the front. This allows for easy fitting over the thickness of the back shoulder. Sometimes a small dart is placed at the back shoulder for this purpose, instead of allowing extra length.

(f) Armhole and sleeve crown

(i) Measure the back and front bodice armholes between shoulder and underarm fitting points. Add these two measurements together to find the full size of the bodice armhole.

(ii) Measure round the fitting line of the sleeve crown. This measurement should be about 25-40 mm more than the bodice armhole to allow the sleeve to be eased into the armhole.

5 Straight grain lines and the alteration of patterns

1 Straight grain lines

On every pattern part there is a straight grain line. This line is always marked on each piece of the pattern, and should be found before attempting to use the pattern for cutting out. These straight grain lines come on the pattern where the warp threads of the fabric run in the cut out garment, and must be accurately placed when laying pattern pieces onto fabric. Always arrange for the warp threads to come in a garment where the greatest strain comes in wear, as they are strong threads and stand up to this strain. The straight grain of the fabric must be planned to come in special positions on the garment so that it will hang straight and untwisted in wear. Use the straight grain lines, therefore, very carefully as guides in cutting out a garment correctly.

Some pattern parts have a straight edge which has to be placed to a fold of fabric. This edge usually takes the place of a straight grain line.

If the pattern needs altering, pay special attention to the straight grain lines so that their position is not moved when making the alteration.

To set a straight grain line parallel to the selvedge, set a pin at one end of the straight grain line, and measure the distance from this point to the selvedge. The opposite end of the straight grain line is then pinned the same distance away from the selvedge (38). The pattern is now balanced with the warp grain and is ready for pinning onto the fabric for cutting out.

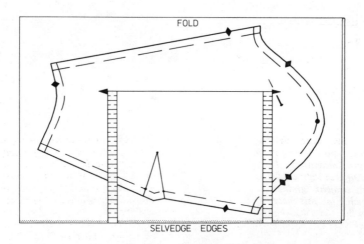

FOLD

SELVEDGE EDGES

38 *This figure shows a sleeve laid on fabric with the straight grain line being pinned and measured to the selvedge*

36

2 Pattern alterations

A Skirt patterns

(a) Altering a skirt pattern in length

A printed line is marked on bought patterns to show the best position for an alteration in length, and any necessary length alterations should be made in the position indicated. All length alterations are made at right angles to the straight grain line (39a).

The pattern is lengthened by cutting it across at right angles to the straight grain line, and inserting a strip of paper to add the extra length required (39b).

A pattern is shortened by pleating away the unwanted length. The pleat is made at right angles to the straight grain line, and equal in width to half the amount to be shortened, ie to shorten a pattern 25 mm, the pleat must be 12.5 mm in width (39c and 39d). In actual fact it is wiser to make the pleat 12 mm wide. Half and quarter millimetres are too small to handle accurately in this type of alteration, and the resulting loss is too small to affect the fitting. This applies to all the following alterations.

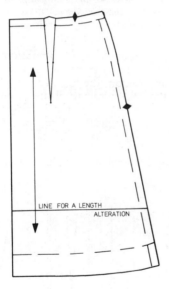

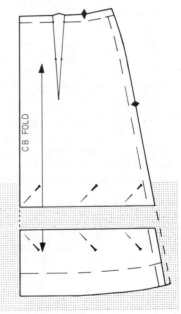

39a *This skirt pattern shows the line for a length alteration. Note that it is at right angles to the straight grain line which, in this case, is parallel to the centre back*

39b *The pattern lengthened by inserting a strip of paper and pinning it in place in the indicated position. The dotted lines show the centre line ruled straight across the insertion and the side seam line continued over the insertion to the hem level. The hem line is slightly widened to meet the new lower side-seam line. This keeps the hem width in proportion to the skirt length*

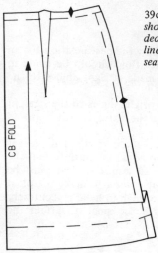

39c *The skirt pattern shortened by a pleat folded along the alteration line. This brings the side-seam out of alignment*

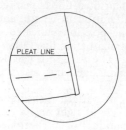

39d *The pattern folded back below the pleat to straighten the side-seam line, and to keep the hem width in proportion to the skirt length*

(b) Altering a skirt pattern in width

The pattern, if bought by the hip measurement, should not require alteration. If the waist is inaccurate in size, this can be attended to by adjusting the darts and/or the side seam curve in fitting. If, for any reason, the hip size of the pattern does need reducing or enlarging, either the pleating or insertion method can be used. Such an alteration is always made parallel to the straight grain lines (40a and 40b). However, care must be taken when working out the width of the pleat or insertion. Consider the following points:

(a) The hip measurement circles the body.

(b) In a two-piece skirt, each pattern section represents half the back or front of the skirt, ie one quarter of the whole.

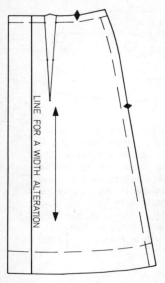
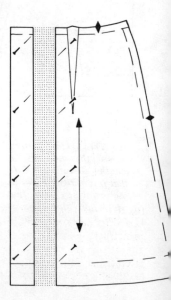

40a *This skirt pattern shows the line for the pleat or insertion. It is parallel to the straight grain line. Notice that it is placed to avoid the dart*

40b *This skirt pattern has been cut and widened by inserting a strip of paper and pinning in in place in the alteration position. The width of the insertion equals a quarter of the total extra amount required. Cut off the insertion strip level with the pattern edges at waist and hem lines*

Therefore the width of pleat for reducing size, must be half of one quarter of the total amount to be removed.

Example:

Hip measurement of body   965 mm
Hip size of pattern   1015 mm
Amount to reduce pattern   50 mm

Divide this 50 mm between the front and back of the skirt, ie reduce each half of the skirt by 25 mm. Following point (b) above, each pattern section must be reduced by 12.5 mm. Call this 12 mm for convenient measuring. Therefore the width of pleat must be 6 mm in each skirt section.

To enlarge a pattern 50 mm on the whole hip measurement, the width of the insertion must be a quarter of the total amount required. Therefore 12mm must be inserted into both the back and front patterns.

(c) Altering a gored skirt pattern

This type of pattern has a straight grain line down the centre of the pattern, not parallel to an edge (41).

To alter in length, the pattern is pleated, or cut, straight across its full width at right angles to the straight grain line, as shown by line AB in figure 41.

To alter in width, draw a new straight grain line, shown as a dotted line in figure 41. Extend the original straight grain line to waist and hem edges, and use this as the guide line for width alterations.

Refer to figures 39b, 39c and 39c for guidance in aligning the side edges of the altered pattern.

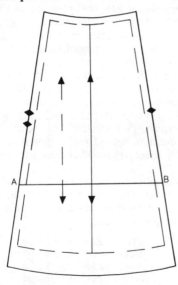

41 *Line AB is placed for length alterations. The new grain line is drawn for width alterations*

(d) Altering skirt patterns of any other style

If a skirt pattern of any other style requires alteration, apply these same basic principles, pleating or inserting extra width of paper as necessary. If the alteration is made at right angles to the straight grain line for length alterations, and parallel to the straight grain line for width alterations, the result will be satisfactory.

Sometimes two alterations may be made in one pattern. For example, a skirt may be made both shorter and narrower or longer and wider, etc. In this case the two alterations must be made at right angles to each other.

B Bodice patterns

The alterations follow the same basic principles outlined for shirt alterations, ie the use of pleats or insertion strips, and the method of calculating these.

(a) Shortening or lengthening a bodice pattern

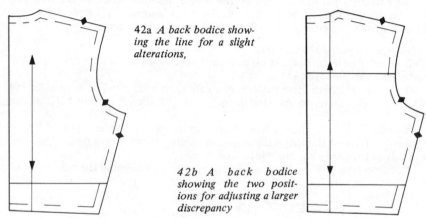

42a *A back bodice showing the line for a slight alterations,*

42b *A back bodice showing the two positions for adjusting a larger discrepancy*

Pleats or slashes used to alter the length of a bodice must be made at RIGHT ANGLES TO THE CENTRE BACK OR FRONT LINES (42a, 42b)

If only a small amount has to be reduced, make the alteration below the bust line. If 25 mm., or more, has to be removed from, or added to, the length, the amount should be divided equally and half the alteration made below, and half above, the bust line. This is done to prevent the armhole from being too low and the side seam too short. Plan carefully the width to make the pleats for shortening, and the amount to spread for lengthening. Extend the straight grain lines of the pattern if necessary, so that they pass across the alteration positions (42a and 42b).

The length alterations disrupt the smoothness of the original side seam lines and the armhole edges of the pattern. This must be dealt with, and new lines drawn as necessary (43a and 43b). Alterations to a front bodice should be made in the same way and in matching positions.

43a *A side seam edge broken by a pleat shortening the lower part of a bodice. For thin figures make a new side-seam line joining the underarm and waist points (broken line in figure). For thicker figures, reshape the waist corner (dotted line in figure). Adjust the fitting lines accordingly*

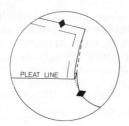

43b *An armhole edge broken by a pleat shortening the upper part of a bodice. For small sizes correct the armhole line by following the inner dotted line. For larger sizes, follow the upper broken line*

(b) Reducing or adding width to a bodice pattern

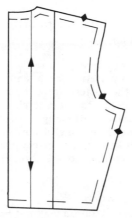

44 *A back bodice pattern with a line showing the width alteration position*

The line for the pleat or slash must come PARALLEL TO THE CENTRE BACK OR FRONT LINES. It should cut the bust line at right angles and should come from the shoulder line, avoiding any dart which may be there. When altering the bodice patterns add or remove ¼ of the whole amount from each pattern, eg if the bust measurement needs reducing 50 mm remove 12 mm from the back pattern and 12 mm from the front pattern. The pleat, therefore, will be 6 mm wide on each pattern section. If the bust measurement needs enlarging 50 mm, insert a strip of paper to widen each section of the pattern by 12 mm. As in the previous skirt example, 2 mm have been lost in the calculation, but this is such a small amount that it will not affect the fitting.

When reducing the width of a bodice pattern, the shoulder line will become misshapen. This must be trimmed according to the shoulder and neck size of the wearer (45a and 45b). The fitting line must also, be adjusted to suit the final shoulder line.

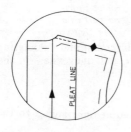

45a *For narrow shoulders and thin neck, cut away the outstanding piece (broken line in figure)*

45b *For wide shoulders and neck, redraw the shoulder line (broken line in figure)*

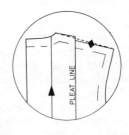

Cutting and spreading a pattern does not make such a noticeable discrepancy in the shoulder line as pleating to reduce width. The shoulder line can be corrected across a widening alteration by drawing a new line to join the neck and armhole points. Adjust the fitting line accordingly.

At the lower edge of the bodice with alteration, reshape the waist line if necessary, by drawing a new line to join the centre back or the centre front line to the side seam line. If there is a waist dart, fold this and pin it in its stitched position before drawing the new waist line. Adjust the fitting line accordingly.

C One-piece dress patterns

This style combines the skirt and bodice patterns into one, making a full length dress pattern from shoulder to hem.

(a) Altering the length of a one-piece dress pattern
Find the waist position as marked on the pattern. Check, and compare with your own measurements, the length of the pattern from the centre back of the neck to the waist, and from the waist to the hem level. It will then be possible to judge whether the pattern needs lengthening or shortening above or below the waist line or whether it needs altering in both positions. It is important for fitting that the waist line is kept in the correct position. Having made this decision, alter the pattern according to the directions given for skirts and bodices.

(b) Altering the width of a one-piece dress pattern
This must be planned carefully, as an equal alteration may not be required for both bust and hip measurements. Decide how much the pattern needs enlarging or reducing at these two positions. Calculate and carry out the alteration needed for the smaller of these two amounts. For example, if the bust needs reducing by 40 mm and the hip by 50 mm, base the alteration on the 40 mm measurement. The additional amount still to be removed from the hip measurement can be dealt with in fitting.

Width alterations should be made parallel to the centre front and the centre back lines, as these are parellel to the straight grain lines. If a dress has side gore patterns, the alterations should be made parallel to the straight grain lines marked on these sections of the pattern.

After making width alterations, measure the resulting waist line and check it against your own waist measurement. The side seam line may need an adjustment over the waist line, or, if the discrepancy is small, this could also be dealt with in fitting.

Smooth out any unevenness in the seam lines as already described for skirt and bodice patterns.

D Sleeve patterns

These alterations are based on the pleating, width insertion and calculating principles already given in this section. Smooth out any unevenness in the seam lines as already described for skirt and bodice patterns.

1 Length alterations
(a) Long sleeves (46a and 46b)
Both these diagrams show the alterations lines placed at right angles to the straight grain lines.

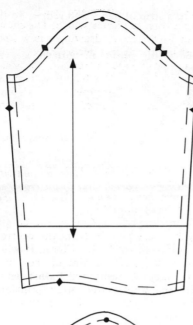

46a *The alteration line for a straight sleeve to be worn either loose or cuffed*

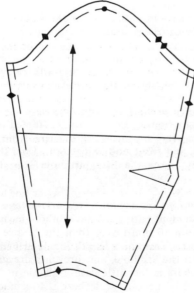

46b *A fitted sleeve with elbow dart. To keep the dart in the right position, the alteration may need dividing, half being placed above and half below the elbow line*

(b) Three-quarter sleeves
These are altered in the same positions as long sleeves.

(c) Short sleeves
(i) Straight short sleeves without seam shaping
To shorten   Fold back the lower edge to make the seam lines the length required. Remember to allow a turning allowance for finishing the lower edge.

To lengthen   Pin the lower edge to a strip of paper and redraw to the length required.

(ii) Shaped short sleeves
These sleeves usually have a shaped facing cut in one with the sleeve, so they cannot be altered at the lower edge (47).

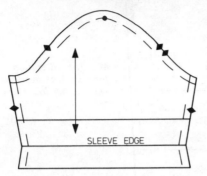

47 *The alteration line is placed at right angles to the straight grain line so that the pleat or insertion is clear of the crown and the lower edge*

After making the alteration, remember to reshape the seam lines and the seam fitting lines between the underarm and the lower edge fitting line.

2 Altering the size of the sleeve crown
This must never be done without careful measuring of the sleeve crown and the bodice armhole, as the size of these must be suitably related for a satisfactory sleeve setting.

(a) To find the size of the sleeve crown   measure round the sleeve crown fitting line, using the tape measure on edge so that it follows smoothly round the curve. Note this measure.
(b) To find the size of the bodice armhole   (any necessary alteration in length must have been made to the bodice, in case it has affected the size of the armhole (refer 42b)). Using the tapemeasure on edge, measure the armhole fitting lines on the back and front bodice patterns. Find the sum of these two measurements as they make the total armhole size. Note this measurement.

(c) Comparing the sleeve crown and bodice armhole measurements
Compare the sleeve crown measurement with the total armhole measurement. The sleeve crown should be 25 mm-50 mm bigger than the bodice armhole. The average difference is 37.5 mm. This extra length in the sleeve crown is required for easing the sleeve into the armhole, and prevents dragging across the top of the arm in wear. If there is too little ease available in the sleeve crown, an insertion alteration will be necessary; if there is too much ease, a pleating alteration will be required. If an alteration is necessary, the best place for it must be found.

(d) Deciding the position of the alteration
Measure across the base of the sleeve crown, between the fitting points, as shown by the broken line in figure 48. The measurement across the base of the sleeve crown should equal your own top arm measurement (taken loosely) + 50 mm.

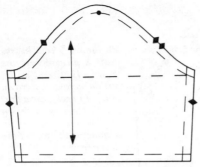

48 *Position for measuring the width of the crown*

If this measurement is correct, the sleeve crown needs altering in depth only; if it is incorrect, the sleeve crown needs altering in width. Whatever alteration is made, check the new sleeve crown measurement carefully and adjust, if necessary, until it is a suitable length for setting into the bodice armhole.

(e) Marking the alteration line
(i) for depth alterations extend the straight grain line to the top of the pattern and make the alteration at right angles to this line.
(ii) for width alterations if the straight grain line is in the centre of the sleeve, extend it for use as above: if it is not, rule a line parallel to it through the centre of the sleeve and use this as the alteration line.
(f) To alter the depth of the crown
Make a pleat (49b), or an insertion (49c) of the required size across the crown, basing it on the prepared alteration line (49a). After the alteration is made, the pattern edge and the fitting line will need adjusting over the sleeve crown.

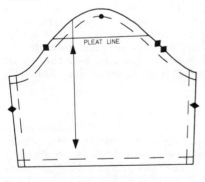

49a *Rule a line across the sleeve crown at right angles to the straight grain line, setting it above the level of the back and front crown balance notches*

49b

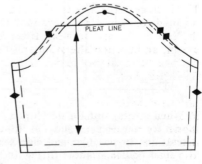

45

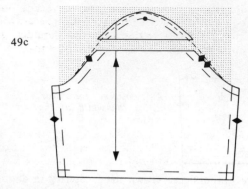

49c

49b and c *These figures show a pleat across the crown (49b), and an insertion across the crown (49c). In each case a dotted line has been drawn to show the necessary reshaping of the top of the sleeve crown*

(g) To alter the width of the crown

Make a pleat, or insertion. of the required size down the centre of the sleeve, basing it on the alteration line, and fixing it with small pieces of *Sellotape*. After the alteration is made, the pattern edge will need smoothing over the top of the sleeve crown. Adjust the fitting line accordingly (50 and 51). Trim away the surplus pattern over a pleated alteration, and the surplus paper across an insertion, to keep a smooth line across the top of the crown.

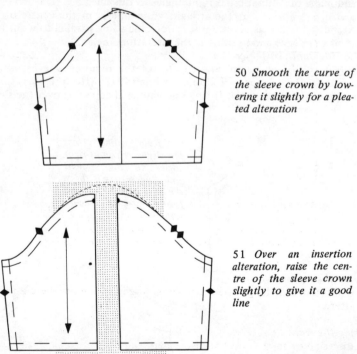

50 *Smooth the curve of the sleeve crown by lowering it slightly for a pleated alteration*

51 *Over an insertion alteration, raise the centre of the sleeve crown slightly to give it a good line*

When cutting out for developed figures, it is often wise to reserve enough fabric for the sleeves and cut them out after the bodice has been fitted. Alterations to shoulder and side seams often alter the size of the armhole. The final bodice armhole fitting line can be measured and compared with the sleeve crown. This can be adjusted accordingly, and the sleeve cut out correctly. It is important to cut out a sleeve with the right size crown, otherwise it is impossible to get a smooth setting over the shoulder. A gathered or puckered setting shows a very poor standard of dressmaking.

E Trouser patterns

Trouser patterns should be bought by the hip measurement and, therefore, should not need altering for hip fitting. Guide lines are given on trouser patterns for lengthening or shortening above or below the crotch line.

(a) Altering the body length (52)

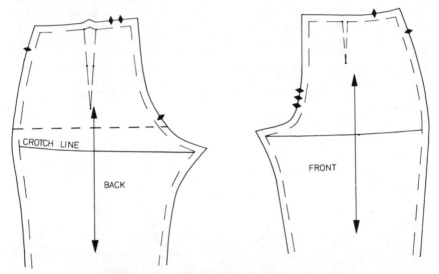

52 *The crotch line runs across the pattern from the fitting point of the leg and body seams. The alteration line comes a short way above the crotch line and is shown here with a dotted line running at right angles to the balance line*

(b) Altering the leg length

The leg is shortened or lengthened just above the hem line or where directed on the pattern.

(c) Altering the waist line

A small discrepancy in the waist measurement can be dealt with by adjusting darts and seams in fitting.

To make a major alteration to the waist size of a trouser pattern, decide on the amount required to remove from or add to the pattern waist measurement, and work out one eighth of this amount. Figures 53a and 53b show how to deal with the necessary alteration.

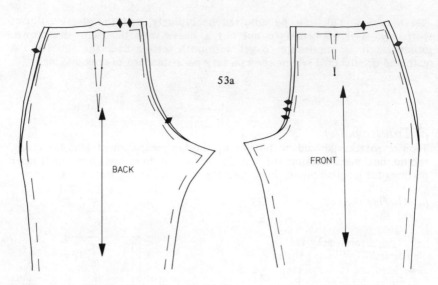

53a and b At the waist edges of the centre and side seams, remove ¼ of the amount to decrease the waist (53a). Add ¼ of the amount to increase the waist (53b). At the side seam, raise the waist point 6 mm, and reshape the waist-line before drawing the new side-seam line

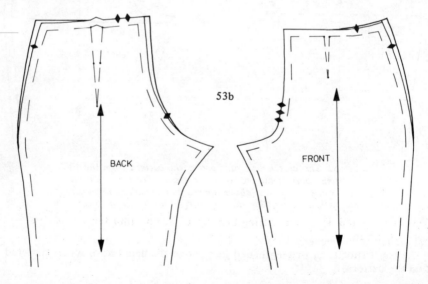

Whichever alteration is made, the new cutting lines must be drawn smoothly into the original cutting lines. Adjust the fitting-lines accordingly.

If the thigh measurement is large in proportion to the hip, allow extra turning in the crotch/thigh area, so that a suitable adjustment can be made in fitting.

6 Laying patterns for cutting out

The size of the pattern must be tested, and any necessary alterations made before the lay is attempted.

Choosing the lay

Study the lays given with the pattern and mark the one provided for your particular size of pattern and width of fabric.

If any alterations have to be made to the pattern, it may be necessary to replan the lay a little, but always study the suggested lay first and base the new plan on it. The suggested lay will indicate positions for the various pattern parts, correctly set in relation to the grain and fold of the fabric. It is important that these placings are not radically changed, although they may have to be spread further apart or moved closer together.

Use of grain

Before carrying out even the simplest dressmaking, it is necessary to understand what is meant by the term 'grain of fabric'. This is the straight thread whether it is warp or weft. The threads running the length of the fabric, parallel with the selvedge, form the warp grain. This is usually stronger than the weft grain, which runs at right angles to the warp grain across the fabric.

When a length of fabric is bought, it is cut off the roll across the weft grain. The straight grain line on a paper pattern is usually intended to run in line with the warp grain, ie parallel to the selvedge. The warp and weft grains cut across each other at right angles. A line running diagonally between the two grains is known as the crossway of the fabric (54).

 54 *The positions of the warp and weft grains in a piece of fabric. One corner has been folded back to indicate the direction of the crossway*

Preparation of fabric

(a) Press the fabric carefully on the wrong side to smooth out any creases. Press parallel to the selvedge, ie with the stonger grain, to prevent stretching the fabric. Be careful that the iron is not too hot for the type of fabric.

(b) Study the cut edges of the fabric, ie the weft edges, and trim one of them straight with a weft thread (55). It may be necessary to pull a weft thread as a guide for cutting straight.

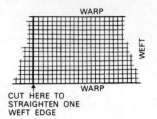

55 *The weave of fabric magnified to show the position for straightening a weft edge*

(c) When the weft edge has been straightened it should form a right angle with the selvedge at each corner. If it does not, it means that it has been pulled diagonally out of shape in manufacture. This occurs chiefly in cottons, but sometimes in other fabrics. To straighten the fabric and re-align the grain, pull diagonally in the opposite direction, until the weft threads are straight and at right angles to the selvedge (56).

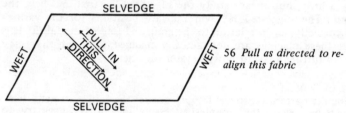

56 *Pull as directed to re-align this fabric*

Pressing with an iron is sometimes helpful. If the fabric proves to be obstinate, it may be impossible to re-align the grain without spoiling the finish of the cloth. In this case, it will have to be cut as it is, and one must hope that the finish is strong enough to support the weave during wear.

It is obviously wise to study the alignment of the grain before buying a length of fabric, and to refrain from choosing a badly distorted piece as this presents a great problem when cutting out on double fabric. However, if the problem does arise, the following points will help in preparing and using fabric which is badly out of alignment, and which does not pull back into shape:

(i) Ascertain that the meterage bought is fully adequate.

(ii) Straighten the weft edges. Lay the fabric on the table and flatten it carefully, keeping the selvedge edges level. Continue doing this as far as possible along the length of fabric then, following the pattern lay, pin and cut out as much of the pattern as will fit onto this part of the fabric.

(iii) Now re-set the fabric. Work from the same edge if possible, but if this will not flatten, begin at the other weft edge, and setting from there proceed as before.

(iv) Finally set the remaining portion of fabric and finish cutting out the last pieces of the pattern.

(d) If the fabric is plain, there will be no difficulty of surface or design, but if there is a nap, pile or one-way design, great care must be taken to place all pattern parts facing in the same direction. It is a good idea to place pins about every 450 mm along the selvedge with the heads facing the chosen way of the nap, pile or design. It can then be seen at a glance, in which direction to place the pattern parts throughout the length of the lay.

The use of the straight grain line

A straight grain line is marked on all pattern parts, and must run with the straight grain of the fabric.

Usually the warp grain runs from the top of the garment to the hem, and from the shoulder to the wrist, ie where the greatest strain comes in wear. It is, however, placed across yokes and along the length of straight collars, cuffs and belts. (Read the section on straight grain lines on page 36).

If the grain is ignored, the garment will neither hang properly nor fit well.

When pinning the pattern onto the fabric, place the straight grain lines of the pattern over the warp grain of the fabric, and pin through the straight grain line at each end to ensure correct placing (refer to figure 38). When the straight grain line is set, the pattern edges can be pinned firmly onto the fabric. Place the pins in the turning allowance of the pattern to prevent pin-marking the fabric, but do not let the points come outside the cutting line of the pattern.

Using a folded edge

Certain edges of certain pattern parts must be placed to a fold of fabric so that the cut-out section is a whole part and not two half parts. Notice which edges these are and place them correctly.

Bought patterns have special signs to mark the edges, which are to be placed to a fold of fabric.

When pinning the pattern on to the fabric, see that the fold is straight with the grain of the fabric. Place fold edge of pattern exactly along fold of fabric and pin to keep it accurately placed. Use as few pins as possible to avoid marking the fabric (57 and 58).

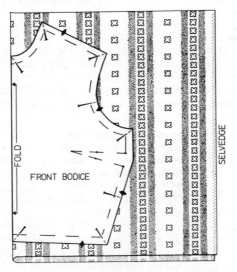

57 *A front bodice pattern set to a fold of fabric*

51

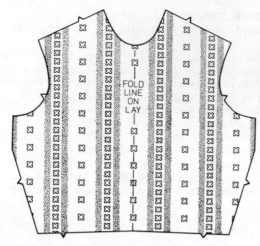

58 *A whole front bodice is cut when the centre front line of the pattern is placed to a fold of fabric (Thread marking of fitting lines and darts omitted)*

The economical use of fabric
(a) By carefully planned folding

Fabric is sold either open to its full width and rolled on a roller, or folded in half lengthways and baled over a flat support of cardboard.

59 *Ready-folded fabric. The meterage required is measured off along the warp, and the length is cut off across the weft*

Garments are frequently cut out on double fabric, and sometimes the ready-folded fabric can be used as it is. Cloth which has been sold from a roll will need folding for a double lay. When folding fabric it is essential to fold straight with the warp grain, and align the weft grain. This careful folding will also keep any stripes or checks over each other on the double layer (60 and 61).

60 *Fabric folded carefully so that the fold comes in line with a warp thread, thus bringing the weft threads exactly over each other*

61 *Fabric folded carelessly so that the fold is not in line with a warp thread. The weft threads, therefore, are not aligned*

Examples of methods of refolding fabric (62, 63 and 64)

62 *This folding gives a double part with fold for the width required. The widest possible single strip is left over*

63 *This folding gives two double parts and two warp folds. It is useful for taking small pattern pieces which have edges needing a fold*

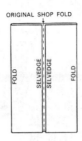

64 *Folding across the weft gives the widest possible double fabric as the full width of cloth is doubled. This is useful for laying very wide pattern parts. It may only be used when no warp fold is required. If the fabric has a one-way design, it must be slit along the weft fold and the top layer turned round so that the design faces the same direction on both layers of fabric. Keep either both wrong or both right sides of fabric touching, so that pairing sections are cut out*

(b) By dove-tailing pattern parts

Dove-tailing a pattern lay is only possible on plain fabric, or on fabric which has a reversible design (65), as the pattern parts are set in opposite directions in order to economise in meterage (66). Dove-tailing may never be done on fabric which has a one-way design, a pile or a nap. The treatment of such fabric will be dealt with later.

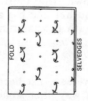

65 *A reversible pattern. The design faces up and down along the warp, and presents the same appearance from either end of the length of cloth*

53

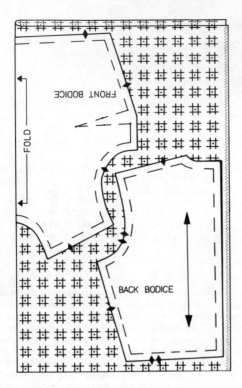

The treatment of one-way fabrics

One-way fabric has a nap, a pile or a non-reversible pattern, and requires careful attention when planning pattern lays.

(a) Napped fabrics

These are brushed on the right side after weaving to give a hairy finish which smoothes in one direction only. The direction of the nap can be found by passing the hand up and down the fabric. When the nap is brushed downwards the fabric feels smoother and has a lighter, shinier appearance. It is usual to cut napped fabrics with the nap running downwards from neck to hem.

(b) Pile fabrics

Pile fabrics such as velvet, velveteen, needlecord, corduroy, fur fabric and towelling, are woven in such a way that some of the yarn lifts at an angle from the basic cloth. When we look 'up' the pile, the fabric appears darker and richer; when we look 'down' the pile, the fabric appears lighter and shinier. The direction of the pile can be tested as for napped fabrics. Cut velvet-type fabric with the pile running upwards from hem to neck to give the richer effect. Fur fabrics and towelling are cut with the pile running downwards.

(c) Non-reversible patterns

67 *This is a simple example of a non-reversible fabric with a design which lies in one direction throughout. The pattern lay must be planned so that the design faces the same way in all parts of the garment, ie upwards to the waist line, the neck line and the top of the sleeves*

Most patterned fabric is non-reversible and the arrangement of the design can be noticed if the fabric is studied carefully (67). Very often a patterned fabric has a design of considerable depth, which is repeated along the length of the fabric. In this case select a conspicuous unit of the design and look for it in other places on the length of fabric. Almost always it will be apparent that this unit, wherever it appears, faces in the same direction. Each unit in the design will probably be found to have its own position and direction in the whole design. Decide in which direction the design looks more pleasing, and

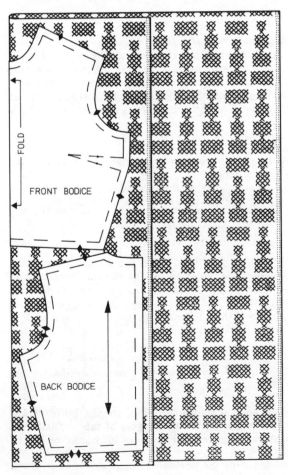

68 *The lay of the bodice pattern of a dress on one-way fabric (pins omitted). The neck lines both face the same direction. Notice the extra meterage required in comparison with the lay of the same pattern on reversible fabric where it may be dove-tailed (refer figure 66). The fabric has been refolded as suggested in figure 62, leaving a strip of single fabric alongside the bodice. This should be used for cutting some small part(s) of the garment*

69 *The printed stripes on this fabric are not reversible as a solid stripe is always to the left of a dotted stripe, and a dotted stripe is always to the left of a grained stripe. Care must be taken to keep this order throughout the garment. When laying the garment pattern, the top edge of each section must face the same direction. It would be impossible to dovetail the pattern lay on this fabric.*

cut the garment with the chosen direction of design running from top to bottom.

As all one-way fabrics are non-reversible, it is essential to cut all parts of the garment in the same direction to prevent variation of appearance throughout the garment.

A longer length of fabric is always required for cutting out on one-way cloth. An extra ¼ or ½ metre is usually needed.

The arrangement of design when using patterned fabric

Study the pattern design carefully and plan the best arrangement of it on conspicuous parts of a garment. Try to avoid centering a large design over either the bust or the back hip line. This is especially important for larger figures. Choose attractive arrangements of design in the following positions:
(a) Down the length of the garment at the centre front and the centre back lines.
(b) Down the centre of the sleeves.
(c) At the centre front of a collar.
(d) On patch pockets. Try to match these to the design in the area of the garment to which they are to be stitched.

Use the balance notches on the paper pattern to balance the design over seam lines. Refer to figures 66 and 68 and note the identical placings of notches in the seams.

The treatment of plaids

There are two types of plaid. These are shown in figures 70a and 70b.

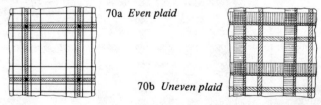

70a *Even plaid*

70b *Uneven plaid*

Even plaids must be folded so that the same colour stripes, both vertical and horizontal, come over each other on the two layers of fabrics, and with the fold in the centre of a block of pattern, or on a carefully selected line of the plaid.

Uneven plaids can be folded with the horizontal stripes over each other, but it is impossible to do this for the vertical stripes. The centre front, centre back or centre sleeve lines must come in the centre of the plaid block. Having chosen the line to use, the fabric must be folded in the centre of the selected area.

The pairing balance notches across seams, etc must be placed on the same horizontal, and if possible on the same vertical, lines of the plaid.

The treatment of stripes and checks

Care must be taken when folding the fabric to follow the principles already outlined for non-reversible patterns (68), and for plaids (70a and 70b). The balance notches for pairing seams must be set on matching areas of the stripe or check. In this way the stripes and checks will meet in the correct chevron formation at seams, and will balance across openings (71a,b,c 72 and 73).

71a *Skirt cut out correctly, but carelessly tacked. The left-hand side seam has been tacked to the right-hand centre seam*

71b *Carefully balanced stripes in the correct chevron formation*

71c *Badly matched stripes. The chevron formation is there, but the solid stripes meet the open stripes*

72 *Carefully balanced stripes matching across a bodice opening. The stripes are also balanced on the collar and on the sleeves*

73 *A check pattern balanced across a bodice opening. The check is also balanced either side of the opening, down the length of the bodice and on the sleeves*

Laying patterns for pairing sections of a garment

Pairing sections of a garment are identical parts required for left-hand and right-hand sides. They include the following:

Collar sections if a collar is divided at both back and front.

The two sections required for facing a neck either side of a neck opening.

Armhole facings

Sleeves

Sleeve edge facings

The parts divided by a long opening in a dress or blouse.

The two front side gores and the two back side gores of a gored dress or skirt.

Pockets if set evenly balanced on either side of a garment.

Pairing sections must always be kept identical in grain. The balance notches of the seams should come on the same level of design on a patterned fabric.

To achieve the required left-hand and right-hand sections, the fabric must be used in one of the following ways:

(a) Folded or laid double for the cutting-out, with either both wrong sides or both right sides touching.

(b) As a single layer and the two sections cut out separately, but with this essential precaution: lay the pattern suitably, mark the uppermost side of the paper pattern and cut out the section. When preparing to cut the second section, turn the paper pattern over and lay it with the marked side downwards on the fabric. Unless this is done, the two sections will be cut out for the same side of the body.

7 Cutting out and preparing for fitting

Cutting out

Choose a table for cutting out which is not too wide to reach across easily. A smooth, unpolished one is ideal.

Keep a special pair of scissors for cutting out so that they retain their sharpness. These should be large scissors with one broad blade and one pointed blade. One handle should be large enough to take the first and second fingers. This is the handle attached to the broad blade. The thumb goes into the handle attached to the pointed blade. The pointed blade should be slipped under the fabric, bringing the broad blade uppermost while cutting. Scissors are specially designed to be used in this way for cutting. The pointed blade lifts the fabric only very slightly off the table, and the broad blade, as it closes down, gives a firm cut (74).

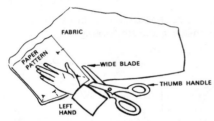

74 *This diagram shows the left hand steadying the fabric and the scissors in position for cutting. The right hand has been omitted to allow the thumb handle to be labelled*

Open the blades wide and take long, even cuts to prevent jagged edges.

If it is necessary to cut through a fold, place the broad blade inside the fold, steady the fabric with the left hand and pull the blade into the fold while cutting. This gives a clean-cut edge.

Cut the larger parts of the garment first and move round the table to reach all parts easily. Never move the fabric if it can possibly be avoided.

If the pattern includes a turning allowance which is adequate in width, cut out round the edge of the pattern, exactly reproducing the straight lines, angles and curves. Cut all the notches to give outstanding points of fabric to mark the notch positions and aid the construction of the garment. Double or triple notches can be cut in one continuous line across the points of the notches (75).

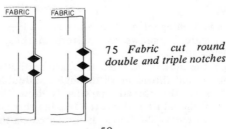

75 *Fabric cut round double and triple notches*

For heavy-weight or fraying fabric, it is necessary to widen the turning allowance to provide enough fabric for fitting and for strong seams. The extra turning width must be marked with tailor's chalk outside the cutting line of the pattern, and the garment sections cut out along the newly marked line. Take great care to reproduce all angles, curves, notches etc, so that the cut edges are accurate in shape.

Transferring pattern marks to the cut-out Garment

It is necessary to transfer the marks which guide the construction of the garment, from the pattern to the cut-out garment. Examples of these marks are fitting lines, snipping points, opening lengths etc.

This marking can be done in a variety of ways. Dressmaker's carbon paper is available, but should be used sparingly as it tends to mark the fabric indelibly. It is not wise to use it if a good standard of finish is desired. Tailor's chalk is another marking agent, but it brushes off easily, so the marks only last a short time. The clearest and most lasting marks are made with needle and thread. Use a contrasting colour from the fabric, but always use pale coloured thread on light fabric so that the thread colour will not mark the fabric.

Marking stitches

1 Thread marking

This is used when a particular line needs marking from the pattern onto a garment, eg the lines of a pleat, to ensure accurate folding.

(a) On double fabric (76a and b)

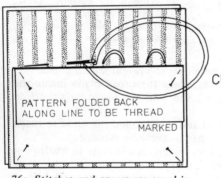

76a *Stitches and spaces are equal in length, but a loop is left at each stitch*

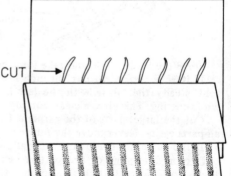

76b *Separate the two layers of fabric as far as the looped stitches will allow, and cut the threads between the layers of fabric*

The marking and folding of a pleat gives a good example of the use of thread marking. Figure 77 shows the pattern markings which need transferring to the fabric.

To thread mark the pleat, fold back the pattern first along one pleat line, then along the other, and thread mark through the double fabric close to the folded edge. When all the thread marking is done, remove the pattern, separate the layers of the fabric and cut the tacking threads.

To form the pleat, crease the fabric as indicated on the pattern, using the thread marking as a guide, and fold this line to meet the second line of thread marking. Pin and tack the pleat in place (78).

PLAN OF PLEAT ON PATTERN.

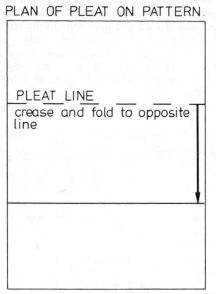

PLEAT LINE
crease and fold to opposite line

77 The plan of the pleat on the paper pattern

78 The prepared pleat

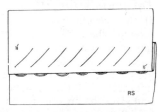

RS

(b) On single fabric
If the pattern has been cut out on single fabric, looped thread marking stitches are not required as there are no layers of fabric to separate. In this case, fold back the pattern as previously described, but mark the line with ordinary tacking stitches about 12 mm-25 mm long.

2 Tailor tacking
This is used to transfer printed guide points from a pattern to cut-out fabric, eg snipping positions, opening lengths etc.
(a) On double fabric
Thread the needle with double cotton and follow the working illustrations in figure 79.

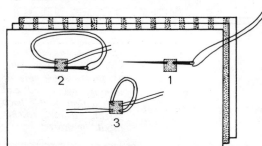

79 Making a tailor tack through printed marks on a paper pattern. 1 and 2 show the stitch in progress; 3 shows a finished tailor tack. Make the ends slightly longer than the loop

When the tailor tacking is finished throughout a pattern section, cut the loop and unpin and lift off the pattern. Separate the layers of fabric carefully so that the top layer is not pulled off the cut thread, and snip the tailor tack between the layers of fabric.

An alternative way to work the tailor tacking is to make the loop a little shorter than the cut ends of thread, and leave the loop uncut. The pattern then has to be torn off the tailor tack. The two layers of fabric can be separated as far as the loops allow, and the thread cut between the layers. This makes a firmer tack which does not slip out of the fabric as easily. If tearing the pattern is undesirable, the pattern can be folded back at the printed mark and a looped tailor tack made as just described, stitching through the double fabric close up to the printed mark on the folded edge of pattern. Leave the loop uncut and proceed as before.

(b) On single fabric
Looped stitches are not required. Transfer the mark from the pattern to the fabric by means of a back stitch 3 mm - 5 mm long .

Preparation for fitting

If the pattern has been chosen carefully for size, tested in all parts, and altered where necessary before cutting out, it is possible that very little, if any, alteration may be required afterwards. It is essential, however, that a careful fitting should be made before any final stitching is put on to the garment. This allows any adjustments to be made which could improve the appearance of the garment on the wearer and fit it to her particular figure, and gives the dressmaker confidence that her work will be satisfactory.

All tacking for fitting must be done on the fitting lines of the seams or processes. Otherwise it is not possible to test the finished size of the garment when it is being fitted. Tack the edges or parts together carefully and accurately, matching all balance points. Tack seams from their upper towards their lower points, eg armhole to waist, waist to hem, as this is the way they hang in wear.

It is not wise to make tacking stitches very long, as they must hold the fabric firmly. The more springy or slippery the fabric, the shorter the tacking stitches need to be.

Fasten on and off very firmly so that the tacking holds during the fitting. For a long line of tacking the method shown in figure 80 is a good one to use: for a short line, use the method shown in figure 81.

80 *For a long line of tacking, begin about 25 mm from the outer edge with a back stitch. Run towards the edge. Reverse the work and run beside these stitches, proceeding with tacking stitches after the first 25 mm. Fasten off the tacking as the beginning*

81 *For a short line of tacking, begin and end with a firm double back stitch. These stitches should be short*

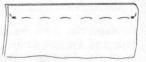

Preparing fullness for fitting
1 Gathers
Find the position of the gathers. This should be indicated by balance notches. To work the gathering, use small, even running stitches worked in matching cotton. Work one row on the fitting line to control the setting of the gathers. Work a second row 6 mm above the fitting line to control the turning of the setting. Leave about 15 cm of cotton hanging at either end of the gathering so that any necessary adjustment may be made easily after fitting (82).

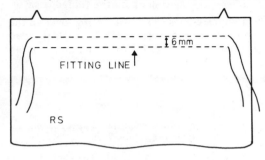

82 *Gathers prepared for fitting*

2 Tucks
A tuck is a narrow fold of material which is even in width along its length. It is stitched to hold the fullness in a decorative way.

For fitting, tack the tucks on right or wrong side, according to style required by pattern (83).

The various ways of arranging and stitching tucks are dealt with in the section on the treatment of fullness page 81.

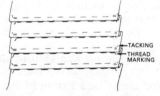

83 *Tucks tacked ready for fitting*

3 Darts
Tack all darts on the wrong side of the garment. Look up the section on dart-making on page 75.

4 Pleats
Place and pin the pleats in position. Tack them as shown in figures 77 and 78.

5 Other forms of fullness
Shirring, smocking etc must be prepared, and fixed in position, before a fitting can be made accurately.

Preparing lines for testing grain position
The following lines should be marked, as it is important to check that the fabric grain is correctly placed at these positions:
The centre front of a skirt, bodice or one-piece dress
The centre back of a skirt and bodice

The centre line of sleeves
Preparing seams for fitting
Tack seams on their fitting lines with the fabric right or wrong side out, according to the type of seam to be used.

Here is a guide for this:
Wrong side out for   Plain open seam.
Right side out for   French seam,
                           Double machine-stitched seam.

For an overlaid or lapped seam which comes at a waist setting, overlap the edges so that the fitting lines come over each other. Tack through the two fitting lines (84). For a yoke setting, tack ready for machining, as an alteration is not often required.

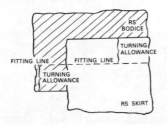

84 *An overlaid (or lapped) seam tacked ready for fitting*

The front shoulder edge is often a little shorter than the back. This ensures a smooth fit at the front and allows slight ease over the back shoulder. Pin the shoulder edges together at neck and armhole fitting points and at the seam balance point. Stretch the front evenly to fit the back, and tack along the fitting line.

Leave any openings free so that the garment may be put on easily, but mark the fitting lines of the opening clearly so that they can be pinned together accurately to show the complete seam line.

Preparing neck, armhole and sleeves for fitting
Neck and armhole fitting lines should be clearly marked so that they can be checked in fitting.

Sleeves should be prepared ready for the second fitting of the garment. Mark the sleeve crown fitting lines and the crown balance points. On long, fitted sleeves, the elbow darts should be marked and tacked. Lastly, tack the sleeve seams.

8 Fitting

The fitting of the prepared garment is one of the most important parts of dressmaking. No final machining should be done until the garment has been fitted in front of a mirror and, if possible, with the help and advice of another person. Occasionally no alteration is required; sometimes a major alteration proves to be necessary; more often than not some slight adjustments are needed to give a better appearance to the garment, and lift it from the 'home-made' to the 'hand-cut' class. Even if it is difficult to arrange for a fitting, the difficulty must be overcome and this vital stage of dressmaking attended to.

Preparation for fitting
1 Wear a bra for fittings above the waist as it gives support to the figure and a foundation for fitting the garment.
2 An underslip is helpful for all dress fittings as it enables the dress to hang smoothly.
3 Wear shoes of a suitable type for the dress or skirt, as the height of the heel affects the hip line.
4 When shoulder pads are used in fashion garments, they should be used in the fitting, as they give form to the shoulder line and, therefore, affect the hang of the garment.

To fit a garment
Be very careful not to overfit the garment. Consider the fullness in the style and do not mistake it for surplus material to be fitted away. Remember, too, that there must be some ease on all round body measurements.

Taking in a seam or letting out a seam in one section usually necessitates one or more alterations in another section of the garment eg lifting a shoulder seam will raise the underarm fitting point of the side seam and also raise the neck line. This will probably necessitate altering the armhole and the neck fitting lines.

Always inspect and alter the garment from the shoulders down towards the hem line.

Fit the garment carefully on the right-hand side. Only pin the left-hand side to keep the balance even.

For a first fitting it is not necessary to have the sleeve tacked in place. Before any alterations are pinned, a general observation should be made. Study the fit of the whole garment first, and then proceed with the fitting in the following order:

1 Fitting shoulder seams
Fit these so that the fabric grains of the bodice run straight down the centre

65

front and the centre back, and across the back width and the chest width lines (85). The shoulder lines themselves should lie smoothly without wrinkles. If there is a shoulder pad, decide whether it is too thick or too thin before altering the seam line. Notice the position of the back and chest width lines.

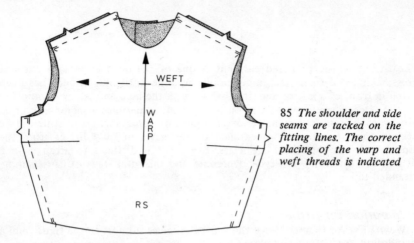

85 *The shoulder and side seams are tacked on the fitting lines. The correct placing of the warp and weft threads is indicated*

If the bodice is loose with the bust-line too low, re-pin the shoulder line, making a wider turning allowance and thereby lifting the shoulder. This will place garment bust-line in its right position on the body.

If it is necessary to adjust the shoulder seam it may need to be lifted more at the armhole edge than at the neck edge if the wearer has very sloping shoulders or is fat across the back of the neck (86). This alteration changes the size of the armhole and neck, and necessitates another fitting for these fitting lines to be corrected.

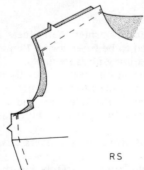

86 *A shoulder seam line fitted to suit a sloping shoulder*

2 Fitting the bust-line

Examine the position of the bust-line of the garment. It should lie over the bust line of the body.

All bodice darts should point towards the bust, and the fullness they provide should give well-placed accommodation for the curve of the bust.

If the fit is not satisfactory the adjustment usually has to be made at the shoulder and/or the underarm seams. It may be necessary sometimes to lengthen darts a little, but the point of a dart should never come right to the bust point as the cup-like shaping provided by a dart comes just beyond its point (87).

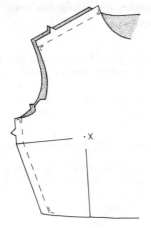

87 *Both the underarm and the waist dart point towards the bust point, which is shown here as X*

If the line of the underarm is too low, try lifting the shoulder seam to raise the dart. This will also raise the bust line and the waist line and may necessitate re-shaping, probably lowering the waist fitting point at the side seam. Alternatively, if the line of the underarm dart is too high, try lowering the shoulder seam and readjust the side seam as necessary. If the underarm dart appears too short, lengthen it. To shorten or lengthen a dart, refer to page 71 figures 100 and 101.

For a prominent bust line, the underarm dart may need reslanting. This is a very frequent alteration. Keep the original position at the side seam, but raise the point of the dart to suit the bust line, making it come about 25 mm short of the bust point. Conversely, a low bust line may need the point of the dart lowered.

3 Fitting underarm seams

These should hang smoothly and straight and without any strain. They should stand away from the body slightly at the underarm point if a sleeve is being

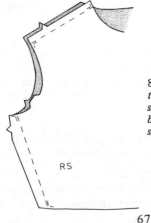

88 *This side seam has been altered to fit a very flat bust line. The size of the armhole has obviously been reduced, which will necessitate further fitting*

set. The fit at the underarm point should be fairly tight for a sleeveless dress.

If there is a dart coming into the underarm seam, see that it points towards the bust line.

A person with a slight bust measurement may need this seam line almost straight from waist to underarm point (88).

4 Fitting the waist line

The position of the waist line will depend on fashion and the style of the garment. It is usually over the body waist line, but is raised or lowered on occasions as a fashion feature.

Wherever it is set, the waist line must appear to lie in an even line round the garment. It should fit easily, not tightly, or the bodice will pucker and show signs of strain over the ribs.

(a) Fitting a dress with a waist seam.

At the first fitting, the measurement round the waist line should be checked and altered if necessary. Also mark a new waist line if the original one is either too high or too low. The dress should be 50 mm - 75 mm bigger round than the body waist size if the style is a fitted one. This prevents strain and allows comfortable movement of the arms in wear.

(b) Fitting a one-piece dress

If the waist line is shaped, notice whether the waist shaping suits the figure. Re-shape the side seam line if necessary, working on the principles illustrated in figures 89, 90 and 91.

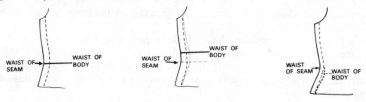

89 *The waist shaping of the side seam as set by the pattern*

90 *The waist shaping of the seam has been raised as the body waist-line is above the waist-line of the pattern*

91 *The waist shaping of the seam has been lowered as the body waist line came below the waist line of the pattern*

(c) Fitting a skirt

The waist line should fit fairly tightly, but not so tightly that puckers appear across the skirt just under the waist line (92). The skirt waist line should be about 12 mm - 25 mm bigger than the body measurement. This allows the skirt to be slightly eased into the band, petersham or facing, and prevents straining.

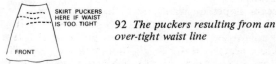

92 *The puckers resulting from an over-tight waist line*

The waist should be reduced or enlarged at seams and/or darts. A dart made 3 mm wider at the top, reduces the waist line by 6 mm. Never alter one dart only, as darts are always paired. If you decide to reduce or increase a skirt waist line at the back dart positions, alter both darts, sharing between them the desired amount for alteration (93).

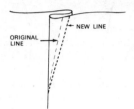

93 *This figure shows a dart made wider in a waist reduction alteration. The pairing dart will require an identical alteration*

It is essential that the waist line alterations are evenly balanced, so that the centre front and centre back lines remain in their true positions, eg Figure 94 shows a skirt with four seams ie side, centre front and centre back seams, and a dart either side of the centre back seam. If a large amount has to be removed take in each seam and each dart a little. If only a small amount, eg 12 mm, needs to be removed, take in each dart 3 mm *or* each side seam *or* each centre seam, according to which will give the best appearance. An enlargement should be balanced in the same way.

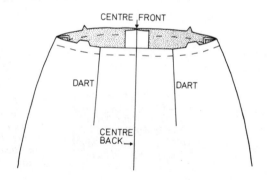

94 *A skirt waist with six possible alteration points*

5 Fitting the hip line
(a) Fitted skirts
The side-seam slopes outwards from the waist to provide width for the hip line. The skirt should appear to fit fairly tightly at the hip, but should be 75 mm - 100 mm bigger round than the body. This prevents sagging at the back and wrinkling across the front. If the hip line is too tight, the skirt will be unsatisfactory in wear (95 and 96): if it is too loose, the attractive line of the skirt will be lost. If the hip line is too tight, let out the side seams (97a): if it is too loose, straighten the curve of the side seam (97b).

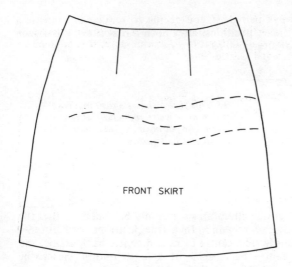

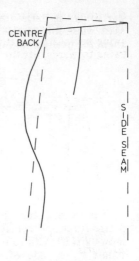

95 *If it is too tight round the hip line, a skirt will crease across the front in the position shown here*

96 *At the centre back, a skirt will sag after sitting if the hip line is too tight. It will also drop at the centre back waist line. The dart, too, will be pulled out of alignment*

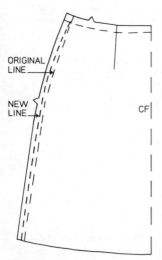

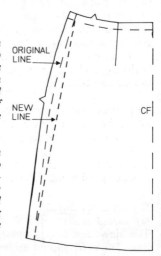

97a *The seam has been let out to enlarge the hip line. The waist remains the same size, but the hem width has been increased to keep the balance of the seam line below the hip*

97b *The seam has been taken in to reduce the hip line. In this case an alteration was not necessary at the waist. The altered hip line is smoothed along to the original hem line*

(b) Full skirts

When easy-fitting or loose skirts are fashionable, they may be shaped by gathering, pleating or by a wide flare shaping. When fitting, check that the fullness falls in soft folds over the hip line. The fullness must be smoothly distributed at the waist and flow evenly from the waist setting.

6 Fitting the side seams of a skirt

These should hang straight from the waist to hem. If the side seam appears to swing backward, lift the front waist a little (98). Alternatively, if it appears to swing forwards, lift the back waist a little (99).

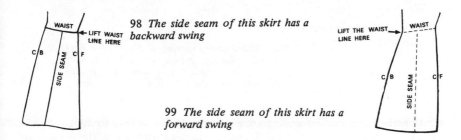

98 *The side seam of this skirt has a backward swing*

99 *The side seam of this skirt has a forward swing*

7 Fitting fullness
(a) Darts

Any dart should provide adequate shaping for the body curve it is accommodating. Most darts have a straight fold line set along a straight grain of fabric, and a straight stitching line which slopes to meet the folded edge of the dart at a point. Occasionally a long, curved dart is provided to give a special fitting to a body curve.

Bodice darts all provide room for the bust curve. They should point towards the bust points. Skirt darts provide room for the hip curve. They should point towards the widest curve of the hip. The pointed end of the dart should approach, but never quite reach, the extreme curve of the bust or hip.

Darts are the flattest form of fullness provision. Therefore the dart itself should lie flat to the body and not stand away from the body at the pointed end. If it does stand away from the body here, it may mean that it has been tacked inaccurately in a curved line. this must be corrected. It may mean that the dart is too long. In that case it must be shortened.

If the point of the dart does not come near enough to the extreme curve it is fitting, and the garment seems too loose over the bust or hip line, lengthen the dart a little.

To shorten and lengthen darts

To shorten a dart, measure the required length down the fold of the dart and reshape from this point to the original width (100).

To lengthen a dart, measure the required length along the fold of the dart, and continue in line for the required length. Reshape the dart from this point to its original width (101).

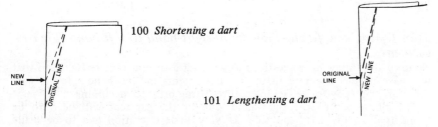

100 *Shortening a dart*

101 *Lengthening a dart*

(b) Gathers

Gathered fullness should drape softly and fall in a suitable position on the body. It should not appear to bunch inwards, or fall outwards, neither should the bust nor hip line strain the fullness. If it appears to give a better appearance, move the gathers a little to the left and/or the right as required (102).

102 *Gathers prepared for setting into the shoulder yoke of a smock. Both ends of each thread have been left free to allow for a fitting adjustment if necessary*

If gathers are worked as suggested in figure 102, it is easy to unpick or add a few stitches at one or both ends, eg to move gathers nearer the neck edge, just add more stitching at this end of the gathering. Unpick a few of the stitches at the armhole end if a flatter finish appears better here.

(c) Pleats

Soft pleats should fall in even folds down their whole length. Pressed pleats should hang straight and unstrained over bust and hip lines. If they do not, it may be necessary to make them a little narrower in width. The alteration should be evenly distributed across back, or across front, or all round garment.

(d) Tucks

Tucks should be placed in an attractive and suitable position on the body, and the slight fullness they provide should be even in arrangement. Unless the worker is prepared to spend time in preparing and making the tucks accurately, it is better to use some other form of fullness reduction.

Tucks are usually set in groups. These groups may always be reset if a better appearance is thus obtained.

(e) Smocking

Before preparing smocking corrugations on an older person's garment it is wise to run a gathering thread on the fitting line above the suggested smocking area, and try on the garment to see if the fullness falls in a desirable position. Remember that the fullness will be more controlled after the smocking is worked.

If it would suit the figure better to adjust the placing of the block of smocking, this is better done before tacking out the corrugations. It can also be seen what depth of smocking would suit the style of the garment for the individual wearer.

Transferring new fitting-lines from right-hand to left-hand side of garment

None of the following suggestions apply to a disproportionate figure, as that will have needed accurate fitting on both right- and left-hand sides. It will, therefore, be ready for re-tacking and re-fitting prior to machining.

All alterations to the right-hand side of the garment will need to be transferred to the left-hand side. If very little alteration had to be made

(103), the garment may be placed flat on a table and the new line pinned on the left-hand side, copying it accurately by measurement from the right-hand side. Place bodice flat on a table. Measure distance from original underarm point to the new seam position there, and measure the distance up from waist edge where the new line joins the original line. Pin alteration line on left-hand side.to correspond with right-hand side. Tack both new side-seam fitting lines and the bodice is ready for machining.

If much alteration had to be made, the line marked by pins in fitting must be thread marked and clipped apart. The garment must then be folded and pinned so that the altered right-hand edge comes over the corresponding left-hand edge, and the alteration line thread marked again (104). This will transfer it accurately to the left-hand side.

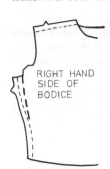

RIGHT HAND
SIDE OF
BODICE

103 *The side seams of this bodice have been straightened in fitting. No other alteration was required in this case, therefore the alteration can be transferred by measurement to the left-hand side*

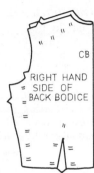

CB

RIGHT HAND
SIDE OF
BACK BODICE

104 *A back bodice folded in half down the centre back, showing thread marks taken from pinned alteration lines at shoulder and at underarm seams and at dart. The corresponding thread marks to those shown on the seam edges here are on the right-hand front bodice. Thread mark again along these alteration lines to transfer the new fitting lines of the shoulder, the side seam and the dart to the left-hand side of the back bodice. The marks must also be transferred to the left-hand side of the front bodice in a similar way*

All altered lines must be tacked together so that re-fitting is possible if necessary and, later, to act as a guide for the machining. Slight alterations need not be re-fitted, but alterations which have necessitated thread marking should be re-fitted to ensure satisfaction before machining.

The second fitting
When the alterations and final stitching following the first fitting have been dealt with, the second fitting should be made. At this stage the neck and armhole fitting lines should be checked and newly marked if necessary.

(a) Setting a new neck fitting line
Pin a line in the desired position from the centre back to the centre front, round the right-hand side of the neck. Check the new height of the neck at the centre points, and make sure that the line travels smoothly over the shoulder seam.

(b) Setting a new armhole fitting line
Work on the right-hand armhole.
1 Set a pin on the shoulder line. Check the shoulder length measurement

from the final neck point to the newly set pin and adjust, if necessary, to get the shoulder length correct.

2 Set pins at the chest width and back width points of the armhole and check to ensure that they are accurately set.

3 Set a fourth pin at the required underarm position.

4 Pin round between these four pins to give a smooth line to the new armhole.

If the figure is in proportion, this new line can be transferred to the left-hand armhole. If the figure is unequal in balance, make a similar alteration to the left-hand armhole.

Transferring new neck and armhole lines

Fold the bodice in half so that it is folded straight along the centre back and front lines, bringing shoulder and side seams over each other, with wrong sides touching. This places one armhole inside the other, and the neck line is folded getween the centre back and the centre front. Work with the alteration pins on the outside.

The shoulder and underarm seams should also be pinned together. Now set the alteration pins through both layers of fabric (105). Thread-mark along these pinned alteration lines. Remove all the pins. Separate and clip the thread-marking stitches and open out the bodice.

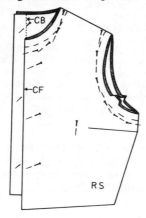

105 *A bodice pinned in half from the centre front. In this case a new neck line has been pinned, raising the line at the shoulder and lowering it at the centre front. There is also a new armhole line, raised at the shoulder, to keep the shoulder line accurate in length, and lowered at the underarm. The original neck and armhole lines can be seen*

Fitting sleeves

This is dealt with in the section on sleeves, page 252, as some guidance on sleeve construction is required before sleeves can be fitted satisfactorily.

9 The treatment of fullness

Darts
When a dart is stitched and pressed, the fabric no longer lies flat on the table, but takes on a curved shape. This type of shaping is useful in dressmaking, and a dart can be used to fold away excess fabric which is required for fitting a prominent area of the body, eg the bust, but which would give a surplus width in a nearby, flatter area, eg at the side seam. Darts, therefore, are useful in the following places:

(a) In a front bodice for fitting the bust line (106), and in a back bodice for fitting the shoulder or back neck area (107).

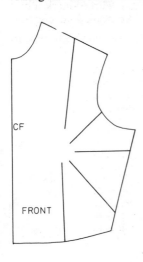

106 The bust can be fitted by making a dart in ONE of the positions shown. If a tight-fitting bodice is required, the dart from the waist can be used along with a shoulder, armhole or high underarm dart

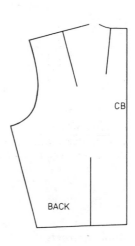

107 The back shoulder area is fitted by a dart in ONE of the positions shown. A neck dart is used for a back with a rounded, fat neck line: a shoulder dart is used to fit a back with prominent shoulder blades. A back waist dart can be used with either a neck or a shoulder dart if a tight-fitting bodice is required

(b) In a long, tight sleeve for fitting the elbow (108).

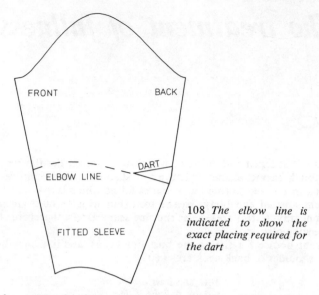

108 *The elbow line is indicated to show the exact placing required for the dart*

(c) In a front skirt for fitting over the tummy line (109), and in a back skirt for fitting over the hip line (110).

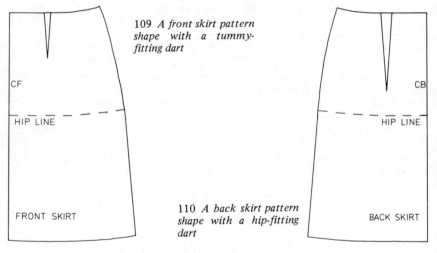

109 *A front skirt pattern shape with a tummy-fitting dart*

110 *A back skirt pattern shape with a hip-fitting dart*

Making darts

A dart shape is marked on a bought pattern by printed lines forming a cone. The point is set inside the pattern: the wide end comes at the outer edge of the pattern and runs into the turning allowance.

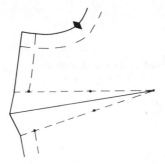

111 *The appearance of a*
dart on a printed pattern

The printed balance spots are transferred to the cut out garment with tailor tacks. When the tailor tacking is finished, the dart is folded in half longways and pinned and tacked ready for machining. The tacking should be worked from the raw edge, through the tailor tacks to the point (112). The tailor tacks should be removed before machining the dart.

SEAM FITTING LINE

WS

112 *A dart tacked ready*
for machining

Use as short a machine stitch as is suitable for the fabric. This sews as much thread as possible into the dart, giving flexibility and preventing the dart from puckering. Work the machine stitching from the wide end towards the point. Stitch slowly so that the work is under control and a good line is stitched, as it is important for the dart to give a smooth fit to the garment.

To fasten off the machine stitching, leave at least 100 mm of cotton at the beginning and end of the dart. At the open end fasten off the cotton by tying three firm knots. At this end the dart is fixed later into a seam, waist band or neck finish, and is finally neatened then.

At the point, bring both threads to the underside of the dart. Thread them into a needle and whip over the last 12 mm of machine stitching (113). Sometimes the machining is reversed for the last 12 mm, but this is not advisable as it tends to cause puckering at the point of the dart.

WS

113 *The machined point*
of a dart with the thread
ends whipped over the
last five stitches

Very firmly woven fabric does not always press smoothly round the point of a dart unless the machine stitching is specially shaped in this area. Stitch as usual to within 25 mm of the point, then guide the machining gently towards the fold so that the last four or five stitches come closely alongside the folded edge (114). Fasten off in the usual way.

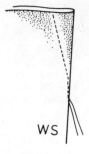

114 *A dart with a finely tapered point to facilitate smooth pressing on difficult fabric*

WS

The shape of the dart stitching line

The basic shape of a dart stitching line is straight from point to wide end. This shape presents no problems in stitching and pressing. Some darts, for reason of position and/or shaping, require special attention in making. The following information gives some guidance for handling various types of dart:

(a) Double-pointed or fish darts

When a one-piece dress pattern is made, the pattern incorporates the bodice and skirt into one front section and one back section. In this case the bodice and skirt have to be joined together, and a long, double-pointed dart results, which cuts across the waist line. This is sometimes called a fish dart (115a and b). This type of dart is usually longer below the waist line than it is above.

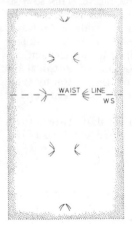

115a *A double-pointed dart, tailor-tacked across the waist line. The widest part comes at the waist line*

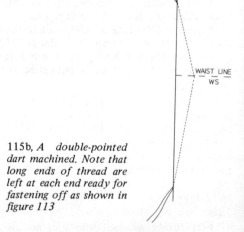

115b, *A double-pointed dart machined. Note that long ends of thread are left at each end ready for fastening off as shown in figure 113*

As the greatest width of a double-pointed dart comes within its length, ie at the waist line, it is impossible to press it flat without snipping it at its widest point (116a and b). If the fabric is inclined to fray, the snipped edges must be overcast or loop stitched.

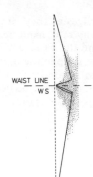

116a *A double-pointed dart snipped at the waist line. Note that the snip comes very close to the machining*

116b *An enlarger diagram of the waist line neatened with loop stitching*

Some fabric may be too firm to lie flat even when it is snipped at the waist line. In this case the fold of the dart must be trimmed away parallel to the machining, to leave a turning of 10 mm, and then slit through the fold to within 25 mm - 30 mm of the point. The dart will now press open and lie flat (117). The raw edges must be overcast if the fabric tends to fray.

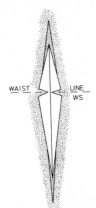

117 *A double-pointed dart cut and pressed open*

(b) Curved darts

A fitted bodice may require a curved or contour dart to give shaping between the bust and the waist, and follow the rather hollow line of the body in this area. This is specially the case for a prominent bust line. A curved dart will not press flat unless it is trimmed. Cut away the dart as shown in figure 117, leaving a turning of 6 mm - 10 mm according to the stretchability of the fabric. Overcast the cut edges together.

(c) Long darts

These are sometimes called french darts, and are used for bust shaping, usually on straight, one-piece dresses. They run towards the bust point from either the waist or the hip line, according to style and fashion. Very often the stitching line of the dart is curved. Long darts are wide at the seam end, and must be trimmed after stitching so that they can be pressed open flat nearly to the point on the same principle as shown in figure 117. Hand overcasting

79

may be the best method of neatening the trimmed edges as they run across the fabric grain and, therefore, are very stretchy. At any rate, hand neatening is essential near the point on account of the shaping and the narrow width.

On thin, fraying fabrics it may be better not to press open the dart. Trim away the dart, leaving a turning of 10 mm - 12 mm beyond the stitching, stopping when the fold is reached. The double raw edge should be neatened together by zigzagging or overcasting. Press the turnings upwards (118).

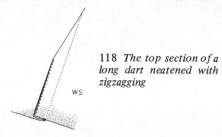

118 *The top section of a long dart neatened with zigzagging*

(d) Darts on transparent fabric

A wide dart, showing through transparent fabric, looks unattractive. In this case the dart is better made as a narrow french seam. The method of work is shown in figures 119a and b. Refer also to the seam section, page 104.

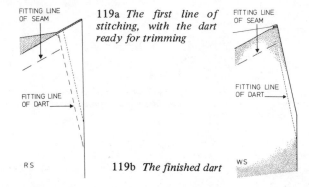

119a *The first line of stitching, with the dart ready for trimming*

119b *The finished dart*

(e) Sleeve crown darts

These are only used when square sleeve crowns are fashionable. They are very short darts, usually only 25 mm in length from the fitting line. Their shortness and position make the shaping very accentuated, and they require careful pressing over a pad.

Pressing darts

All darts should be pressed after stitching to smooth the line of machining and to flatten the fold. Do not press beyond the point of the dart or the fabric will be creased.

Before setting the dart into the seam, etc, it must be pressed flat onto the garment, ie either upwards or downwards according to position. The outline shape of the pattern edge across the width of the dart determines which way the dart is meant to be pressed, and this direction should be followed. To ensure which way to press the dart, study the edge of the fabric at the width end of the stitched dart. Try folding the dart both upwards and downwards, and notice which way it sets in line with the edge of the garment (120a and b).

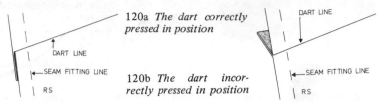

120a *The dart correctly pressed in position*

120b *The dart incorrectly pressed in position*

If there is any doubt, press according to the following guide:
Press waist, shoulder, neck and sleeve crown darts inwards towards the centre line nearest the dart.
Press underarm darts downwards towards the waist so that they cause no bulkiness near the armhole seam. If, however, they are narrow, they are better pressed upwards as they are less conspicuous that way.
Press armhole darts upwards.
Press elbow darts downwards.

When pressing check that the dart is flat on both the right side and the wrong side. On the right side it should be creased back sharply along the line of stitching.

A pressing pad is useful for pressing darts, as it allows them to follow their natural contour, and facilitates the smooth pressing of the fabric round the point.

Tucks

A tuck is a narrow fold of fabric machined parallel to the fold along its whole length. In dressmaking the width of tucks varies from pin-tucks, which are about two threads wide, to any width required according to fashion.

They can be worked straight with the warp, straight with the weft, or sloping across the fabric grain. In any case the fold of the tuck should be straight in itself, and the line of stitching parallel to the fold (121). Fasten off the machine threads on the side of the tuck which will be pressed downwards onto the garment.

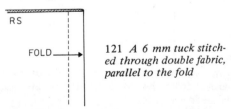

121 *A 6 mm tuck stitched through double fabric, parallel to the fold*

As tucks are always pressed flat, the double fold of the tuck, therefore, needs its own width to lie on, so that the total amount of fabric used in a tuck is 3X its finished width. Therefore a 6 mm tuck uses up 18 mm of fabric.

Tucks may be placed so that the fold of one tuck lies along the line of stitching of the previous tuck (122a). In this case the spacing of the tucks is measured as shown in figure 122b.

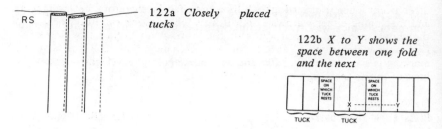

122a *Closely placed tucks*

122b *X to Y shows the space between one fold and the next*

When machining, work on the upper side of the tuck. This brings the better side of the stitching to the top. The stitching must be done with great care and precision. Inaccuracy spoils the finished appearance. The beauty of tucking lies in the evenness and straightness of the folding and stitching.

Sometimes tucks are placed a little way apart (123a). In this case the width between the lines of stitching equals twice or three times the width of the finished tuck, according to the spacing desired (123b).

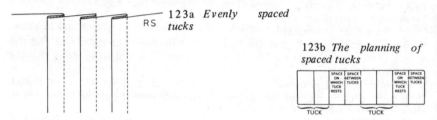

123a *Evenly spaced tucks*

123b *The planning of spaced tucks*

Tucks are rarely worked singly. They are usually worked in a group or in spaced groups of two or more. Tucks of this type are most often used as a decorative way of taking in fullness or, in the case of children's clothes, to provide extra fabric which can be let out later to allow for growth.

Pin tucks

These are so named because they are no wider than a pin. They may be used only on very thin fabric, eg nylon organza, nylon chiffon, fine lawn etc, and are purely decorative, being too narrow to provide fullness. Fold the fabric along the line of the tuck and tack it in place. Machine or run by hand as close to the fold as possible (124).

124 *A pin tuck*

Inverted tucks

These are folded and stitched on the wrong side of a garment, so that the tuck itself is not visible from the outside, but appears as a stitched line from which the fullness falls in a soft fold.

Very attractive tucks can be stitched on modern sewing machines. Directions for working these will be found in the machine manual, giving details for the particular make of machine concerned.

Checking tuck guide lines

When making a tucked garment from a bought pattern, the guide lines for the tucking should be thread marked onto the garment fabric. Slight inaccuracies often occur when transferring tuck lines onto fabric, therefore, before tacking and machining either warpway or weftway tucks, check carefully to see that the thread marking is accurate with the fabric grain. Adjust it if necessary. For tucks which slope across the fabric grain, check that each line of thread marking is straight in itself. For all tucks check for equal spacing between the lines of thread marking.

Pressing tucks
Press each tuck along the line of stitching on the under side of the fold, taking care not to stretch the fabric. Then press the tucks to one side so that the fold lies away from the centre line of the garment. If necessary, use a pressing muslin to protect the right side of the fabric and to prevent shining. Do not press short tucks beyond the line of machining.

If the fold of a tuck impresses the underlay of fabric, slip a strip of clean paper under each tuck as it is pressed flat.

Pleats
Pleats are a means of arranging fullness to give style to a garment and to allow freedom of movement in wear. Pleats may be pressed or unpressed according to the type of fabric and style of the garment. Pressed pleats should hang straight, with sharp edges, and require firm, heavy, fairly smooth fabric. A heavily textured fabric is unsuitable as it distorts the edge of the pleat and breaks the line of the sharply creased fold. Unpressed pleats look their best on soft fabric with a good draping quality.

Pleats formed on checked or striped fabric should be carefully planned in width to balance with the arrangement of the checks or stripes, so that an orderly appearance results. Haphazard pleating on such fabric is unbecoming, but attractive arrangements are possible with thoughtful preparation.

A smart appearance is obtained only if sufficient fabric is allowed to make suitably deep pleats. A garment with much pleating can be an expensive one in yardage of fabric.

It is necessary to fit pleated garments fairly easily so that the pleats are not pulled open in wear. A pattern for a pleated skirt should be bought by the hip measurement, so that the fit is correct at the widest part. It is wiser to adjust for fit at the waist-line, and avoid alteration at the hip line.

The outer and inner folds of pleats may be edge-stitched by machine to sharpen the fold and facilitate pressing, especially after laundering. It is unwise to introduce much pleating into a garment which will be frequently washed as, even if edge stitched, pleats take time to press to perfection. Heat-set, permanent pleating, done commercially, does away with this problem. Certain synthetic fabrics can be permanently pleated with a hot iron.

Most pleats are planned to hang with the warp grain, as this ensures their straightness and gives a good line to the pressed edge of the pleat. Sometimes, however, a pleat is shaped to be wider at its lower edge than at the top. In this case, the outer fold of the pleat will run slantwise across the grain. Such a style is suitable only for firm fabric, otherwise the edges of the pleats will stretch and drop in wear.

The pleat lines must be marked out accurately from the pattern after cutting out, see page 61. When the pattern is removed, check that the pleat lines are straight with the fabric grain, or straight in themselves if they slope across the grain. Adjust the lines if necessary.

It is helpful to tack out the pleat lines in different coloured threads. Use one colour for the fold line (usually a solid line on the pattern), and a second colour for the placing line (usually printed as a broken line on the pattern).

Types of pleating
The following describes and illustrates the three basic pleat formations. In each figure the direction of the warp grain is shown by a solid arrow and the balance of the weft grain across the pleat is shown by a dotted arrow.

(a) Knife pleats
Knife pleats form the simplest form of pleating. The pleats are equal in width and all the folded edges face in the same direction. It is usual for the pleats to meet and form a continuous line round the garment (125). Sometimes, however, they are arranged in groups, divided by plain panels of fabric.

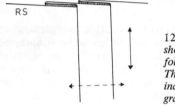

125 *Two knife pleats showing their similar folding and close placing. The dotted arrowed line indicates the aligned weft grain*

(b) Inverted pleats
An inverted pleat is formed by folding two equal width knife pleats to face each other (126).

(c) Box pleats
A box pleat is formed by the reverse formation of an inverted pleat, and consists of two equal width knife pleats folded away from each other (127).

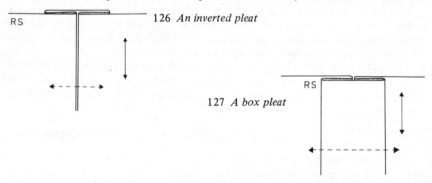

126 *An inverted pleat*

127 *A box pleat*

Preparing and tacking pleats
Pleats must be prepared and folded with the garment placed right side up and flat on the table. For this reason it is best to prepare pleats section by section, or to leave one seam unstitched so that the fabric can be kept flat for preparing and handling the pleats (128).

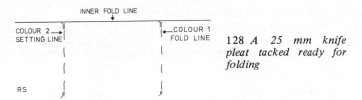

INNER FOLD LINE

COLOUR 2 →
SETTING LINE

COLOUR 1
FOLD LINE

RS

128 *A 25 mm knife pleat tacked ready for folding*

Fold and pin the fabric along the fold line. Set the pins slant-wise, as this keeps the folded edges smoother. Check that the fold is straight with the warp grain. Tack through the double layer of fabric about 5 mm-10 mm in from the fold, according to the thickness of the fabric.

Bring the tacked fold to lie along the placing line, and pin it in position. Check that the weft grain is kept even across the pleat and the single fabric as the pinning proceeds, and that any checks are accurately aligned (125). Cross tack the pleat in position (129).

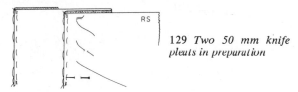

RS

129 *Two 50 mm knife pleats in preparation*

The stitching of pleats

Knife pleats arranged in groups, inverted pleats and box pleats are often placed in skirts to give styled extra width at the hem line. Sometimes the pleats are arranged throughout the full length of the skirt, but are stitched for part of their length to give a flat fitting over the waist to hip line. This stitching can be machined on the right side, but may be worked on the wrong side if preferred. In either case the machine thread ends must be fastened off securely.

1 The right side stitching of pleats
(a) Knife and box pleats
On light-weight fabric, machine close to the folded edges for each type of pleat (130a). On heavier-weight fabric, machine 5 mm - 6 mm inside the folded edges. At this spacing the machine-stitching needs pointing off at the lower edge (130b).

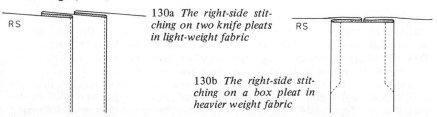

RS

130a *The right-side stitching on two knife pleats in light-weight fabric*

RS

130b *The right-side stitching on a box pleat in heavier weight fabric*

(b) Inverted pleats
Machine 3 mm or 6 mm either side of the centre line, according to the weight of the fabric. The turning point may be rounded (131), squared or pointed.

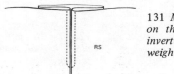

131 *Machine stitching on the right side of an inverted pleat in light-weight fabric*

(c) Strengthening the end of the right side stitching
Some form of strengthening is necessary at the end of the machine stitching to prevent the fabric from tearing away at this point. There are three possible methods:

(i) A fabric stay
Cut a 40 mm square of firm lining fabric. Tack it to the wrong side where the stitching will end or turn, so that it is machined onto the wrong side of the garment to support the end of the pleat stitching (132). Trim the square, and overcast the edges if inclined to fray.

132 *A wrong side stay behind an inverted pleat*

(ii) A tailor's bar tack
A tailor's bar tack is a useful method of strengthening when an inconspicuous result is desired. It is most often used on light or medium weight fabric. Study figures 133a and b in which the stitches have been enlarged for clarity. Use the machine thread, and work four strands 6 mm long over the edge of the pleat just at the base of the machine stitching. These strands should be very close together. Using the eye end of the needle, whip over the strands, but do not stitch into the fabric.

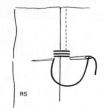

133a *Stranding a tailor's bar tack*

133b *Whipping the strands*

(iii) Arrow heads
When fashionable, arrow heads are often used at the base of the stitching on an inverted pleat in garments of thick fabric. They must be evenly worked as they are conspicuous, forming a decorative strengthening to the pleat. Use buttonhole twist of a matching colour to work the arrowhead.

Tack out the shape of the arrow head: the sides usually measure approximately 10 mm. Run in the thread at the beginning as shown in the first stage of figure 134, and then work from the set of diagrams, following the in and out position of the needle for each stitch. Stab the needle through the fabric from the right side to the wrong side at the right-hand position, and from the wrong side to the right side at the left-hand position.

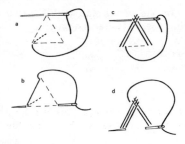

THE FINISHED
ARROWHEAD

134 *The stages in work-ing an arrow-head*

2 The wrong side stitching of pleats

The lines for the machine stitching must be tacked for the length required. Before machining, open out the fabric with the right side uppermost, and check that the tacking has been set straight with the warp grain, and that the weft grain runs smoothly across the tacked area. If the fabric lacks firmness, a small square of lining fabric can be set at the base of the stitching line, so that the last 25 mm of machine stitching, and the fastening off, come in the reinforced area.

(a) Knife pleats

Fold the fabric wrong side out, bringing together the fold and setting lines of the pleat. Pin, tack and machine along the tacked line. Remove the tackings and press the stitched line (135). When the fabric is folded back to reveal the right side, the machine stitching will be hidden (136).

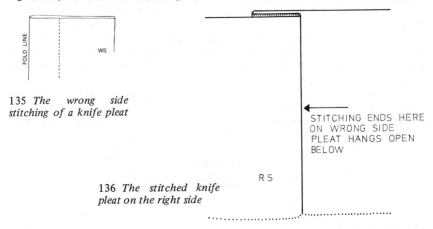

135 *The wrong side stitching of a knife pleat*

STITCHING ENDS HERE ON WRONG SIDE PLEAT HANGS OPEN BELOW

136 *The stitched knife pleat on the right side*

(b) Box pleats

Each box pleat is stitched as two separate knife pleats on the wrong side. The stitched knife pleats are then folded inwards towards each other, and the box pleat is formed with the stitching invisible on the right side.

(c) Inverted pleats

Fold the fabric wrong side out, bringing together the two fold lines of the pleat. The temporary fold thus formed, comes along the setting line. Pin, tack and machine together the two fold lines. Remove the tacking and press the stitched line (137). Open out the fabric to reveal the right side, and flatten the stitched line over the setting line (138). On the wrong side, tack the two folded edges of the pleat onto the skirt, keeping the weft grains aligned.

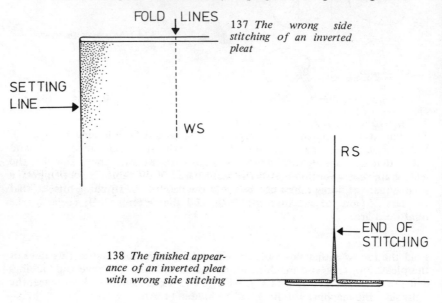

FOLD LINES

SETTING LINE

WS

RS

137 *The wrong side stitching of an inverted pleat*

END OF STITCHING

138 *The finished appearance of an inverted pleat with wrong side stitching*

Pleats formed over seams (139, 140 and 141)

It is sometimes more economical in cutting out to plan for a seam to come within a pleat, but it should be hidden from view when the garment is being worn.

The tension of the machine stitching used for making and neatening the seam must be carefully adjusted so that it is sufficiently loose to prevent any possibility of puckering. Neaten the raw edges of the seam turnings with either machine zigzagging or by hand overcasting.

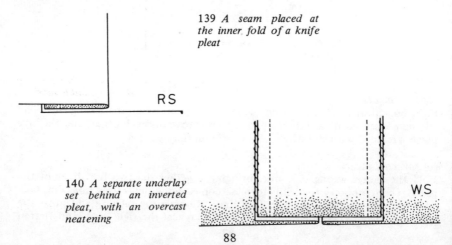

139 *A seam placed at the inner fold of a knife pleat*

RS

140 *A separate underlay set behind an inverted pleat, with an overcast neatening*

WS

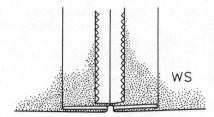

141 *An inverted pleat folded to meet over a seam. Machine zigzagging used to neaten the turnings*

It is not possible to place a seam as satisfactorily in a box pleat. If it is necessary to have a seam, it is best to put it into the garment lay under one side of the box pleat, so that it is not set within the pleat itself where, in any position, it would give unwanted bulk.

Pleats set below a seam

1 A shaped pleat below a seam

Figure 142 shows a front skirt pattern with centre front and side front panels forming a shaped pleat at the lower end of a seam. A section of the pleat is included in the pattern of each panel. The back, or underlay, of the pleat has a separate pattern piece. The seam is made from the waist edge as far as the solid spot, along the one-notched edge.

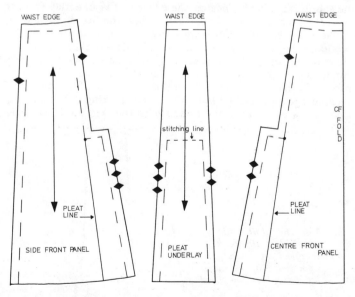

142 *The front pattern of a skirt with a shaped pleat below a seam*

Machine and press open the seam. This brings the two pleat sections into position on the wrong side of the skirt. The two folds are tacked below the seam and pressed lightly (143).

89

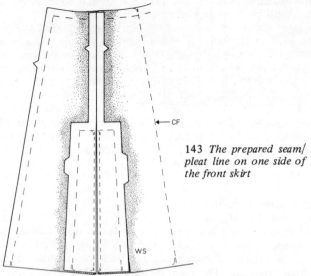

143 *The prepared seam/ pleat line on one side of the front skirt*

Remove the tacking stitches along the pleat and fold lines and press firmly to sharpen the fold. The seam/pleat line is now ready for applying the pleat underlay.

If the fabric frays badly, neaten the edges of the underlay from the waist edge as far as the stitching line. Check that the stitching line is clearly marked. Pin the pleat underlay from its centre point, to the top edge of one pleat section. The stitching line of the underlay is then tacked along the fitting line at the top of the pleat section, the solid spot coming to the centre of the underlay stitching line. Care is needed to ensure accuracy of placing at the centre. Continue the tacking down the outer edge of the pleat to the hem line. Machine along the tacked line. Repeat this tacking and machining on the other side of the pleat. Tack the underlay to the skirt along the waist fitting line (144).

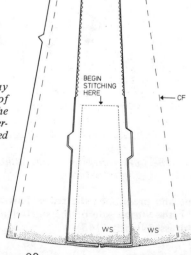

144 *The pleat underlay attached at the back of the pleat. In this case the upper edges of the under- lay have been neatened*

Press the machined area of the pleat and trim the raw edges down either side. Neaten with machine zigzagging or hand overcasting.

On the right side, cross tack over the two folded edges of the pleat. Work a tailor's bar tack at the base of the seam to hold together the edges of the pleat. Alternatively an arrow head could be worked if suitable.

If the pleat underlay promises to give unwanted bulk between the top of the pleat and the waist line, lining fabric could be used in this area instead of the garment fabric. Cut across the underlay pattern 15 mm above the stitching line. Cut out the lower part in garment fabric, and the upper part in lining fabric. Allow a 15 mm turning for the join on each piece. On the upper section allow 5 mm turnings on the two side edges. Turn under the 5 mm turnings and machine edge stitch to prevent fraying. Machine the two sections together, using the 15 mm turning allowances, and press the turnings upwards onto the lining fabric. Attach this prepared underlay as already described (145).

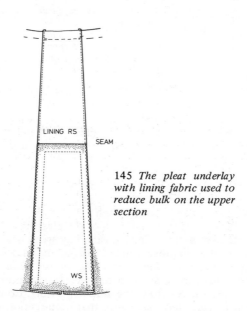

145 *The pleat underlay with lining fabric used to reduce bulk on the upper section*

2 A straight pleat below a seam

A central pleat at back or front is sometimes cut with a seam in the upper half, but the centre line of the pleat is laid to a fold of fabric. When the seam is made, and the pleat folded into place, it is machined across the top from the centre to each side as for a shaped pleat below a seam (146).

Matching the skirt grain, prepare a strip of lining fabric to fit between the waist edge and the machined line across the pleat. Allow 5 mm turnings on the two long edges for machine edge stitch neatening. Allow a 10 mm turning at the lower edge, which should be turned and tacked before neatening the side edges.

Tack the centre of the prepared strip along the seam line, with wrong sides together. Tack along the waist fitting line and hem the lower edge along the machined line (147).

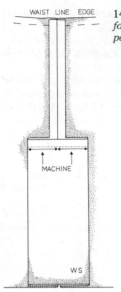

WAIST LINE EDGE

MACHINE

WS

146 *A straight pleat folded and stitched in position below a seam*

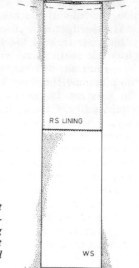

RS LINING

WS

147 *The finished pleat on the wrong side, showing the strip of lining fabric used as a support between the waist and the top of the pleat*

Pressing pleats

If the garment hem has not been made, leave the pleats unpressed over the hem area. If the hem is finished, press the pleats to the end.

Use a steam iron and a dry pressing cloth, or a dry iron with a damp pressing cloth, and a dry cloth for final pressing. Do not use too much moisture.

Place the tacked pleats right side up on the ironing board. Press lightly at first on both the right side and the wrong side, just to set the pleat folds, working first with steam and then through a dry cloth.

Remove the tacking from a small area of the pleating at a time, eg one box or inverted pleat, two or three knife pleats. Lay strips of dry cloth under the fold of each freed pleat to prevent indenting the underlay of each pleat. Press both sides, but more firmly than before. Again use steam pressing followed by dry pressing. This should sharpen the pleat folds and remove any marks left by the tacking stitches from the initial pressing. Continue until all the pleats have been pressed, but make sure that each section is quite dry before moving on to the next. If necessary, support the completed areas on a chair while finishing the pressing.

Hang the garment to cool off and air. Cross tack coarsely over the pleat folds to keep the pleats in position while finishing the garment.

Gathering

When fashionable, gathering provides a loose, soft way of reducing fullness to fit into a smaller area, eg a very full sleeve must be reduced in size at the crown to fit into a bodice armhole. Gathering is suitable only for light-weight fabrics as it should fall in soft folds below the setting line. It looks bunchy and cumbersome on thick or stiff fabric. The finished appearance is attractive only if the degree of fullness suits the type of garment and the fabric. The following table of proportion gives a guide to planning the degree of fullness:

Slight fullness . . . use half as much again as the required finished length
Average fullness . . . use twice as much again as the required finished length
Maximum fullness . . . use 3X as much again as the required finished length

Gathers are easy to launder as the point of the iron will press right into the inset line of the gathering.

Gathers should be sewn along the weft way of the fabric. In this direction they complement the weave of the fabric, drawing it up in the direction of the weaving movement and allowing the folds to hang with the warp grain which provides better drapability.

The stitching of gathers

The extent of the gathering is usually marked by printed directions or notches on the pattern. Gathers are never worked across a turning allowance, so work accurately within the marked positions.

Using thread marks, divide the area to be gathered into 2, 4, 6 or more even sized sections, according to length. Approximately 45 cm is long enough for a gathering section. This keeps the threads of a manageable length for drawing up, and simplifies the even setting of the gathers. The plain area, eg a yoke or band, into which the gathers are to be set, should be divided into the same number of sections (148). These, too, must be equal in length, but the lengths will be shorter according to the proportion of the gathering.

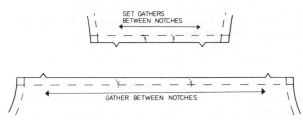

SET GATHERS
BETWEEN NOTCHES

GATHER BETWEEN NOTCHES

148 *This figure shows the sections marked both on a length for gathering and on the plain edge to which it will be set. In each case the space between the notches has been divided into three equal sized sections*

The gathering must be stitched evenly and smoothly along the fitting line. This is usually parallel to a raw edge. One way to help keep a good line of stitching on a straight edge is to fold over the edge of the fabric along the fitting line and press firmly (149a and b). The crease will act as a guide when working the stitches if the turning is folded to the side which is uppermost while the gathering stitches are being worked.

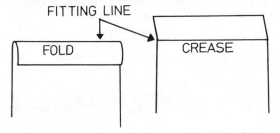

FITTING LINE

FOLD   CREASE

149a *The turning allowance folded to crease along the fitting line*

149b *The crease along the fitting line to guide the gathering stitches*

If the gathers have to be placed along a curve, eg the crown of a sleeve, it may be necessary to tack along the fitting line as a guide for the gathering.

Gathers should always be worked provisionally before fitting. Refer to page 63.

When placing gathers avoid working over seams and other double parts to prevent bulkiness, and to keep the setting smooth.

Use sewing thread which matches the fabric for the stitching of gathers. Work one row of gathers on the fitting line and a second row 3 mm - 6 mm above the fitting line. This second row controls the turning, making the setting easier and the finished result flatter, as it is left in permanently to hold and control the fullness of the turning within the finished seam or band. In fact, there is no need to remove the gathering stitches on the fitting line, unless they happen to show when the seam is finished.

Leave 80 mm - 100 mm of thread hanging at the ends of each line of stitching to hold firmly when beginning to draw up the gathering.

(a) Gathering by machine
Use a long stitch and, if necessary, loosen the upper tension, but this is rarely required on the newer machines. The fabric draws up more easily on the under thread, and the side of the drawn threads gives a smoother area for setting the seam or band, and keeps the fullness better controlled along the fitting line. Therefore stitch with the fabric right side down in the machine.

The use of machine attachments for gathering
Most machine manufacturers supply a gathering foot. These are very useful and give a quickly worked line of gathering. However the degree of fullness is limited. Follow the machine instructions for using the foot, and test it out on spare fabric so that the amount of fullness can be judged. It will vary according to the length of stitch used and the thickness of the fabric.

(b) Gathering by hand
This is rarely done nowadays, but can be useful for short areas and for very fine fabric on which the machine stitching may be too strong for the single fabric.

On modern fabrics running stitches worked on the right side give the best result. To ensure even gathering, the stitching must be worked regularly, with stitches and spaces equal in size. The finer the fabric, the smaller the stitches must be.

(c) Drawing up gathering threads
Fasten off very firmly at the end of each section. Hold the hanging threads at the other end of the stitched line, and ease the fabric along the two gathering threads, pulling gently and evenly. Draw up the gathered lines section by section, reducing each section to the approximate size to fit the space into which it will be set finally. When the gathered line seems short enough, secure the threads temporarily by winding them round a pin set into the turning allowance. If a pin would mark fine fabric, hold the threads with a small piece of sellotape. Test the length of the gathered section against the section to which it will be attached, and adjust as required. When the length is correct, fasten off the threads.

(d) Fastening off gathering threads
Both machine and hand gathering must be firmly fastened off when the correct placing and fullness are established.

(i) Machine gathering threads
Draw the right side thread through to the wrong side. Tie one knot, then thread the two ends into a needle and whip over the back of the stitching for 5 mm - 6 mm.

(ii) Hand gathering threads
Fasten off on the wrong side with two or three fine back stitches.

Spreading the gathers
It is essential that gathers are spread evenly, and time must be given to doing this. Ease the gathers along the gathering threads until they are regular in appearance with neither plain nor bunchy patches. Pin the gathered and plain fitting lines together at the marked sections, and arrange the fullness smoothly within each section. Adjust until the appearance is satisfactory and the gathers arranged in unbroken evenness along their whole length.

Setting gathers
Gathers can be set into an overlaid or lapped seam, see page 111, the gathered section always forming the underlay. This method, with the machine stitching showing on the right side, is rarely used nowadays. It is more usual to arrange the seam so that the machine stitching is invisible on the right side, see page 113. Gathers are fixed more easily if upright tacking is used (150). The seam is then machined along the fitting line, and the straight edge, or overlay, lifted up above the gathers. The two most usual ways of neatening the seam on the wrong side are:
(i) by machining the two turnings together 5 mm - 6 mm outside the fitting line, trimming the turnings close to the stitched edge and zigzagging over the raw edges.
(ii) by trimming the gathered turning to 4 mm - 5 mm, folding the flat turning over to form a hem which is hemmed to the fitting line (151a and b).

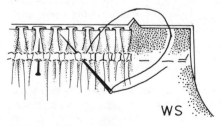

WS

150 *Straight tacking along the fitting line, turning into upright tacking along a section of the gathering*

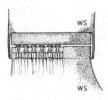

151a *The gathered turning trimmed, and the flat turning prepared for folding over and hemming to enclose the gathers*

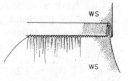

151b *The flat turning hemmed on the wrong side*

Setting a circular band to a short gathered sleeve
(a) Preparation of band
The band should be cut with the warp grain running along its length, and with a turning allowance on all four edges. Fold the band in half along the weft and join the two short raw edges together with a plain, unneatened seam. Trim the turnings to 5 mm and press them open flat.

On one circular raw edge pin the turning to the wrong side and tack it close to the fold. Trim the turning to 5 mm (152). It is less likely to fray if trimmed at this stage.

152 *The band with finished seam and tacked, trimmed turning*

(b) Attaching the band to the sleeve
Slip the band inside the sleeve to bring the right sides facing, the raw edges together and the seams over each other. Pin the band and sleeve together with the fitting lines matching (153a). Tack and machine along the fitting line. Trim the turnings to 5 mm.

Fold the band to bring the prepared edge over to the wrong side and pin it down above the machine stitching (153b). Tack and hem it in place. These hemming stitches will not show through to the right side as they are worked on the turning just above the machining, or into the machining itself.

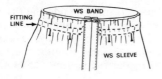

153a *The band pinned to the sleeve*

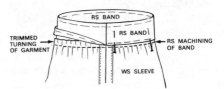

153b *The setting of the band on the wrong side*

Shirring
Shirring is formed by working three or more rows of gathers exactly under each other. Both the stitching and the spacing must be absolutely even or the effect is spoilt. Shirring is only satisfactory if used on soft, fine fabric, as it should have a very soft appearance on the right side. It can be worked by hand or by machine, providing the machine stitching is not too strong for the fineness of the fabric.

The fastening off at the ends of each row needs care, as the wrong side stitching required may be visible through the fabric. In this case a pin tuck (page 82 figure 124) has to be worked down each side of the shirred area (154).

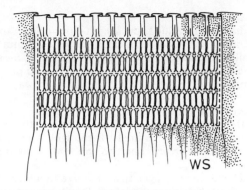

154 *A section of a shirred area, showing a pin tuck at each side*

WS

Spread the shirring into complete regularity throughout all the rows, or the attractive effect will be lost.

It is usual to support shirring by a stay on the wrong side. Prepare a strip of self fabric to fit behind the shirred area. Balance the grain with the garment and allow 5 mm turnings on all edges. Fold and tack the turnings along the two shorter sides, and then along the two longer sides. Set the prepared stay behind the shirred area and hem it finely round the four sides, sewing into the back of the pin tucks and the top and bottom rows of shirring.

Set the shirring as directed for gathers.

Frills

Soft fabric which drapes well is necessary for the making of frills, as they should always hang in folds and not stand out stiffly from the garment. For example, fine cotton lawn and nylon chiffon are two fabrics which are suitable for frilling; cotton poplin and nylon organza are not.

The use of fabric grain when cutting frills

Frills always fall more softly if cut with the weft grain along their length and with the warp grain hanging downwards in wear, following the same principle as for gathered fabric explained on page 93. It is essential that frills are cut straight with the fabric grain if they are to gather evenly and hang attractively in wear. A paper pattern for a frill is not satisfactory, as it is difficult to pin it exactly with the fabric grain. It is better to prepare the fabric for cutting by measuring the depth required and pulling a thread, unless the grain can be seen and followed easily in cutting.

Planning the width of frills

Outstanding frilling round a neck-line must be narrow, otherwise it will droop and lose its line; 25 mm - 40 mm is wide enough.

Frillings set into small sections of a garment, eg a collar or pocket, must be narrow, 12 mm - 20 mm, or they will give an overweighted appearance.

A frill can be any width up to 75 mm. If cut wider than that it is called a flounce. The preparation and setting are the same, therefore no particular information is required for flounces.

A frill is usually made from single fabric with some type of suitable finish along the lower edge. On very thin fabric a frill can be folded and made

97

double, with a fold along the lower edge.

When the required width has been decided, the length for cutting can be calculated. Single frills are cut the finished width required plus 10 mm for setting, plus an adequate turning allowance for the lower edge finish chosen. Folded frills are cut twice the finished width required plus 20 mm to provide two 10 mm turnings for setting when the frill is folded in half lengthways.

Calculating the length of frilling to be cut

Measure the exact length of the garment edge to which the frill is to be set, and then decide on the amount of fullness required for the frill. A wide frill usually has more fullness than a narrow one, to prevent a skimped appearance.

Frills are usually cut 1½, 2 or 3 times longer than the edge to which they are to be joined. The thinner the fabric the fuller the frill may be, but guard against too much fullness as a bunchy frill loses essential daintiness. It is wise to gather about 30 cm of frilling and draw it up to find the most pleasing appearance. Measure the gathered length resulting, in relation to its original flat length, and work out the degree of fullness required.

Probably several lengths will have to be joined to procure the necessary length of frilling, so include a seam allowance when cutting the lengths. Join single frilling with a fine French seam; for folded frilling use a narrow, single seam with the turnings pressed together.

If the frill is to be set round a corner or sharp curve, eg a collar or pocket, allow a little extra fullness at these points, so that the frilling is not skimped.

When using a machine gathering foot for stitching a frill, a measured test strip must be stitched first to guide the length calculation.

Planning the garment turnings for frilled edges

This varies according to the setting method chosen, so the construction and setting of the frill should be decided before cutting out the garment if possible. If in doubt, leave 20 mm - 25 mm, then there will be enough for any type of setting. Remember that the lower edge of the frilling forms the final edge of the garment in most cases, and check that this will come in the right position on the garment.

If an original design is being altered and a frill added, allowance must be made for the width of the frill, so that neither extra width nor length is added to the garment. The original fitting line of the garment must be moved inwards, eg at a neck line, or upwards, eg at a hem line, to ensure the correct fit of the garment. This point also applies if the width of a frill is being altered and made wider or narrower than suggested in the original design.

Some suggestions for lower edge finishes for frills

Frills must be edged lightly to allow them to hang in soft flutes. The lower edge must be finished before the frill is set. If the frill is to be set onto a circular edge, eg a hem line, it must be joined into a circle before the edging is worked. Hand finishes, eg shell hemming, whipped rolls, etc, look pretty and used to be popular, but are slow to work on a long strip. They are not much used nowadays for this reason. The following suggestions offer some suitable finishes:

(i) Machine a hem using the narrow hemmer. Use a short machine stitch. It looks more attractive and makes the guiding of the fabric easier as it passes more slowly through the machine. Practice using the hemmer first, as the fabric must be fed accurately into the hemmer, ie not more than 6 mm, or the hem becomes uneven. Read the machine manual directions for the use of the hemmer before working the practice piece.

The blind hemmer foot can also be used to make a suitable edging for a frill.

(ii) Machine a rolled hem, using the roll-hemmer with a zigzag stitch. Try first using a zigzag setting 3½ and No. 2 stitch length. Adapt these settings if necessary to suit individual fabrics.

(iii) Machine scallop the edge, using the scallop embroidery cam or setting. First test to see how the fabric responds to this. Sometimes a strip of organdie or nylon organza tacked to the wrong side gives the necessary support to a fabric for a satisfactory finish. Trim away both frill edge and backing to the scalloping on the right side, and the backing fabric on the wrong side.

(iv) Tack a narrow hem and hold it with a fine machine embroidery stitch.

(v) Edge the frill with lace. Allowance must be made for the width of the lace when calculating the width to cut the frilling strips. Take into account the turnings required for setting the lace. Tack a narrow hem 2 mm - 3 mm wide to the right side of the frill. Tack the lace edging over this and machine to secure lace and hem to the frill (155).

155 *The arrangement of hem and lace, showing the position of the machine stitching*

(vi) Attach narrow ribbon or ornamental braid to the edge. Fold a single turning to the right side, making it a little narrower than the ribbon. Set the ribbon along the frill edge, and machine along each side to enclose the turning (156).

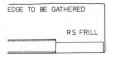

156 *The arrangement of the turning and the machined ribbon*

These last two finishes are decorative, but add to the cost of the garment. Work out this additional cost before deciding to use these edgings.

Refer to the gathering section on page 92 for guidance in preparation, stitching, drawing up the threads and spreading the gathers.

Using a machine gathering foot
This is a very useful foot and is well worth trying as it is quick and effective. Two lines of test stitching must always be worked first to ascertain the best stitch length to use. The thinner the fabric the fuller the gathering will be. A thin fabric may gather adequately at No. 1 setting, whereas thicker fabric may need a setting of 2, 3 or 4.

When preparing a broderie anglaise edge for frilling, use a light gathering or the embroidery design is spoilt.

Two lines of gathering should always be stitched when using the machine gathering foot, as the frill appears fuller after the second line has been stitched. Stitch along the turning first 3 mm outside the fitting line, and then along the fitting line, otherwise the fabric is awkward to handle in the

99

machine, and the turning would be more tightly drawn up than the fitting line.

Setting frills
(a) Plain settings
The setting methods described for gathers can also be used for setting frills. Press the turnings away from the edge of the garment, and the frill will fall into place.

(b) Decorative settings
Either ribbon or braid can be used on the right side to give a decorative effect. Choose the width carefully so that it does not overwhelm the frill. Allow 10 mm turnings both on the frill and on the garment edges. Prepare the frill in the usual way. Place the right side of the frill to the wrong side of the garment. Pin, tack and machine along the fitting line and also along the second line of gathering, to join the turnings together (157a). Trim away the surplus turning close to the second line of machining. Press the turnings flat, using the side edge of the iron, and then press it upwards onto the garment.

Place the ribbon or braid to cover the turning, setting it so that it can be machined along the fitting line of the frill at its lower edge, and onto the single fabric of the garment along its top edge (157b).

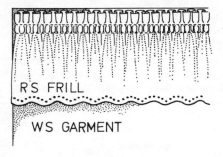

157a *The frill set to the garment edge with two lines of machine stitching*

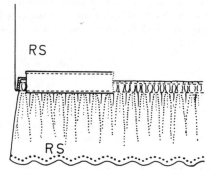

157b *A section of the ribbon machined over the trimmed turnings*

A folded frill
Frills on sheer, plain fabrics are often made double so that there is a fold along the lower edge. This gives a neat strong edge which cannot fray out with wear.

Cut the frilling twice the finished width plus two turnings. If joins are necessary, machine the two lengths of frilling together across the width. Trim the turnings to 3 mm - 4 mm and press them both to one side. The turnings will show through to the right side on sheer fabric, but pressing the turnings together makes the shadow as narrow as possible.

Fold the strip in half along its length, with the right side outside. Tack the double fabric together at the open edge to hold the layers firmly for stitching the gathers. Gather and set the frill as desired.

Easing

Easing is a means of shortening the length of an edge of fabric without any apparent reduction of fullness. It can be done only to a limited extent, and the length which can be eased away depends on the softness of the yarn and the flexibility of the weave or knit used in making the fabric. The easing movement compresses the weave or knit and, with careful pressing, the fabric can be flattened, or shrunk to the reduced size. Soft woollen cloth is ideal for reduction by easing: glazed cotton is impossible to ease because of the hard yarn and the welded nature of the finish. The area for easing is usually marked on a bought pattern, and the position setting it is shown on the corresponding edge. Easing is useful in the following example positions:

(i) When setting a plain sleeve crown,

(ii) when preparing the elbow section of the seam in a fitted sleeve,

(iii) when providing shaping, without the use of a dart, along the back edge of a shoulder seam,

(iv) over the bust line area when preparing a panel seam styled from the shoulder or armhole,

(v) when preparing to stitch the hem on a curved hem line.

Preparing the section for easing

It is helpful to divide the two edges into even-sized sections as suggested for gathering on page 93. Work throughout with the section for easing uppermost.

(a) On off-grain edges, and on soft fabrics with a fairly loose weave, easing can be done by careful handling. Pin the two sections together at the marked points, setting each pin through the fitting line and bringing it out through the turning, and at right angles to the fitting line (158). The amount for easing is now regulated, and can be compressed by curving the fabric over the forefinger and setting further pins in the same way.

158 *The preparatory pinning for easing by manipulation*

(b) An adapted method is necessary on firm, closely woven fabric, which is more difficult to ease. In this case it is better to stitch along the fitting line. This should be done with a line of very fine running stitches along the entire length of the section to be eased. The fabric can then be eased back along the thread to the required length. If this is evenly done along fine running stitches, the fabric will not appear to be gathered. Press the turning outside the easing to smooth and flatten the fabric.

Stitching an eased seam

Tack the seam and, along the eased section, curve the fabric over the forefinger and use shorter tacking stitches than usual.

Machine the seam, taking particular care not to let any small pleats form while machining. Stitch slowly, using the two forefingers to smooth out the fabric in front of the machine foot on either side of the fitting line.

The use of ribbon cord and elastic to reduce fullness

Ribbon, cord or elastic can be threaded through a widely cut garment of light-weight fabric to give the appearance of fit with fullness. For example, the neck line of a peasant style bodice is reduced by facing the neck edge and threading it with either cord or narrow ribbon to draw up the fabric, and a bow is tied to hold the fullness to the required size: a widely cut nightdress can be drawn to size at the neck line in the same way, and further shaped by setting a casing at the waist level to be threaded with either ribbon or elastic.

(a) Ribbon tie-strings

A folded hem may be used on straight edges, but a wrong side crossway facing (see page 122) is necessary on a curved edge.

Before a crossway facing is set, two buttonholed slots must be worked through single fabric either side of the centre front line, on the right side of the garment. They must be spaced sufficiently far apart to allow for tying the ribbon. At a neck line, they must be made just below the neck fitting line to allow for setting the facing. The slots are worked as buttonholes but with two round ends, and should be just wide enough to fit the ribbon.

Both edges of the hem or facing should be machined as it gives a more attractive appearance in use, and strengthens the upper edge against the rub of the ribbon. Allow the width of the ribbon plus 1 mm - 2 mm between the two lines of machining. Measure carefully to find the finished width of crossway facing required, and then allow two turnings (159).

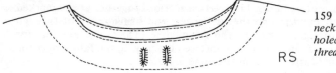

159 *A crossway faced neck edge with buttonholed slots ready for threading with ribbon*

A casing for ribbon set at the waist line of a nightdress, has a straight or crossway strip fixed by machine to the wrong side (160). Before this is applied, two buttonhole slots, about 25 mm apart, must be worked at the waist line either side of the centre front, on the right side of the nightdress (161).

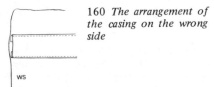

160 *The arrangement of the casing on the wrong side*

161 *The slots, with threaded ribbon, on the right side*

If a ruffle is required at a ribbon threaded edge which is straight, a wide hem may be turned with a casing formed by two lines of machine stitching at the lower edge (162).

162 *A section of a hem prepared for threaded ribbon to form a ruffle*

A ruffle on a curved edge is made in one of the following ways:
(i) By applying a facing either on the cross or cut to shape, to act as the wide hem in figure 162. This can be done only on thin fabric or the seam along the edge would give unwanted bulk.
(ii) By making a thin, narrow edge finish, eg machine scalloping, along the raw edge and applying a crossway casing below for threading the ribbon.

(b) Elastic
Elastic is sometimes used with a nightdress waist line casing instead of ribbon. The casing is made as already described (160), but a 15 mm gap should be left at the centre back on one edge of the casing to allow for threading the elastic. The gap can be back stitched from the right side after the elastic has been inserted.

If an elasticated waist line is used on a child's skirt or shorts, a hem or crossway facing is used for the casing. A slot is needed for the threading of the elastic, and is placed at the centre back on the wrong side.

(i) A slot in a hem
Machine or back stitch a rectangle 15 mm - 20 mm long across the centre back to hold the first turning of the hem in place. Machine the hem beginning and finishing either side of the stitched rectangle, and then machine the top edge of the hem (163). Insert the elastic through the stitched slot.

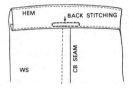

163 *A stitched slot at the centre back of a hem prepared for threading with elastic*

(ii) A slot in a crossway facing
Machine or back stitch the turnings of the strip along the straight grain, and arrange them to meet edge to edge. Machine both edges of the facing before threading the elastic (164).

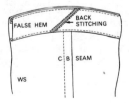

164 *The diagonal slot formed in a crossway facing*

(iii) Joining the elastic
When calculating the length of elastic to cut, arrange for a 25 mm overlap for joining. Pin the overlap and either oversew the double edges, or machine zigzag across the overlap. Begin and finish 15 mm either side of the overlap, making a line of zigzagging 55 mm long.

10 Seams

A seam is a method of joining together two pieces of fabric. The raw edges are either completely concealed or strengthened by protective stitching. There are many types of seams. It is therefore necessary to choose the right seam for the nature of the fabric and the use of the garment. Unless the seam is to form part of the decoration of a garment it should be as inconspicuous as possible. Any stitching which does show on the right side must be very evenly and neatly done. All seams must be made with strict attention to the fitting lines so that the garment is made to the required size.

Before cutting out it is necessary to decide on the type of seam to be used at joining edges, and the finished width required, so that adequately wide seam turnings can be allowed to provide for the fraying of the fabric, and also to leave sufficient width of turning for the making of well-finished seams after the frays are trimmed away. Whenever possible leave 25 mm turnings for seams as this gives a useful width of fabric, and allows for some fraying. Very badly fraying fabric needs wider turnings, especially in areas where much handling and snipping is required in construction. Heavy fabrics, eg tweeds, should be made up with wide seam turnings, as these give a smoother line after pressing. As the usual turning allowance on bought patterns is 15 mm, the extra width required must be allowed for when cutting out.

All garment seams should be tacked on the fitting-line, so that they can be accurately fitted to test the finished size of the garment.

French seam

This seam may be used on thin fabrics only and therefore is useful for lingerie, children's wear, blouses and occasionally for thin dresses. If carefully worked it is ideal for thin, fraying fabrics as the raw edges are completely enclosed. It is not suitable for shorts, trousers or pyjamas as it is too bulky at the crotch, where leg and body seams cross. No stitching is visible on the right side of a french seam.

Method of making a french seam

Tack the edges together along the fitting line with the right sides outside. Machine outside the fitting line for the width of the finished seam. This should be 5 mm for fraying fabrics, but can be narrower for non-fraying fabric (165a).

Trim the turning outside the machining so that it is a little narrower than the finished width of seam (165b).

Press open the trimmed turnings with finger and thumb or an iron. This ensures a perfect finish to the seam. The raw edges are now just clear of the fitting lines (165c).

If the fabric frays badly, press open the turnings before trimming. In this case great care must be taken to avoid snipping the garment as the single turnings are trimmed.

Turn the garment to the wrong side and fold back the seam, creasing sharply along the first line of stitching. This brings the fitting lines over each other. They are first tacked and then machined together (165d).

Press along the length of the seam, and then press it flat onto the garment, turning it towards the back (165e). If this rule is followed, all seams will face in the same direction, and will remain untwisted along their length.

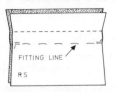

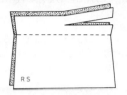

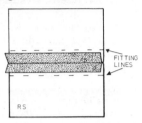

165a *A French seam showing the tacking on the fitting line, and the first line of machining worked on the right side*

165b *Trimming the first turning*

165c *The opened turnings lying within the fitting lines*

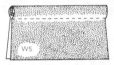

165d *The second line of machining, which is worked on the wrong side along the fitting line*

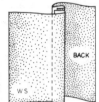

165e *The french seam pressed into its final position*

Making a french seam in a curve

If the seam is curved, eg the underarm seam in a short kimono sleeve, the first turning must be trimmed and snipped before it is pressed open flat (166a). Leave the tacking along the fitting line while trimming and snipping the turnings, as it helps to support the stretchable line of the curve.

After the second row of stitching has been worked, the seam must be snipped across its width once, or twice if it is a deep curve, and the raw edges loop stitched to strengthen (166b). When the garment is turned right side out, the seam can open and set flat.

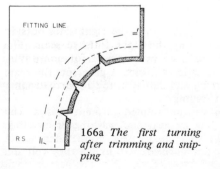

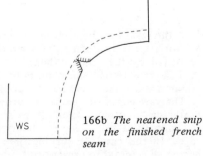

166a *The first turning after trimming and snipping*

166b *The neatened snip on the finished french seam*

Plain or open seam

This is the most generally used seam in dressmaking as it is very flat in finish and may be used on any but transparent fabrics. It is used for skirt, bodice and sleeve seams.

A plain seam needs a turning allowance of 25 mm to give a satisfactory finish to the seam. On heavy fabric a turning allowance of 40 mm is required for a good result. No stitching is visible on the right side of a plain seam.

Method of making a plain seam

Pin and tack the edges together along the fitting-lines on the wrong side of the fabric, matching any balance notches. Machine along the fitting-line and remove the tacking (167a). Press the turnings open flat on the wrong side (167b).

167a *The machining on the fitting line*

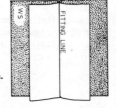

167b *The turnings pressed open flat*

If the seam is used on stretchable fabric, eg crimplene, it is necessary to tape the shoulder seams. This prevents the shoulder line from stretching in wear, causing the sleeve setting line to drop. Use ribbon seam binding; ribbon or even a 12 mm wide strip of lining fabric, cut from a selvedge edge, for the taping. Cut it equal to the shoulder length plus neck and armhole turnings.

Tack the seam along the fitting line as previously described. Then tack the taping strip along the seam, setting the centre of the strip over the seam fitting line. Machine the seam along its fitting line, stitching through the tape and the two layers of garment fabric (167c). Press the seam open flat, enclosing the tape under one turning.

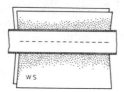

167c *A section of a taped seam with machining in position*

If the seam is to be enclosed within a lining, the edges of the seam turnings do not require neatening. This would be a waste of time as they are fully protected by the lining. When a lining is loose inside a garment, the seam turnings require neatening, on both lining and garment, for abour 230 mm - 300 mm above the hem line to prevent fraying.

The raw edges of the seam turnings in an unlined garment always need neatening to protect them from fraying in wear and washing or cleaning. Occasionally a crimplene is found which is completely non-fraying at cut edges. In this case the turnings need not be neatened, unless they roll and neatening is found to prevent this.

Width for finished seams
This is variable according to the type of fabric, but this seam is never satisfactory if it is very narrow in its finished width. The following list gives a guide for the finished width of *each turning* of the seam:

Thin fabrics	10 mm
Medium-weight fabrics	20 mm
Heavy fabrics	25 mm-30 mm

Wrong side finishes
When a suitable wrong side finish has been chosen for the seam, trim the two seam turnings even in width, making the width suitable for the type of fabric and finish to be used.

(a) Neatening with machine zigzagging
Whenever possible use machine zigzagging to neaten seam turnings as this is quick and effective. The zigzagging must always be tried out on spare fabric to find the most suitable spacing and bight. Trim the turnings evenly to the finished width required before stitching and zigzagging (168 and 169).

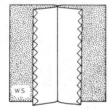

168 *Plain machine zigzagging worked over the edge of the seam turning. The right-hand drop of the needle should come just over the raw edge of the turning*

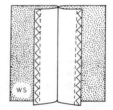

169 *If the zigzagging frays or flutes the edge, try stitching a line of straight machining about 3 mm inside the edge of the turning and zigzag over this and the raw edge*

Zigzagging is unsuitable for use over the edge of thin fabric as it causes the edge to disintegrate, but it can be effective if it is worked as shown in figure 170. This is particularly useful as a quick finish for lining fabrics which usually fray badly. Trim each turning of the seam 3 mm wider than the finished width required, eg trim Tricel to 15 mm, allowing 3 mm for the neatening turning, and 12 mm for the finished width of each turning of the seam.

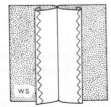

170 *A single turning 3 mm wide folded to the underside of the seam turning and the edge zigzagged for the width of this turning*

These methods show the most common ways of neatening plain seams by machine. By studying your machine manual, you will probably find other finishes suggested. These finishes will vary according to the make and type of machine, and it is always worth while trying out the methods suggested, and to make full use of the scope of your machine.

(b) Neatening by overcasting
This is a hand method of neatening which can be used on slightly fraying fabric, eg flannel, if a machine zigzag stitch is not available. Overcast the edges after trimming them to the required width. Before overcasting, a line of straight machining may be stitched just inside the raw edge. This gives a firmer finish to the seam. Hold the raw edge with the right side of the turning facing you as you work the overcasting. The overcasting may be worked from right to left or from left to right, according to the direction of the fabric threads along the raw edge. Examine the raw edge and notice which way the threads unravel so that the overcasting holds them down in their natural direction (171a, b, c & d).

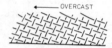

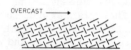

171a *When the warp threads come away from the seam edge in this direction, overcast from right to left*

171b *When the warp threads come away from the seam edge in this direction, overcast from left to right*

171c *Overcasting a seam edge in a left to right direction*

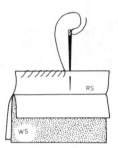

171d *On this seam, a line of machining has been worked close to the raw edge of the seam turnings, and the over-casting is being worked from right to left*

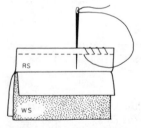

(c) Neatening with edge-stitching
This is satisfactory for thin and medium-weight fabrics, eg Terylene/cotton mixtures, most cotton dress fabrics. Trim the turnings to 15 mm. Crease a single fold to the underside of the turnings, leaving the finished turning 12 mm wide from the fitting line. Machine close to the folded edge (172).

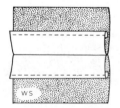

172 *The seam with an edge-stitched finish*

(d) Neatening with binding
For badly fraying tweeds, linen etc use a bound finish. For seams cut with the straight grain use paris binding; for sloping seams use bias binding as this is

108

more flexible for setting along an edge which slants across the fabric grain. Take care not to stretch the edge of the seam.

(i) Straight edges
Trim the turnings to the width required. Fold the paris binding nearly in half and tack it over the raw edge, with the wider part on the underside of the turning. Machine close to the edge of the binding on the upper side of the turning (173).

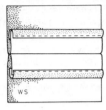

173 *Paris binding machined along a straight seam edge*

(ii) Sloping edges
Press open one turning of the bias binding. Fold over and press the remaining turning to enclose its raw edge (174a). Slip the prepared fold over the edge of the seam turning, bringing the single flap of the bias strip to the underneath of the turning. Machine close to the fold through all layers (174b).

174a *The prepared bias binding*

174b *The binding is shown tacked in place on one turning and machined on the second turning*

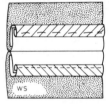

This method of setting the bias strip, edges the seam turning quickly and gives as flat a finish as possible. The surplus raw edge of the strip may be cut away close to the machining if liked.

Handling a shaped plain seam
(a) A waist shaping
If a plain seam is used at the sides of a blouse or one-piece dress, it is often shaped to fit into the waist. It is then impossible to press the seam open flat. After machining on the fitting line, snip across the turning at the waist to within 3 mm of the fitting line. Press the seam turnings open flat and loop stitch the raw edges of the snips (175). The seam turnings may now be neatened as required.

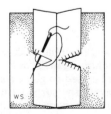

175 *Strengthening the snip at the fitted waist line of a plain seam*

(b) A kimono underarm seam
Refer to the sleeve section page 261.

Setting shaped panels

Dresses with long panel seams curving either from the shoulder or the armhole down to the hem line, require special attention at the panel seam lines. These seams are conspicuous as they provide style lines in the garment, and it is essential to make them smooth and strong.

A plain seam will not always press open flat where the seam curves over the bust line, as the turnings of most fabrics flute, and necessitate notching. This weakens the seam, especially if the fabric frays. Some woven woollen fabric, and wool jersey, can be pressed through a damp cloth and the fluting shrunk away. On these fabrics, a plain seam can be used successfully for panel seams, but in most cases, especially on light-weight or fraying fabrics, a plain seam is not the best choice.

Making the seam on a curving panel line

Pin the seam in the following order:

(i) At the shoulder, or armhole, fitting lines.

(ii) At the balance notches. Between these two pins one edge will appear longer than the other. This is to allow for some easing over the bust line.

(iii) Keeping the fitting-lines together gently ease the more prominent curve along the flatter curve, pinning about 15 mm intervals (176). (Refer page 101.)

(iv) Continue pinning the seam down to the hem edge, keeping the fitting lines flat.

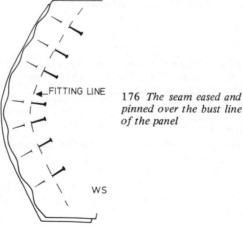

176 *The seam eased and pinned over the bust line of the panel*

Tack the seam along the fitting line and machine as shown in figure 167a. Keep the two turnings together and machine again about 8 mm outside the fitting line (177a). The machine foot can be used to guide a suitable width.

Press the seam flat as stitched, trim away the surplus turning close to the second machining and machine zigzag (or hand overcast) to neaten (177b).

Press the finished seam towards the centre front or the centre back of the garment. The seam is sufficiently narrow to set flat, but is satisfactorily strong (177c).

110

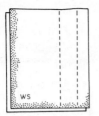

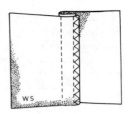

177a *The two lines of stitching on the wrong side*

177b *The seam pressed flat as stitched*

177c *The finished seam*

Lapped or overlaid seam

This is used for fixing yokes, panels and frills. A line of machining shows on the right side and helps to give style to a garment as well as making an essential join.

If both edges to be joined are flat, lay the top part of the garment over the lower part; if one edge is full, lay the plain edge over the full edge. A lapped seam should not be used if both edges are full. The edges of a centre panel should lap over the side panels of the garment.

On the wrong side the finished width of the seam should be not more than 10 mm on thin fabric and 12 mm on medium-weight fabric. This seam is not used on heavy fabric as yokes and frills are unsuitable on thick cloth, and a panel would be set by a different method.

Method of making a plain lapped seam
Fold the full width of the turning allowance to the wrong side along the edge which is to come on the top of the seam, eg the yoke. Tack this turning in place (178a). This side of the seam is called the lap or overlay.

Set the overlay over the underlay so that the fitting lines come over each other. Tack through the three thicknesses. Machine close to the folded edge of the overlay (178b). On the wrong side the raw edges of the turnings come together. Wrong side finishes are dealt with later.

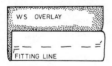

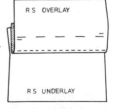

178b *The right side of the seam after machining*

178a *The prepared lap or overlay*

Method of making a lapped seam over gathers
Fold a turning to the wrong side of the overlay and tack as previously described. Draw up the gathers to equal the space between the gathering position markings of the overlay (179a).

Lap the prepared overlay over the gathers on the right side so that the fitting lines come together, the balance points match and the outer edges are level. Tack close to the edge of the overlay on the right side, and machine along the fold (179b).

111

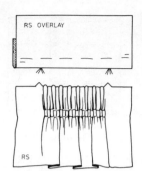

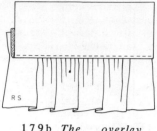

179a *The gathers drawn up to fit the overlay*

179b *The overlay machined in place over the gathers*

Wrong side finishes for lapped seams
(a) For non-fraying fabric

On the wrong side machine the two turnings together 6 mm-9 mm away from the first line of stitching, according to the thickness of the fabric. This compresses the turnings and makes a flatter seam. Trim the turnings to 3 mm outside this machining and zig-zag over the raw edge (180). If a zigzag machine is not available, hand overcasting may be used.

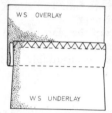

180 *The finished seam on the wrong side. The turnings are pressed up-wards onto the overlay*

(b) For fraying fabric

The upper section of the turning should be cut down to 6 mm or a little less. Fold the under section to form a hem over the trimmed turning. Tack and hem in place just above the machining (181).

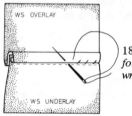

181 *The overlay turning folded into a hem on the wrong side*

Reinforcing a corner in a lapped seam

Sometimes in a child's dress style a yoke and centre front skirt panel are combined. In this case an angle appears in the seam line, making a very weak point unless the corner is reinforced. Use a spare piece of garment fabric for the reinforcement unless it is too thick, when a piece of matching lining fabric must be substituted.

Cut a square of the reinforcing fabric of at least 50 mm, cutting straight with the fabric grains. Place the right side of the square to the right side of the yoke at the corner, matching the grains carefully as indicated in figure 182a. The shaded area indicates that a 12 mm square of the reinforcing material must project beyond the raw edge of the garment at the corner. It is important that the widths at A and B are as wide, or wider than, the seam turning allowance. Tack and machine along the fitting line for the extent of the square (182a).

Cut away the surplus fabric shaded in figure 182a, and snip the corner of the raw edges to the fitting point of the seam. Take care not to cut the machining (182b).

Fold the reinforcing square to the wrong side, and trim the two outer edges to continue with the yoke turnings. The yoke turnings are thus folded in position along their fitting lines and the corner is permanently strengthened.

The overlay may now be finished with zigzagging or overcasting. Any other method of finish would be too bulky at the corner.

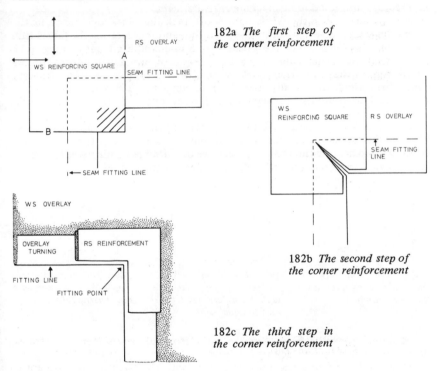

182a *The first step of the corner reinforcement*

182b *The second step of the corner reinforcement*

182c *The third step in the corner reinforcement*

Setting yokes and frills with no right side stitching visible

This is an alternative method which is very popular as it gives a softer appearance to the seam. The join is made, in the first place, as a plain seam, but the two raw edges are neatened together as for a lapped seam.

Make the seam in the following order:

(a) Place the two edges together with the wrong sides outside. Tack and machine on the fitting line.

(b) Press the two turnings together on to the garment. Usually they are turned upwards. Check that the seam is sharply creased back from the stitching on the right side.

(c) Trim and neaten by joining together the raw edges of the seam turnings according to the methods given for a lapped seam.

Double machine stitched seam

This seam is strong and quite flat when finished. It is held by two rows of machining which are both visible on the right side. It is used on garments which are plain in style, eg women's and girls' shirts and pants, simply styled nightwear for women, girls and infants, overalls, jeans and men's and boys' shirts and pyjamas. It is worked entirely by machine on the right side of the fabric and, as can be seen from the examples given, it is suitable for firm but not thick fabric.

Method of making a double machine-stitched seam

With the right side of the fabric uppermost, tack the edges together along the fitting line, using short, firm stitches. On thin and medium-weight fabric trim the turning of the back of the garment to 5 mm, and the front turning to 10 mm (183a). For jeans, trim the back turning to 8 mm and the front turning to 16 mm, as the seam needs to be wider for this type of garment. On very thin fabric which frays badly, trim both turnings to 10 mm and handle them together. This prevents the seam from fraying out with the strain of wear (183b).

Fold the front turning over the back turning so that the raw edge is just clear of the tacking. Tack the front turning in place (183c). If the trimming method shown in figure 183b has been used, a double turning will have been folded over, giving a double raw edge just clear of the tacking.

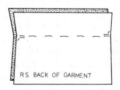
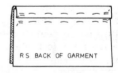

183a *The seam tacked along the fitting line with turnings trimmed*

183b *The seam tacked on thin, fraying fabric, with both turnings trimmed to equal width*

183c *The second tacking, showing a seam with one narrow turning*

Machine along the fitting line with the front of the garment uppermost. Remove the first line of tacking (184a)

Open out the fabric and press the seam onto the back of the garment so that the raw edge is hidden. When pressing, check to see that the underside of the seam is quite flat. Tack and machine close to the folded edge of the turning on the right side (184b).

184a *The first line of machining*

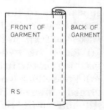

184b *The finished seam*

114

It is important that the final fixing of the seam comes onto the back of the garment where this is possible. If the seam is centrally placed, eg the centre front and the centre back of rompers, it can fall either to right or left, but should follow the same direction on both back and front sections.

When making garments with legs, make the leg seams first and the body seams afterwards. The body seam is then constructed as a continuous line from the front waist, crossing the leg seams at the crotch, and finishing at the back waist.

Turn one of the legs wrong side out and tuck it inside the other leg so that the wrong sides touch and the leg seams come over each other. The body seam is thus placed edge to edge ready for stitching. Tack on the fitting line (185). For this seam it does not matter which turning is trimmed as it is the left-hand and right-hand sides of the pants which are being joined. Make a double machine-stitched seam, taking care to place the second turning carefully over the crotch and to keep the width even.

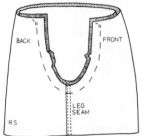

185 *The prepared body seam*

Setting a sleeve with a double machine-stitched seam

The type of garments for which this seam is used usually have plain, shallow crowns to the sleeves, eg a shirt. The sleeves are made and inserted with machined seams. When preparing the sleeve inset seam, trim down the sleeve turning so that the bodice armhole edge folds over on to the sleeve. In this way any ease round the sleeve crown is controlled by the stitching down of the bodice armhole edge.

Run and fell seam

This seam is used for infant's underclothes and nightwear when made by hand. Therefore it has very little use nowadays. It can be used for joining lace as it is a flexible seam and can be very narrow in width.

It is always worked entirely by hand and on the wrong side of the fabric. In those two ways it differs from a double machine-stitched seam, but the actual construction of the seam is similar. Work with the wrong side of the fabric outside, and substitute fine running for the first row of machine stitching and fine hemming for the second row of machine stitching.

Machine fell seam

A machine fell seam is a combination of a double machine-stitched seam and a run and fell seam. It is made on the wrong side of the fabric, and follows the same general principles of construction. The first line of stitching is worked by machine along the fitting line, but the second line is hemmed by hand. It is used when a narrow, flat seam is required without any machine stitching being visible on the right side.

11 The preparation and use of crossway strips

The crossway cuts across the fabric grain with a diagonal slope. The warp and weft threads meet at right angles on the crossway (186). Therefore the crossway stretches as no straight thread pulls along its length. A narrow strip cut from the crossway of the fabric will stretch sufficiently to lie in a smooth line round a curve. It is therefore useful for finishing raw edges which are curved, eg neck-lines, armholes, etc.

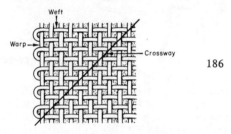

186

A strip cut at any other angle to the selvedge is said to be on the bias. Bias strips do not stretch as much as crossway strips, and will not stretch as well round a curve. Bought bias binding, however, is made from strips cut on the crossway of fabric. This varies in quality. For good results and wearing ability buy fine, soft bias binding which has an adequate turning allowance.

Folding cutting and joining crossway strips
Work on the right side of the fabric when preparing the strips to avoid handling the right side more than is necessary.

(a) Folding on the cross (187)

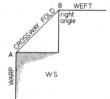

187 *To obtain a crossway fold, take a straight warp edge, the selvedge is suitable, and fold it over so that it makes a right angle with itself and lies along a weft thread. Cut through the fold from A to B, pulling the blade of the scissors right up into the fold. This gives a straight, clean cut*

(b) Cutting and trimming the strips
As the strips stretch easily they tend to lose a little width with handling. It is, therefore, wise to cut them 3 mm-5 mm wider than required.

(i) Cutting (188 and 189)

116

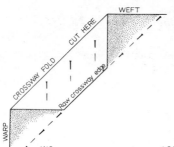

188 *Method 1. Fold over the newly cut crossway edge for the width required, and pin it in place. Mark the cutting line with pins beyond the ends of the raw crossway edge, to guide the cutting. Cut through the fold, and along the raw crossway edge, thus cutting two strips at once. Repeat this until the required number of strips has been cut*

189 *Method 2. This method is useful for fabric which frays easily or is slippery. Measure from the raw crossway edge, for the width of the strip, and mark the cutting line with pins. Cut along this line, following it very accurately*

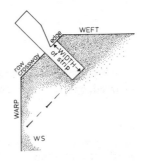

(ii) Trimming (190a and b)

Each strip must be a perfect parallelogram. The long edges are cut parallel along the crossway of the fabric; the width edges must be trimmed parallel and running with the warp, so that the join will not stretch and distort the strip. Place the strips right side up, pull out a warp thread as a guide and cut along this line (190a). Check the trimmed edge to ensure that it is straight with the grain. It is essential to trim the strips in this way otherwise it is impossible to join the strips together neatly, strongly and inconspicuously. When the width edges have been trimmed the strips will fit together in a straight line with all warp threads parallel (190b)

When working on patterned fabric, especially on stripes and checks, arrange the joins to fit the colour plan of the pattern so that an inconspicuous join is made.

190a *Trimming away an unwanted weft edge on a crossway strip*

190b *Two correctly trimmed corssway strips ready for joining*

(c) Joining the strips

Place the right side of the fabric together with the warp edges level, but allow the sharp points to protrude at each end to give a turning width of 3 mm-6 mm. Pin and tack on the fitting line, which runs between the two right angles formed by the two pointed projections (191a). The join can be sewn finally by either running or machine stitching.

Press open the turnings of the join and cut off the protruding sharp points. The join slopes across the strip in line with the warp threads (191b). If several joins are made to provide the length strip required, they must all be parallel.

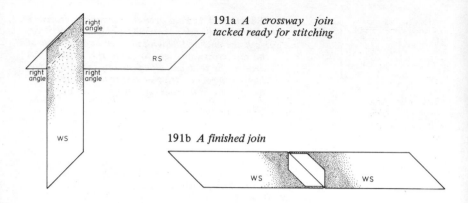

191a *A crossway join tacked ready for stitching*

191b *A finished join*

Binding

Binding gives a neat, plain finish to an edge when a hem is undesirable. The width of a binding is equal on both sides of the garment. No stitching shows on the right side. It may only be used on thin fabric as it gives four extra thicknesses of fabric to the edge being bound. Neither is it suitable for very fraying fabric as the turning has to be narrow, 6 mm at most. A wider binding is clumsy and tends to twist.

When binding an edge no turning allowance is required. If there is one, it should be cut off along the fitting line, and the first row of stitching placed as far below the fitting line as the finished width of the binding.

Binding may be set on to a straight edge, or on to a curved edge of any shape.

When setting the binding by machine, use a slightly easy upper tension and a fairly short stitch to give flexibility to the machine stitching. If hand sewing is used, the running stitches must be fine and not too tightly sewn, otherwise the binding will pucker.

Types of binding
(a) Single binding

Single binding is used on fabric which is non-transparent. The width of the crossway strip must equal 4 X the width of the finished binding plus 5 mm allowance for stretching in preparation. Cut the strips 25 mm wide for a finished binding of 5 mm width.

Place the right side of the binding to the right side of the garment. Pin, tack and stitch as far below the fitting-line as the finished width of the binding (192a). On the right side fold back the crossway strip along the line of stitching (192b). On the wrong side, fold over the edge of the strip to meet the fitting-line of the garment (192c). Tack this turning on slippery fabric. To form the binding, fold over the strip once more on the wrong side. All the raw edges are now enclosed. The folded edge of the binding comes just above the running stitches. Tack the binding in place and hem so that the stitches do not show through to the right side (192d).

To obtain a firm finish the three raw edges, ie one of garment and two of binding, come level and right up into the top fold of the binding. The binding is then evenly padded throughout its width and does not twist in washing.

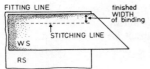
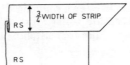
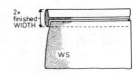

192a *The first line of stitching which sets the finished width of the binding*

192b *The first fold in the preparation of the binding*

192c *The second fold in the preparation of the binding*

192d *The finished binding on the wrong side*

(b) Double binding

This method of binding is used only on very fine or transparent fabric. It gives a narrow, firm finish.

Cut the crossway strip 6 X the finished width plus 5 mm to allow for stretching in preparation. For a finished width of 5 mm, cut the strip 35 mm wide. An even narrower finished width can be achieved if the fabric is delicately handled.

Fold the prepared strip in half lengthways, right side out, and tack through the centre (193a). Tack the strip to the right side of the garment with the three raw edges level. Tack and stitch as far below the fitting-line as the finished width of the binding (193b). Fold the outer edge of the double binding over to the wrong side and tack it just above the first line of stitching. Hem it in place so that the hemming does not show through to the right side (193c).

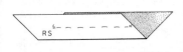
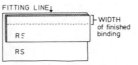
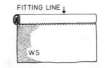

193a *The double strip tacked through the centre*

193b *The double strip with the first line of stitching*

193c *The finished double binding on the wrong side*

Binding curved edges

On a straight edge the strip is applied evenly: it is neither stretched nor eased along the raw edge. When binding is set to a curved edge, it must be either stretched or eased according to the nature of the curve.

On a concave, or inner curve, eg a round neck line, the crossway strip is slightly stretched as it is fixed in place ready for the first stitching (194). This helps to place the finished binding flat and smooth along its outer edge.

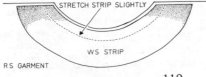

194 *A slightly stretched crossway strip sewn onto a concave curve*

Conversely, on a convex curve, eg a rounded off corner, ease the crossway strip a little in fixing it, to ensure a flat finished binding (195). Only slight easing is necessary, as the line of the first stitching must be unpuckered.

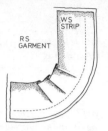

195 *An eased strip stitched to a rounded corner*

Binding angles
(a) An outer angle

Tack the strip up the right-hand side as far as the angle, and fasten off. Ease the strip round the angle, making a tapering fold in the strip (196a). Press the fold to the right and tack the strip from the other side of the angle. Stitch by hand up to the angle on the right with the fold turned to the left, and down from the angle on the left with the fold turned to the right (196b). Ensure that the angle is kept a good shape by making a back stitch when it is reached, and slipping the needle through the fold of the strip at the angle, ready to begin stitching down the second side. Keep the strip pressed to the right and turn the strip to form a binding. When setting the binding onto the wrong side, fold the pleat at the angle to the left before fixing the second side (196c). On both the right and wrong sides there is now a folded line on the bisector of the angle (196d).

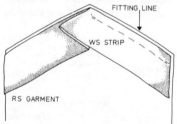

196a *The first tacking with the crossway strip folded to fit the angle*

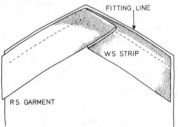

196b *The strip stitched either side of the angle with the fold left free*

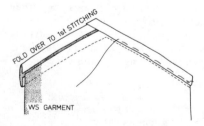

196c *The setting of the binding on the wrong side*

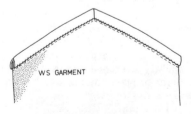

196d *The finished binding on the wrong side. Hem the fold across the width of the binding at the angle if necessaryy*

(b) An inner angle
Make a snip at the angle of the garment, making the depth of the snip nearly equal to the width of the finished binding (197a). The angle will now open out to a straight line, which can be stitched to the crossway strip. The stitching must come close to the base of the snip, but just clear of it (197b). Fold the trip to form a binding, and hem it on the wrong side. Fold back the binding at the angle, and oversew the folds at the point. Back-stitch across the width of the binding in line with the fold of the garment (197c). Flatten the dart formed by the back stitching and hem it down onto the binding (197d).

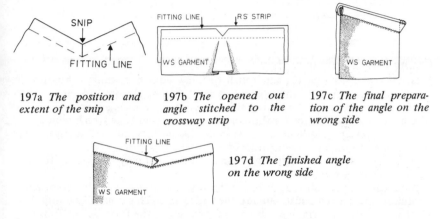

197a *The position and extent of the snip*

197b *The opened out angle stitched to the crossway strip*

197c *The final preparation of the angle on the wrong side*

197d *The finished angle on the wrong side*

The final join if a crossway strip applied to a circular edge
This join must be made parallel to any other joins in the strip, ie sloping with the warp. It must NEVER be made straight across the width of the strip. Arrange for the final join to come over a seam line of the garment, eg. at the underarm seam point of a nightdress armhole.

(a) For single binding
Place the strip in position and begin to tack about 25 mm to the left of the garment seam. Stop tacking about 25 mm to the right of this seam. Make the join so that the binding fits the edge of the garment exactly (figure 198). Finish the tacking.

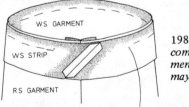

198 *The finished join coming across the garment seam. The tacking may now be finished*

(b) For double binding
The final join must always be made across the single width of the strip and parallel to the warp. Tack the double strip to the garment, beginning and finishing about 75 mm either side of a seam. Release the tacking through the centre of the strip, so that it can be handled in its single width for making the join. The two edges to be joined must be opened out to their full width. Make

121

the join along the warp (199), and press open the join without stretching the strip. Fold the strip back into its half width, finish the tacking and set as shown on page 119.

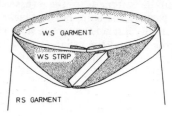

199 *The warp join made across the opened out width of the double binding*

Facing with a crossway strip

A facing also gives a neat, plain finish to a raw edge but, unlike a binding, it shows only on one side of the edge when set. It can be arranged to show either on the right side or on the wrong side. A wrong side facing may be called a false hem, and is useful for finishing a shaped or curved edge which would not set with a plain folded hem, eg a crossway facing may be used to finish the underarm curve on a yoked nightdress.

A facing makes a stronger edge than a binding and may be used on fraying fabric if carefully set.

A narrow turning allowance is required on the garment. Trim the original turning to the desired width outside the fitting line. This is usually 6 mm, but allow more on badly fraying fabric, and trim away the frays before finishing the facing.

The width of the crossway strip required equals the finished width of the facing + two turnings + 5 mm to allow for stretching and loss of width in preparation. The turning allowance on the strip should be the same as that on the garment.

A wrong side facing is fixed by laying the right side of the strip to the right side of the garment. A right side facing is fixed by laying the right side of the strip to the wrong side of the garment (200a). Press the strip upwards away from the fitting line after the first stitching is done (200b).

200a *The facing fixed in place according to the required finished effect. Machine stitching or fine running is used along the fitting line*

200b *The facing pressed back along the fitting line*

To finish a wrong side facing, fold the facing over to the wrong side of the garment, arranging a *very narrow* heading of the garment to show above the facing on the wrong side. Tack the facing close to the top edge (201a). This is essential for getting a sheer edge to the garment. Trim the raw edge of the facing if necessary, and turn it under to make the facing the required finished width, usually 10 mm-15 mm. Tack the facing along the lower edge (201b). This tacking is helpful in keeping the facing exactly even in width. Hem or slip-hem along the lower edge.

201a *A wrong side facing tacked along the top edge*

201b *A wrong side facing tacked ready for final stitching*

To finish a right side facing, fold the facing over to the right side of the garment. Arrange a narrow heading of the facing above the edge of the garment on the wrong side to give a sheer edge finish on the right side (202).

202 *A right side facing tacked at either edge to ensure a good finish*

Fix the facing on the right side with machine stitching for a plain finish (203) or, for a decorative finish, choose an embroidery stitch which is flat and strong. A machine embroidery stitch is suitable. It must be arranged to hold the lower edge of the facing and to secure the turning.

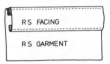

203 *A right side facing with a plain finish of straight machine stitching*

A facing for a circular edge is tacked in place and the final join is made before any permanent stitching is done. This join has already been described on page 121.

Facing curved edges (204 and 205)

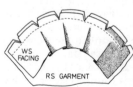

204 *When facing an outer curve, notch the turnings so that they will lie flat when the facing is turned to the other side. Be very careful not to cut the sewing stitches*

205 *When facing an inner curve, snip almost to the sewing stitches. This allows the turning to stretch out and lie flat when it is turned to the other side*

Facing angles
(a) An outer angle
Place the strip along each side of the point so that a dart may be pinned into the strip to shape it exactly to fit the angle. The pins should set the dart along the bisector of the angle.

Fold the dart to the left and set on the strip, as far as the angle, with running stitches along the fitting line. Fold the dart to the right and continue

123

the running stitches the other side of the angle. Stitch the dart in position from the angle, towards the raw edge, but leave the turning allowance free (206). Trim the turning of the dart. Fold the facing over to the opposite side of the garment and finish as required.

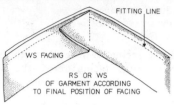

206 *The first setting, with stitched dart on the facing, for an outer angle*

(b) An inner angle

Follow the same principle as for an outer angle, but reverse the shape of the dart. Stitch the dart from fitting line to angle (207). After the strip has been joined to the garment with running stitches, snip the garment turning at the angle nearly to the fitting line. Trim dart, leaving a narrow turning. Turn the facing over to the other side.

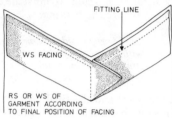

207 *The first setting, with stitched dart on the facing, for an inner angle*

To make a casing for elastic

A crossway facing turned to the wrong side and machined along both its edges is often used as a casing for elastic where the edge is too much shaped to take a hem. The outer edge is machined because it gives a smarter finish and also because it strengthens the edge against the rub of the elastic.

When the facing has been set to the right side, make a loop-stitched slot for inserting the elastic, placing it at the centre back. Turn the facing to the wrong side, tack and machine the edges (208). A loop-stitched slot is difficult to make on some fine, fraying fabrics. If this difficulty is found, a slot may be made as shown on page 103 figures 163 and 164.

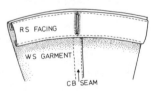

208 *The stitched casing with loop-stitched slot*

A double facing

This method of facing is used on very thin fabrics. It is easier to manipulate and is stronger and more attractive, as there is no turning to show through along the lower edge.

Cut the strip twice the required finished width of facing, plus two turnings. Prepare it as for a double binding (193a).

Tack and machine the double facing along the fitting line, setting it either

124

onto the right or wrong side according to the finish required for the garment edge (209a). Fold the facing to the right or wrong side, and fix as desired. Deal with the top edge of the facing as described on page 123.

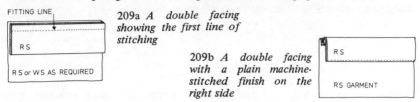

209a *A double facing showing the first line of stitching*

209b *A double facing with a plain machine-stitched finish on the right side*

To give a more decorative finish to a right side facing, a machine embroidery stitch may be used for final fixing or, if suitable, a light frilling of lace may be inserted under the fold before the final stitching is done.

12 Shaped facings

Shaped facings give a neat, strong finish to an edge, eg at neck, armhole, wrist or sleeve edges and at the centre front of button-through shirts and dresses etc. They vary in width according to their position on the garment. Suggested widths are included in the directions which follow later in this section.

The final position of a shaped facing is usually on the wrong side of a garent, as this provides a sheer and inconspicuous finish which is invisible on the right side. Wrong side facings are usually cut from the garment fabric, but can be cut from a lining fabric if necessary.

Occasionally a shaped facing is set onto the right side of a garment to form a decorative finish. In this case it can be made from either the garment fabric or a suitably contrasting one.

A hem may also be finished with a shaped facing, but this is usually referred to as a false hem and is dealt with in the hem section on page 304.

Most shaped facings are supported by interfacing fabric to give a firmer, crisper finish. The choice and handling of interfacings is a wide topic and is dealt with in a separate section on page 140. If this shaped facing section is studied first, it will give basic understanding of points underlying the correct use and handling of interfacings.

Shaped facings reproduce the exact shape of the area they are neatening, and must be cut with the warp and weft grains matching the direction of the garment grains in this area (210a and b, and 211). This gives a perfect setting round the edge when the facing is finished, and the balanced grains ensure that the facing remains flat after repeated washing or cleaning.

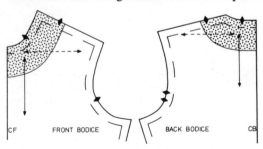

211 The shape, position and graining of an armhole facing marked on a bodice pattern, following the same plan as figures 210a and b. The back armhole facing follows the same principles

210a and b *The shaded areas indicate the shape and position of a round neck facing, marked on the front and back of a bodice pattern. The arrowed lines show the position of the fabric grains for both the bodice and the neck facings. The solid arrow points with the warp and the dotted arrow with the weft*

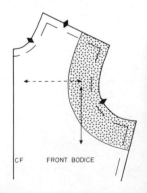

Neck and armhole facing patterns

Making the facing patterns

The area to be faced is exactly reproduced onto spare paper for the facing pattern, unless a dart runs into the edge to be faced. In this case fold out and pin the dart on the garment pattern before making the facing pattern. Do not attempt to make a dart in the facing as this would give unwanted bulk at the finished edge. For example, a dart running into the back neckline would have to be folded out before the facing pattern could be made.

Allow seam, neck and armhole turnings to correspond with those of the bodice. Allow 5 mm-10 mm turnings on the inner edge of the facing. The finished width of neck and armhole facings is usually 40 mm-50 mm.

(a) Neck facing patterns

Pin the neck areas of the bodice pattern onto a piece of spare paper. If a dart has been folded out of the neck, the pattern will no longer lie flat. In this case the edges to be outlined must be pinned flat onto the spare paper, and the remainder of the pattern allowed to lift away from it. Outline the shoulder, neck, centre front and centre back edges. When the patterns are unpinned, the outlines will be visible on the spare paper (212).

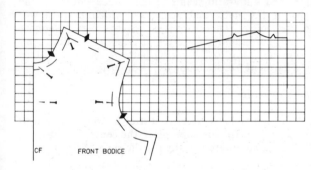

212 *Preparing to make a neck facing patern. On the left, the front bodice has been pinned to spare paper ready for outlining. On the right, the required outline has been drawn round the back bodice pattern*

Label the centre front and the centre back lines and mark the fitting lines at the neck and shoulder edges, and at the centre back if there is a seam in this position.

Mark in the grain lines parallel to the centre front and the centre back. Add together the required finished width of facing plus the inner edge turning allowance. Measuring from the neck fitting line, mark this distance along the shoulder fitting lines, down the centre edges, and at intervals in between. Join the marked points to give a firm outline to the inner edge of the facing pattern (213).

213 *The facing shapes, showing on the left the marked points for the front facing, and on the right the firm outline of the inner edge on the back facing, which is ready for cutting out*

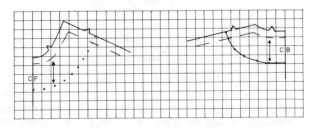

Cut out the two neck facing patterns after checking that notches and fitting and grain lines are clearly marked (214a and b).

FRONT NECK
FACING

214a *The front neck facing pattern*

214b *The back neck facing pattern*

BACK NECK FACING

(b) Armhole facing patterns

An armhole facing pattern is made in a similar way to a neck facing pattern but, in this case, it is the armhole and part of the shoulder and side seams which are outlined. Before outlining the necessary edges, however, draw a grain line in the armhole area of both the back and front bodice patterns, making them parallel to the bodice grain lines. They can be traced off later onto the facing patterns to ensure accurate cutting out.

The problem of neck and armhole facings and bodice fitting

Alterations to the shoulder and underarm seams of the bodice will affect the size and often the shape of the neck and armholes, which in turn will necessitate alterations to the facings. Therefore it is wise to reserve adequate fabric for the facings, and cut them out after fitting the bodice. Any alterations required can thus be made to the facing pattern, and the pattern checked against the altered garment before being used for cutting out.

Cutting out neck and armhole facings
(a) Neck facings

Place the centre front and the centre back edges to a straight warp fold unless there is an opening in the garment. In this case, place the centre line straight with the warp grain and allow an adequate turning for the type of opening.

(b) Armhole facings

When laying the armhole facing pattern, set the grain line accurately by checking its distance from the selvedge or a straight warp edge (215).

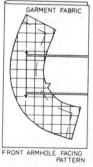

GARMENT FABRIC

FRONT ARMHOLE FACING
PATTERN

215 *The grain line of an armhole facing pattern balanced against a warp edge of fabric*

An armhole facing is usually composed of two pattern sections, viz a back section and front section. These join together at the shoulder and underarm lines to make a whole facing to fit round the armhole. When cutting out the armhole facings on fabric which has a right and wrong side, care must be

128

taken to cut one pair of sections for the left armhole, and one pair for the right armhole. See page 57 for guidance in this.

Occasionally a bought pattern supplies an armhole facing pattern cut in one piece, with the grain balanced to the front bodice. This means that the grain on the back area of the facing is not aligned with the back bodice grain, and can cause the facing to 'wring' after washing or cleaning. It is also impossible to adjust the facing to correspond with an alteration which may have been made in fitting the shoulder lines of the bodice. To ensure a satisfactory set at the back armhole and to make allowance for shoulder fitting, cut across the facing pattern at the shoulder line to make two pattern sections (216).

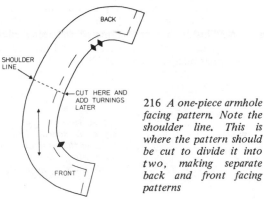

216 *A one-piece armhole facing pattern. Note the shoulder line. This is where the pattern should be cut to divide it into two, making separate back and front facing patterns*

After cutting across the pattern, make any necessary alterations to the shoulder lines and add a seam turning allowance to the two shoulder edges. Pin the back section of the facing pattern onto the armhole area of the back bodice pattern, and mark in the grain line parallel to the grain line on the back bodice pattern.

Making neck and armhole facings
Neck and armhole fitting lines should be stay-stitched if the fabric is inclined to stretch on curved edges.

Before making a neck facing, the shoulder seams of the garment must be finished and pressed, and the neck fitting line checked.

Before making an armhole facing, the shoulder and side seams of the garment must be finished and pressed, and the armhole fitting lines checked.

Make any corrections necessary to the neck or armhole fitting lines, and make sure that they run smoothly over the seams.

Pin the facings, and fit the pinned facing to the garment edge. The seams of the facing should pair with the corresponding seams in the garment; the centre front and centre back lines of a neck facing should match those of the bodice.

Adjust the facing to size if necessary, then tack and machine the facing seams. Trim them to 5 mm-6 mm and press open. Do not neaten the facing seams. This would give extra bulk to the edge and is unnecessary as, finally, the wrong side of the facing is entirely enclosed. On thinner fabrics, fold over the inner edge turnings of the facing to the wrong side, pin, tack and edge stitch by machine to neaten. Trim the turning close to the machine stitching (217).

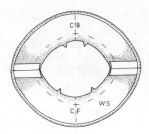

217 *A neck facing show-ing the trimmed shoulder seams and the neatened outer edge turning mac-hined and trimmed*

Alternative inner edge finish;–
On heavier fabrics an edge-stitched turning is too bulky, and tends to cause a ridge on the right side of the garment. In this case, machine a line of straight stitching about 2 mm inside the fitting-line of the inner edge. Trim off the turning allowance close to the machine stitching and machine zig zag over the raw edge, right side uppermost (218).

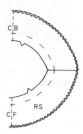

218 *A section of a neck facing in heavier fabric, showing the straight mac-hine stitch and zigzag finish on the inner edge*

Setting neck and armhole facings
Pin the prepared facing to the neckline or armhole of the garment with right sides together, match the fitting lines and pair the seams and the balance notches. Tack and machine the facing to the garment, stitching along the fitting line, and press after removing the tacking stitches.

Layer the turnings by trimming the garment turning to 10 mm, and the facing turning to 5 mm. Light, non-fraying fabric may be trimmed to a narrower width. Shoulder seam turnings should be snipped diagonally at the neck edge. Where the edge is curved, snip nearly to the fitting line at 12 mm intervals. The snipping allows the turning to open out and set flat when the facing is turned to the wrong side (219).

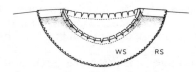

219 *A round neck facing machined in place. In this figure the layered turn-ings are visible at the front and the snipping shows all round the neck*

At the corner of a square neck, the turning must be snipped nearly to the stitching (220). This allows the turnings to stretch out and flatten when the facing is turned to its final position on the wrong side of the garment.

130

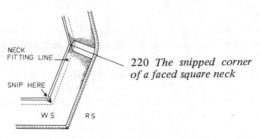

220 *The snipped corner of a faced square neck*

The purpose of a neck or armhole facing is to give a sheer finish to the outer edge. There should be no sign of the facing showing on the right side when the edge is finished. It is necessary, therefore, to press the turnings onto the facing before folding it back to the wrong side, and to roll the stitching line to the inside of the neck or armhole edge to give a smooth, sheer line on the right side. It is difficult to achieve this finish with fabrics which are not easily pressed flat, eg Crimplene, Terylene blends, etc. To overcome this problem, the neck turnings can be under-stitched (machined) to the facing after they have been layered and snipped. Take care to tack them firmly in order to set them flat before machining (221a and b).

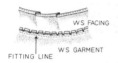

221a and b *Sections of a neck facing showing right and wrong sides, with the understitching set just above the fitting line*

To finish the facing, fold it over to the wrong side of the garment, rolling the fitting-line slightly to the wrong side. This prevents the seam line from showing on the right side when the edge is finally pressed. Tack round the neck or armhole edge and press it very lightly on the wrong side. Pin and hem the inner edge to any seams or darts which it crosses (222). Remove tackings and give a final press to the facing. Use a pressing cloth to prevent shining or marking on the right side.

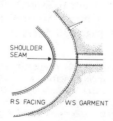

222 *A section of a finished neck facing with the inner edge attached to the shoulder seam and back neck dart. Note, also, the neck edge which shows the fitting line rolled slightly to the wrong side, and the line of understitching*

Setting a collar with a neck facing
Refer to the Collar Section on page 216.

A neck facing with a zip opening
Refer to the Zip Section on pages 168 and 212.

131

Sleeve facings

A sleeve facing can be used to neaten the lower edge of any sleeve except a very short one with scarcely any length of seam. A narrow crossway facing is usually used in this case, or the sleeve is made double.

A sleeve facing pattern may be included with the garment pattern, but if it is not, or you wish to alter the suggested sleeve finish, a facing pattern can be made following the general principles given for making other facing patterns:
(a) Pin the lower edge of the sleeve pattern to paper.
(b) Outline the lower edge of the sleeve and then outline the seam edges for a depth equal to the lower edge turning width, plus the required finished width of facing, plus 5 mm-6 mm turning allowance for the top edge of the facing.
(c) Unpin the sleeve pattern, and join the two side lines of the facing shape with a line drawn parallel to the wrist or lower edge line, making the facing a suitable width for the type of sleeve. An average width is 30 mm-40 mm plus a turning allowance of 5 mm-6 mm on the top edge. Mark in the fitting lines and the grain line, which must lie in the same direction as the grain line of the sleeve. Cut out the facing pattern (223).

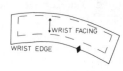

223 A sleeve facing pattern made to finish a long sleeve with a wrist edge which will pass over the hand, without requiring an opening

Cutting out sleeve facings

A sleeve facing pattern must be placed with strict attention to the grain of the fabric, otherwise the faced edge will tend to twist, especially after washing or cleaning.

As the facing pattern is small, it is sometimes fitted into odd pieces of fabric, and the two facings cut singly. If this is done on fabric which has a right and wrong side, remember to cut a pair of facings, ie the paper pattern must be reversed when cutting the second facing.

Making and setting sleeve facings

Fold the facing in half, wrong side out, to bring the seam edges over each other. Tack and machine along the seam fitting line. Trim the turnings to 5 mm-6 mm and press open flat, taking care not to stretch the facing. Neaten the upper edge (ie the edge with the 5 mm-6 mm turning allowance) as directed for armhole and neck facings on page 130. Press the facing. Make the second one to match.

224a A prepared wrist facing with a machined turning at the upper edge. This is the better finish for thinner fabrics

224b A prepared wrist facing with a straight stitch and zigzag finish at the upper edge. This is suitable for heavier fabrics

Setting the facing

Place the right sides of the sleeve and the facing together with seams and balance notches aligned. Tack and machine along the fitting line. Layer the edge by trimming the facing turnings to 5 mm-6 mm and the sleeve turnings to 10 mm (225a). Snip the edge to give flexibility to the turnings (225b). Press round the fitting line.

225a *A sleeve facing machined in place, with the turnings layered*

225b *The layered turnings snipped nearly to the machine stitching*

Fold the facing to the inside of the sleeve, bringing the join just inside the edge to give a sheer finish on the right side. Tack it in place and slip-hem it to the sleeve. Press the edge lightly, remove the tacking and press more firmly, using a pressing cloth to guard against marking the right side (226).

226 *This facing has been slip-hemmed to the wrist edge of a sleeve. The thread has been fastened on and off at the seam, where plain hemming can be worked over the turnings for strength. Note the position of the lower edge seam*

If the inner edge of the facing has been neatened with machine stitching and zig zagging, sew this edge to the sleeve with catch stitching (refer page 146).

Bodice blouse and dress facings with buttoned fastenings

These facings are used in the following positions:
(a) At the centre front or centre back of blouses with a button-through opening.
(b) At the centre front of a button-through dress or housecoat, with or without a waist seam.
(c) At the centre front bodice of a dress which has a buttoned opening from neck to waist line, eg a shirt waister.

The facing neatens and supports the opening edges of the dress from the neck to the waist or hem edge. It can be cut all in one with the dress pattern, or it can be cut as a separate part and joined to the dress at the edge of the opening. In either case an extension is allowed beyond the centre front line to form an overwrap for fastening the opening (237 on page 138).

A front facing cut in one with the bodice (227 and 228)

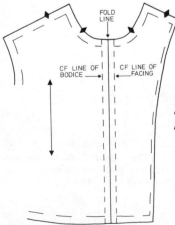

227 *A front facing cut in one with the front bodice pattern*

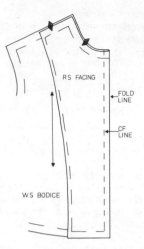

228 *The bodice pattern with the facing section folded back along the fold line as it will lie finally on the wrong side of the bodice. The two centre front lines come over each other, also the neck edges of bodice and facing fit together, and the facing lies partly along the shoulder line. In this case the position of the fabric grains is obviously identical in both bodice and facing*

A front facing cut separately from the bodice (229 and 230)

A front bodice pattern and a separate facing pattern are shown in figure 229. Note the centre front lines, the fold lines and the turning allowance for joining the facing to the bodice. The grain line of the facing is marked parallel to the centre front line to align it with the bodice grain. When the front facing pattern is fitted over the front bodice pattern (230) it is seen to be identical in shape to the centre front area of the bodice, and to have balanced grain and fitting lines.

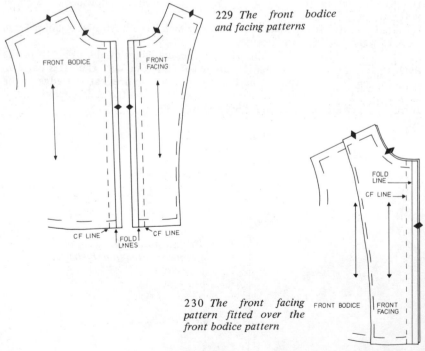

229 *The front bodice and facing patterns*

230 *The front facing pattern fitted over the front bodice pattern*

Setting bodice facings

If the fabric is soft and inclined to stretch, the neck lines of bodice and facing should be stay stitched to prevent stretching out of shape.

The shoulder seams of the bodice should be stitched, neatened and pressed.

Prepare a back neck facing, but do not, as yet, neaten the inner edge. In width the back neck facing should equal the length of the shoulder edge of the front facing. The inclusion of an interfacing is dealt with on page 146.

(a) Setting a front facing with a plain faced neck edge

1a With a front facing cut in one with the bodice, fold the front facings back to the right side of the bodice, turning along the fold line, or

1b With a separate front facing, place the right sides together and pin and tack the front facing to the front bodice along the fold line. The fold line, therefore, becomes the fitting line for this seam.

2 Pin facings and bodice together at the waist line, or lower edge, and set a pin on each front facing at the centre front neck fitting line. This holds the front facings in position for handling.

3 Pin the back neck facings to the front facings at the shoulder lines, and check that the prepared neck facing fits round the neck fitting line of the bodice. The shoulder seams and centre back points should meet exactly. Adjust the shoulder seams, if necessary, to ensure a good fit.

4 Tack and machine the shoulder seams of the facing and press them open flat. Trim the turnings to 5 mm-6 mm.

5 Pin and tack the right side of the facing to the right side of the bodice neck, matching the centre back points, the shoulder seams and the front neck balance notches.

6 The facing is now ready to be machined to the bodice. Work with the facing uppermost in the machine, following either method 'a' or method 'b'.

(a) With a facing cut in one with the bodice, machine the facing to the neck along the neck fitting line, stitching right across from the left front fold line to the right front fold line (231). Fasten off the machine thread ends very firmly and neatly.

(b) With a separate front facing, machine up the left front fold line, round the neck fitting line and down the right front fold line. Turn the fabric carefully at the centre front neck points to ensure accurate and matching corners (232).

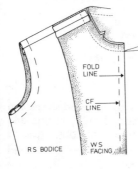

231 *A section of a bodice with a front facing cut in one, showing the machine stitching at the neck*

232 *A section of a bodice with a front facing cut separately, showing machine stitching on the fold line and at the neck edge*

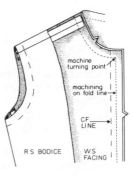

135

7 The inner edge of the whole facing can now be neatened. Fold back the turning allowance to the wrong side along one front facing, continue along the back neck section and then along the second front edge. Press and/or tack the turning and edge stitch by machine (233).

8 Trim the bodice neck turning to 10 mm or less, and the facing neck turning a little narrower. Snip the neck turnings at 10 mm or 15 mm intervals according to the stretchability of the fabric. Take care not to cut the machine stitching. Snip diagonally across the corner of the turnings at the centre front to reduce bulk (233).

If the front facing has been cut separately, the fold line seam must also be resduced. Trim the bodice turning to 6 mm and the facing turning to 3 mm (234).

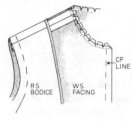

233 *A top front section of a bodice with front facing cut in one, showing the neatened inner edge of the facing and the trimmed and snipped neck edge*

234 *The centre front neck section of a bodice with the facing cut separately, showing the layered turnings at the fold line seam, and the trimmed and snipped neck turnings*

9 Turn the facing over to the wrong side, pushing the edges right out to the machining. The snipping allows the neck turnings to open out and set flat, giving a sheer edge to the neck with thin, well-shaped corners at the centre front.

Gently roll the neck seam line to lie just to the wrong side of the bodice neck. This is only fractionally possible, but it prevents the facing from showing on the right side. If the front facing has been cut out separately, roll the fold line seam just to the wrong side of the front edge of the bodice (235).

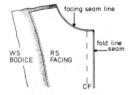

235 *A section of the seam lines at neck and centre front, set just to the wrong side of the bodice*

10 Tack the outer edges of the facing, if necessary, to hold a good shape and press them lightly. Remove the tacking and press more firmly, taking any precautions required by the fabric to prevent shining or marking the edges.

11 Hem the facing across the bodice shoulder seams and to the back neck darts if there are any.

(b) Setting a collar with a shaped facing
See the Collar Section on page 216.

Making patterns for bodice blouse or dress facings for centre front openings

It is useful to know how to extend the centre front of a pattern to provide a facing at this edge. A pattern originally made with a fold at the centre front can be adapted and turned into a pattern for a button-through bodice, blouse or dress. The same principles can be applied to make a button-through opening at the back of a bodice, etc. In this case the alteration is based on the centre back line instead of the centre front line.

In order to fasten, the front opening has to be arranged to overlap. This necessitates adding extra width to the original pattern beyond the centre front line. The centre front lines of the bodice can then overlap to fasten, and keep the bodice the correct size for fitting (236).

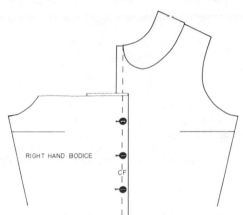

RIGHT HAND BODICE

CF

236 *This figure shows a bodice with a faced front opening. The whole of the left-hand side of the bodice is visible but, for clarity, the top of the right-hand side has been cut away to show the arrangement of the centre front overlap. When the opening is closed, and the two centre front lines meet, the extra width allowed forms a convenient overlap for fastening the bodice*

Width of overlap to allow

To keep the correct size for fitting, and a balanced appearance to the finished bodice, the buttons must come on the centre front line, and fasten the opening in this position (236). The width of the extension beyond the centre front varies according to the width of the buttons, as half of each button will lie outside the centre front. A small margin of fabric should show between the button edge and the outer fold.

For a button with a diameter of 12 mm allow a 10 mm extension
For a button with a diameter of 25 mm allow a 18 mm extension
For a button with a diameter of 40 mm allow a 26 mm extension

When using a bought pattern with a faced front opening, the width allowed beyond the centre front line must be considered when buying the buttons. If the facing pattern is being made, however, the width of the extension can be made to suit any size of button.

(a) A facing pattern cut in one with a bodice pattern

Find a piece of spare paper onto which the bodice pattern will just fit. Overlap and pin the centre front edge of the bodice pattern to the spare paper. Outside the centre front edge, rule a line to give the required allowance for the opening overlap. This will be the fold line for the facing. Extend the neck and waist lines to meet the fold line (237).

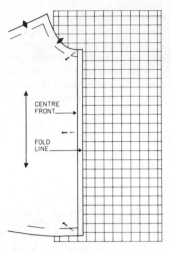

237 *The overlap extension drawn outside the centre front line*

Sellotape the centre front edge to the spare paper, which should then be folded back along the newly ruled line. Pin the pattern to it. Cut from the fold, round the neck line and along the shoulder line for approximately half the shoulder length. Cut along the waist line. Unpin the pattern and open out the spare paper which has now become the facing section of the bodice pattern.

Rule the centre front line of the facing (dotted in 238), making it parallel to the bodice centre front line, with the fold line midway between the two. At the waist, mark a point on the facing about 75 mm from the fold line. Join the facing shoulder line to the marked point, making a smooth curve. Draw the fitting lines on the neck, shoulder and waist edges. The surplus paper is now cut away along the curved line from shoulder to waist, and the pattern is ready for use (238).

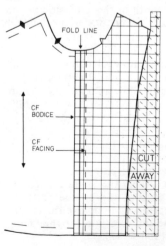

238 *The facing prepared on the spare paper*

(b) A facing pattern cut separately from the bodice
Study figure 229 on page 134, and the appearance of the required facing for a front bodice can be seen.

Prepare the bodice pattern first, by extending it beyond the centre front for the required width of extension plus a turning allowance equal in width to the neck turning allowance. Pin the prepared bodice pattern onto spare paper and outline half the shoulder line, the neck, the front edges and the waist. Remove the bodice pattern. Rule the fitting/fold line, and the centre front line. Draw the curved inner edge of the facing (see previous instructions, figure 238). Cut out the facing pattern.

(c) A facing pattern for a full-length garment
A front facing pattern for a dress or housecoat is made on the same principles as those already described, but the facing, of course, has to extend from neck to hem line.

If the garment has a waist seam, this need not be reproduced in the facing. Overlap the waist fitting lines of bodice and skirt before drawing the fold line, so that the facing pattern can be drawn in one piece.

(d) Making facing patterns for a back opening
These are easily made from the directions previously given, but substituting 'centre back' for 'centre front' when following the text.

(e) Facing a waist line
A skirt or slacks with a faced waist-line also need a shaped facing, but it is not satisfactory unless it is interfaced for added strength and to prevent stretching. For this reason, a waist facing is dealt with in the interfacing section on page 152.

Right side facing
If a decorative right side facing is to be made, follow the directions for pattern making already given.

When setting a right-side facing, the basic principles are exactly the same as for a wrong-side facing, with the following exceptions:
1 In the first place, set the right side of the facing to the wrong side of the garment.
2 When turning the facing over onto the right side, allow the facing to rise slightly above the garment on the wrong side, to give a sheer edge on the right side.
3 Take particular care to make a smooth, flat turning along the inner edge of the facing. Fold the turning to the wrong side of the facing and tack it close to the fold. On a curved edge the turning may need notching. Trim the tacked turnings as narrowly as the type of fabric will allow, to prevent a bulky edge.
4 Hold down the inner edge of the facing with machine stitching or a suitable decorative stitch, according to the type and style of the garment.

13 Interfacings

A crisper, firmer finish can be given to facings if they are set in conjunction with an interfacing. The added firmness of an interfacing also prevents the faced edge from stretching in use.

The position of interfacings

When a firm, crisp finish is required, the interfacing is attached to the garment, but for a softer appearance, it is usually set onto the facing. However for thin, stretch or knitted fabrics, always set the interfacing onto the facing otherwise a hard, conspicuous line will show on the right side of the garment.

Examples of areas which require interfacing are the faced edges of necks and armholes, the edges of button-through openings in dresses, blouses, etc, collars, cuffs, belts and some pockets. Interfacing is also used at the front, sleeve and hem edges of jackets, and it must always be used to strengthen a shaped facing which finishes the waist edges of slacks or skirts.

Types of interfacing

Interfacings are available in different types and weights. It is important to balance the weight of the interfacing with the weight of the garment fabric, as a thin interfacing cannot support a heavy fabric, and a thick interfacing gives a clumsy finish to fine fabrics. As a general rule the interfacing should be a little lighter in weight than the fabric it is supporting, but it must be firm enough to support the fabric adequately. Washable interfacings are essential for use with washable fabrics and, in all cases, the interfacing should be non-fraying.

(a) Woven interfacings

This type of interfacing obviously has warp and weft grains. Examples are fine, closely woven cotton lawn, cotton organdie and nylon organza, which are suitable for use with light and medium weight fabrics. Canvas, holland and tailoring linen give a better result with heavy fabrics. These interfacing fabrics do not have a right or wrong side.

(b) Bonded interfacings

These are made from processed man-made fibres, and have no grain as they are not woven, eg Vilene. They are made in a variety of weights ranging from very thin, suitable for light-weight fabrics, to heavy-weight, suitable for heavy fabrics. These interfacings do not have a right or wrong side.

(c) Iron-on interfacings

Both woven and bonded interfacings are available with one side treated so

140

that they can be ironed-on with a hot iron to the wrong side of the garment fabric. This fuses the interfacing to the fabric it is supporting. The treated side becomes the wrong side of the interfacing fabric. Iron-on woven interfacing is always made from cotton fabric. Examples are Moyseel and Staflex.

Choosing interfacings

It is necessary to consider the fibre content of the garment fabric when choosing an interfacing, eg nylon organza is ideal for use with light-weight synthetic fabrics as it is similar in its washing and drying qualities; cotton lawn and organdie are both satisfactory for interfacing cotton fabrics for the same reasons. Cotton lawn is also useful for interfacing light and medium-weight wool as it is non-slippery, and the washing and dry-cleaning required for wool cannot impair cotton fabric.

Neither woven nor bonded interfacings are suitable for use with lace as they spoil its openwork appearance. In this case, net is the best choice for interfacing as it merges with the background structure of the lace. Pull both the lace and net in directions which correspond to the warp and weft of woven fabric. This will show which is the firmer direction of the mesh in each case, and these can be matched when cutting and placing the net interfacing.

Plain bonded interfacing can be used with knitted fabrics, eg Crimplene and wool jersey. An iron-on, woven interfacing, such as Moyseel, gives a good result on these fabrics, if applied to the facings, as some of the jersey flexibility is retained. Iron-on, bonded interfacing sets jersey too firmly, and its flexibility is lost. This makes the facings too rigid to set well along the garment edges.

Woven interfacings give a smoother finish to folded and curved edges, eg collars, providing the grain is matched with the garment grain. Bonded interfacing does not always set smoothly round the curved fold of a collar. It is inclined to crack and break the required smoothness of the folded edge.

Iron-on interfacings, although very convenient, are not satisfactory for use on large areas, as they are likely to separate from the fabric with wear, washing or cleaning, giving a patchy effect. They can be used successfully on smaller areas such as cuffs and smaller facings which have been cut on the straight grain. Crosscut fabric does not set with its characteristic softness if an interfacing is ironed-on, as it cancels the pliable quality of the crossway. Fabric with a nubbed or hairy finish cannot be supported satisfactorily, as the rough surface does not allow the iron-on interfacing to adhere firmly. The right side appearance of thin fabric, and fabric with an open weave, is often spoilt by the use of an iron-on interfacing, as the colour may be changed and/or an opaque effect may result.

Cutting interfacings

Some patterns contain special pattern pieces for the interfacings. If these are not provided, the facing patterns may be used.

Woven interfacing must be cut with strict attention to the grain line of the pattern, so that the grain of the garment, facing and interfacing all match.

Bonded interfacings, as they have no grain, can have the pattern pieces set in any position which makes for economical cutting. This is the great advantage of bonded interfacing.

In most cases it is safer to cut the interfacing with the same turning allowance as the garment and with the balance notches clearly indicated. The interfacing can then be set quickly and accurately.

Some collars and cuffs are made with a fold along the outer edge, and are cut twice the finished size, plus side and neck or wrist turnings. In this case the interfacing is cut to cover half the collar or cuff (239).

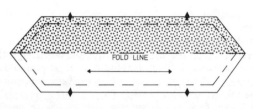

239 *The shaded portion of this collar pattern shows the size of interfacing to cut. Note the three edges where turnings are required. As the interfacing will be catch-stitched to the collar along the fold line, no turning is needed here*

Iron-on interfacings need special care in cutting out, as the adhesive provides a wrong side to the fabric. When cutting interfacing for a back neck which is divided by an opening, both a left-hand and a right-hand section must be cut. Similarly when cutting armhole interfacings, left-hand and right-hand sections must be cut from both the back and front patterns.

Joining interfacings

When a long strip of interfacing is required, eg at the front of a button-through dress or housecoat, it is often possible to save meterage by making a join in the interfacing, but with light-weight fabric, test first to ensure that this will not show through. Allow 5 mm turning on each edge for the join.

(a) Joining plain interfacing

Overlap the edges of the interfacing sections for 10mm, and tack down the centre of the overlap. Machine along each side of the tacking with either straight or narrow zigzag stitching. Trim away the surplus turning close to the machine stitching on either side and press the join (240a and b).

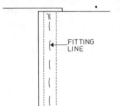

240a *Straight machining stitched either side of the tacking*

240b *The finished seam with turnings trimmed. Zigzag stitch has been used in this case. The fitting line comes down the centre of the overlapping seam*

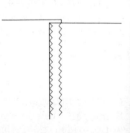

(b) Joining iron-on interfacing

Allow a 5 mm turning allowance on one of the joining edges. Take the strip without a turning allowance, set it in position on the garment and iron it in place. Overlap the second strip for the 5 mm turning allowance, align it in position and iron it in place.

142

Setting interfacings

The following directions guide the setting of interfacings to garments. Once the interfacing is fixed in position, the fabric to which it is attached is handled as a single layer, and the facing is applied as directed in the section on Shaped Facings, page 126. The only exception is for the interfaced waist edge of skirts and slacks. This process is fully described in this section as it is not dealt with elsewhere.

Interfacing garment edges

Careful placing and setting of interfacings are essential if the finished edge is to have a good appearance. The interfacing should neither show through the outer fabric nor make a visible ridge, along its lower edge, on the right side of the garment. Fitting lines and balance notches must be accurately matched so that the interfacing fits exactly into position without being either stretched or eased.

(a) Setting plain woven interfacing

When a woven interfacing is used, the alignment of the fabric grains on garment, interfacing and facing must be checked, and the interfacing set into position before any final stitching is done. This applies to both plain and iron-on woven interfacings (241).

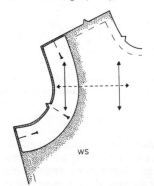

241 A plain interfacing pinned to the armhole of a sleeveless dress. The interfacing is set to the wrong side of the dress. The warp grains (shown by solid arrows) are parallel, which brings the weft grains (dotted arrow) also into alignment. The interfacing is now ready to be tacked to the dress

When thin interfacing is used, it can be sewn in with the garment seam, and the turning trimmed away close to the machining (242). The seam is then neatened and pressed in the usual way. The interfacing is thus held firmly and does not add bulk to the seam.

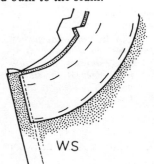

242 Interfacing sewn in with an underarm seam. The turning is shown trimmed close to the machining

If a heavy interfacing is used on a heavy fabric, the seam may be too bulky if the interfacing is machined into it. In this case, the interfacing is trimmed away to the fitting line of the dress seam and is not stitched in with it. After the seam is machined, the turnings are neatened, usually with machine zigzagging. The seam is then pressed open and catch-stitched to the interfacing without stitching through to the dress (243). Work the catch stitch rather loosely and coarsely as it will later be covered by the facing.

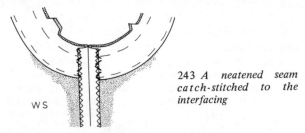

WS

243 *A neatened seam catch-stitched to the interfacing*

(b) Setting plain bonded interfacing

Bonded interfacing is set in exactly the same way as woven interfacing, except that no consideration has to be given to fabric grain.

(c) Setting iron-on interfacing

Iron-on interfacing must not be attached hurriedly. Check first that the garment is smooth and that the grain is not pulled out of alignment by careless setting on the ironing board. If the interfacing is ironed-on thoughtlessly, the garment fabric may be set off grain.

Iron the iron-on interfacing to the garment as indicated in figure 241. In the case of bonded iron-on interfacing there is, of course, no grain to align. Trim away the seam turning allowance before fusing the interfacing to the garment fabric to prevent bulk and hardening at the seam lines.

Use as hot an iron as possible for setting on the interfacing. Test spare scraps first to find a suitable temperature. The interfacing will not fuse if too cool an iron is used. Too hot an iron overmelts the fusing material and spoils the appearance of the right side of the fabric. Use even pressure over the whole area. Do not slide the iron backwards and forwards, as this could cause the interfacing to slip and wrinkle as it is fused to the garment (244).

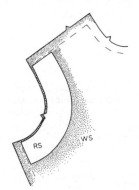

RS   WS

244 *Iron-on interfacing fused to a bodice arm-hole, showing the trimmed edges at the shoulder and underarm seam lines*

The seams can now be made, neatened and pressed open. It is unwise to trim away the interfacing turnings at neck and armhole edges. The adhesive may weaken with repeated washing or cleaning, so it is best to hold it by the machine stitching at these edges. It is then permanently fixed, and will retain its support of the faced edges throughout the life of the garment. If it will pull off easily from the fabric of the turning allowances, it can be cut away close to the machine stitching.

Setting neck and armhole facings to interfaced edges

As the interfacing is already firmly attached to the garment fabric by tacking or fusing and seaming, the neck and/or armhole edges of the garment can be handled as single fabric. The facings are set as directed in the section beginning on page 129.

Interfacing neck and armhole facings

The facing pattern can be used for cutting out the interfacing. When using a woven interfacing fabric, careful attention must be paid to the alignment of the fabric grain when cutting and setting the interfacing. Bonded interfacings require no grain alignment.

(a) Plain interfacing

This is tacked to the facing sections before they are joined to make either a complete neck or a complete armhole facing. With thin interfacing, the sections are joined and the seams tacked as shown in figure 242. Heavier interfacing is treated in a similar way to that shown in figure 243, but remember that facing turnings are not neatened, so the zigzagging of the seam turnings is not required in this case, and the catch-stitching is worked over the raw edge of the facing turnings.

(b) Iron-on interfacing

The woven type must be matched in grain with the grain of the facing. All iron-on interfacing requires the same care in setting as outlined on page 143, but substitute 'facing' for 'garment' when reading these guiding points. The shoulder turning of a neck interfacing, and the shoulder and underarm turnings of an armhole interfacing are trimmed away before ironing the interfacing to the facing sections. Leave neck and armhole turnings intact for the reasons already given above.

Once interfacing is ironed in place, the facing sections can be joined together. The facing is then handled as a single layer of fabric, and is attached as in the section beginning on page 129.

Interfacing buttoned openings on dresses and blouses etc

The main purpose of using an interfacing on these openings is to give support for the fastenings, and to provide a crisp, sheer edge to the opening. To choose the best method of application, the type of fastening to be used must be considered. For bound buttonholes, set the interfacing onto the garment, as it forms a protective layer between the garment and the binding fabric. Either plain or iron-on interfacing can be used with bound buttonholes (see page 141 for guidance on the choice of interfacings). When making hand or machine worked buttonholes, set the interfacing onto the facing, as this helps to strengthen the back of the buttonholes. Plain interfacing gives a softer finish to hand-worked butt~ ;holes, but either plain or iron-on interfacing is satisfactory with machine wo.ked buttonholes. These points apply whether the facing is cut in one with the garment, or whether it is cut separately and joined on later.

(a) Attaching the interfacing to the garment
(i) Plain interfacing used with a facing cut in one with the garment: The interfacing is cut without a turning along the long, curved edge, and is set onto the bodice so that it fits up to the fold line. It is tacked to the bodice at neck, shoulder and waist fitting-lines, and catch-stitched along the folded line (245 and 246a, b and c).

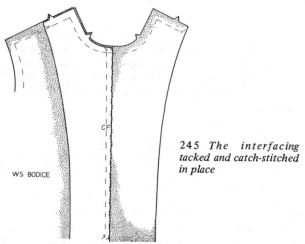

245 *The interfacing tacked and catch-stitched in place*

Catch stitch(246a, b and c).
Catch stitch is used to hold the interfacing in place at the fold line. This is necessary to prevent it from curling back in wear, washing or cleaning. The stitch is worked alternately into the interfacing and the garment, picking up a very small amount of fabric with each stitch. When stitching into the garment fabric, the needle picks up a very small stitch just outside the fold line, ie in the facing section. When the facing is folded back into position the stitches do not show from the right side of the garment.

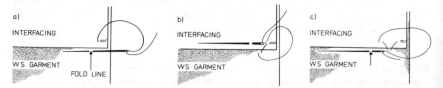

246a,b and c *The working of a catch stitch. When fastening on and stitching into the interfacing, be very careful not to stitch through to the garment*

(ii) Plain interfacing used with a facing cut separately: In this case the interfacing is cut with the same turning allowance as the facing, except on the long, curved edge, where no turning allowance is required. It is tacked to the wrong side of the garment along the shoulder, neck, fold line and lower edge. It must be set absolutely flat to the garment so that there is no possibility of puckering. The facing is then set to the right side of the garment and tacked along the fold line. Check that this, too, is flat, and that the fabric grains of the garment, facing (and interfacing if a woven type) are all aligned. The three layers are joined together by machining along the fold line. Press to flatten the machined line. Trim away the interfacing along the machine stitching (fold line) and layer the other two turnings, making the bodice turning slightly wider than the facing turning (247).

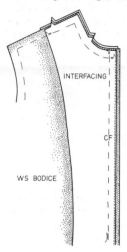

247 *The facing and interfacing machined to the bodice along the fold line. The turnings have been suitably trimmed. The tack-marking of the centre front line is seen showing through the interfacing*

(iii) Iron-on interfacing used with buttoned openings:
Iron-on interfacing, if suitable for the fabric, is set in a similar way to plain interfacing, but catch stitching should not be required at the fold line as in figure 245, unless the texture of the garment fabric does not allow the interfacing to adhere very firmly. In that case the interfacing can be catch-stitched along the fold line, and this will keep it permanently attached to the fabric.

When the facing is cut separately, no turning should be required at the fold line of the interfacing. Otherwise the interfacing and facing are dealt with as in figure 247. However, a turning can be used if it would appear to give a better result for the reason given above.

The catch stitching or use of a turning at the fold line does not make iron-on interfacing suitable for rough textured fabric, but it does make it useable on fabric with a very slightly uneven surface.

(b) Attaching the interfacing to the facing
In all cases cut the interfacing the same size as the facing, including all turning allowances. Match the fabric grains when using woven interfacing.

(i) A facing cut in one with the garment
(a) Plain interfacing
Method 1   The interfacing is tacked to the wrong side of the facing at neck, shoulder and waist edges, cross-tacked (see figure 248) down its length and catch-stitched at the fold line. Keep the catch stitching on the facing side of

the fold line so that it does not show on the right side of the bodice.
Neatening the long raw edge:
On light-weight fabric trim off 5 mm from the interfacing, fold over the facing to enclose the interfacing, and edge stitch by machine (248).

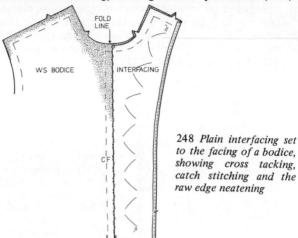

248 *Plain interfacing set to the facing of a bodice, showing cross tacking, catch stitching and the raw edge neatening*

On heavier-weight fabric edge stitching a turning will be too bulky a finish. In this case machine the facing and interfacing together, and zigzag over the raw edges to neaten (249).

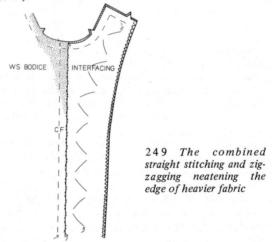

249 *The combined straight stitching and zig-zagging neatening the edge of heavier fabric*

Method 2 Light-weight fabric which frays is better interfaced by this method. Place the interfacing onto the right side of the fabric. Pin, tack and machine them together along the long raw edge, using a bare 5 mm turning. Slightly trim the turning of the interfacing (250a).

Press the line of machining and fold the interfacing back to the wrong side of the facing, creasing sharply along the stitching. Pin along the edge and cross-tack the interfacing to the facing to keep it flat. Trim the straight edge of the facing if necessary, so that it can be catch-stitched to the facing just clear of the fold (250b).

148

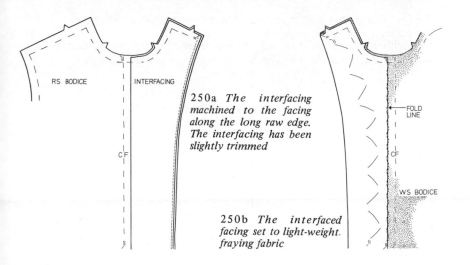

RS BODICE   INTERFACING

250a *The interfacing machined to the facing along the long raw edge. The interfacing has been slightly trimmed*

CF

250b *The interfaced facing set to light-weight fraying fabric*

FOLD LINE

CF

WS BODICE

(b) Iron-on interfacing
The interfacing is cut the same size as the facing, and is pinned to the wrong side of the facing, setting it evenly along the fold line. Iron over the area of the interfacing, and leave it until cold. Zigzag the long curved edge. This setting is almost similar in appearance to figure 249 when finished, but the catch stitching and the straight line of machining are not required.

If zigzagging does not give a good finish, a similar method to that shown in figure 248 can be used but, before ironing it in place, trim away 5 mm at the long curved edge of the interfacing. Iron-on the interfacing and leave it to cool. Fold over the free edge of the facing, tack it in place and edge stitch by machine. The finished appearance is almost similar to figure 248, but without the catch stitching.

(ii) A facing cut separately from the garment
(a) Plain interfacing
Plain interfacing is tacked to the wrong side of the facing at neck, shoulder and waist edges, and cross-tacked (248) down its length. The outer edge of the facing can be neatened as shown either in figure 248 or figure 249, according to the type of fabric. Alternatively, for light-weight, fraying fabric, place the interfacing onto the right side of the facing. Pin, tack and machine them together along the outer edge, using a bare 5 mm turning. Fold over the interfacing so that its wrong side touches the wrong side of the facing, creasing sharply along the machine-stitching. Tack the two layers together along shoulder, neck and centre front lines, and cross tack down the length (251)
(b) Iron-on interfacing
Iron-on interfacing is ironed on to the wrong side of the facing, using the technique outlined on page 144. Before fusing the interfacing, however, the finish for the long curved edge must be decided. The same methods are used as already described, ie edge stitching (the finish shown in figure 248) or zigzagging (the finish shown in figure 249).

149

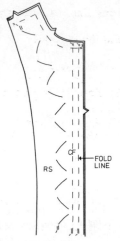

251 *The facing and interfacing joined together along the long edge. The prepared facing is ready for setting to the bodice*

The interfaced facing is handled as a single layer, and is set as explained on page 135.

Interfacing collars cuffs and belts
Interfacing collars — see the section on page 204.
Interfacing cuffs — see the section on page 269.
Interfacing belts — see the section on page 282.

An interfaced waist facing
A faced waist line gives a neat, flat finish to skirts and slacks, but it is most unsatisfactory in wear unless it is interfaced to give firmness and to prevent stretching. A firm, woven interfacing such as tailor's holland is the best choice for woollen fabrics, as it retains its strength after washing or cleaning. If a bonded interfacing is used, it must be the heaviest weight suitable for the garment fabric. An iron-on interfacing may be strong enough for cotton fabrics, but is not satisfactory for heavier cloth.

A facing can be substituted for a waist band, and a facing pattern made if one is not supplied with the garment pattern. Read the directions for making a neck facing pattern on page 127, to revise the principles of facing pattern making.

(a) Making a waist facing pattern
Fold out any darts at the waist edge of the back pattern, and pin them securely.

Pin the centre back line onto spare paper for about 100 mm, and smooth the prepared waist edge so that it can be pinned flat onto the spare paper. The lower part of the pattern will not lie flat because of the pinned darts. Pin the side seam flat for about 100 mm. Outline along the centre back line, the waist line and the side seam line, and unpin the pattern. Draw in the side seam and waist fitting lines. Label the centre back line and mark a grain line to correspond with that on the garment pattern. Draw the lower edge of the

150

facing 80 mm below the waist fitting line. Cut out the back waist facing pattern.

Make a front waist facing pattern in the same way.

(b) Cutting out the waist facing and the interfacing
Cut out the waist facing from the garment fabric, setting the grain line accurately, and allowing the same turnings as used on the garment. Mark the fitting lines.

Cut out the interfacing following the directions for cutting the facings, unless a bonded interfacing is used. In that case there is no grain to align, but the turnings will be required.

(c) Interfacing and making the facing
(i) For a garment with a side opening: Place the interfacing to the wrong side of the facing on both back and front sections. Pin the layers together, keeping them flat and smooth.

If an iron-on interfacing is being used, begin the fusing at the centre and move the iron slowly first to one side and then to the other.

Tack plain interfacing down the centre front and the centre back lines and along the waist edges. Tack close to the lower edge of the facing (252).

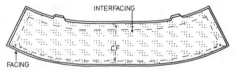

252 *Plain interfacing tacked to the front waist facing of a skirt*

Join the back and front facings together at the right side seam. As the interfaced side of the prepared facing will be set to the wrong side of the garment, the turnings of the seam must come on the interfacing side of the facing. Trim away the interfacing close to the machine stitching and press open the seam turnings. Trim the turnings 5 mm narrower than the garment seam turnings to graduate the thickness.

Machine the interfacing and the facing together close to the lower edge, and zigzag to neaten.

(ii) For a garment with a centre back opening: The back facing is composed of two sections, one to fit to the left and one to the right of the opening. When using fabric with a right and wrong side, care must be taken to cut left and right sections for the back facing.

Refer to the previous directions for guidance in preparing the front facing and for fixing iron-on interfacing if this is being used. Tack plain interfacing to the facing along the fitting lines at the centre back, waist and side seam edges. Tack close to the lower edge of the facing (253).

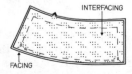

253 *Plain interfacing tacked to the right half of the back facing*

Join the back and front facings together at the side seams. Trim the interfacing, press and trim the seam turnings and neaten the lower edge of the facing as described in the previous directions.

(d) Setting an interfaced waist facing

(i) To prepare the garment waist line: All darts and seams running into the waist line must be stitched, neatened and pressed, and the zip fastener machined in place.

If a skirt is to be fully lined or half-lined at the back, the lining must be tacked to the skirt along the waist line and hemmed in place either side of the zip (see page 172). The lined skirt is then handled as single fabric.

Check that the waist fitting-line is clearly marked and in the correct position.

(ii) To finish the waist edge: Open the zip and pin the prepared facing to the garment, setting the right sides together and matching the balance notches and seams. For a side zip, the left-hand seam turnings of the facing should be outstanding, and for a centre back zip, the centre back turnings of the facing should be outstanding. Tack and machine the facing round the waist fitting line, between the two sides of the zip. Remove all the tacking except along the facing turnings either side of the zip (254).

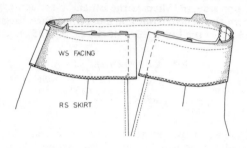

254 *A skirt with a centre back zip which is shown open. The facing has been machined round the waist fitting line from centre back to centre back. Note that the facing turnings are left outstanding either side of the sip. The facing and interfacing are still held together by tacking stitches along the centre back line*

Trim away the interfacing close to the machining along the waist line, and close to the tacking along the outstanding turnings.

At the waist edge, layer the turnings by trimming the facing turning to 10 mm and the garment turning to 15 mm. Snip the seam turnings diagonally on both the facing and the garment where they cross the waist turning (255).

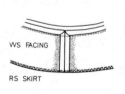

255 *A section of the waist line, showing the facing machined in place. At the waist, the interfacing is closely trimmed and the other two turnings are layered. Note the diagonal trimming at the top of the side seam turnings*

Turn up the facing away from the garment, folding it back sharply along the line of machine stitching, and tack the waist turnings to the facing. This necessitates snipping the waist turnings at intervals to ensure a flat setting. Press firmly along the waist-line to flatten it as much as possible.

Understitch the waist turnings to the facing about 5 mm outside the machining on the waist fitting line, continuing across the outstanding turning above the zip (256). This secures the edge of the zip tape.

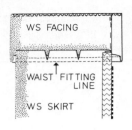

256 *This figure shows the top section of one side of the zip on an unlined skirt. The waist turnings have been layered and understitched to the interfaced facing. The outstanding turning has been snipped diagonally to remove bulk at the top of the fastening*

Fold the full width of the outstanding turning to the wrong side. Tack it in place and press to sharpen the fold. Herringbone the folded turning to the facing, thus flattening this area as much as possible (257).

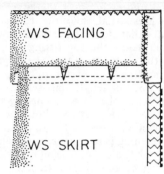

257 *The herringboned turning of the facing*

Turn the facing to the wrong side of the garment, folding it back along the waist fitting line, but bringing the seam just to the wrong side to give a sheer edge on the right side. Pin and tack the facing in position round the waist and down the side of the zip. Finally pin and tack along the lower edge, keeping the facing and garment perfectly flat. Hem the facing down each side of the zip. On an unlined garment, stitch the lower edge of the facing to darts and seam turnings. If a skirt is lined, hem the facing to the lining along the lower edge. Press the facing area thoroughly on the wrong side, taking care not to mark through to the right side.

14 Openings

The top of an opening always comes at a small part of the body eg neck, wrist, waist, so that the garment will fit neatly at these places, but open adequately to allow easy dressing and undressing over the larger parts of the body eg head, hand, bust or hips. It is essential, therefore, to plan the length of an opening carefully and make sure that it is long enough for its purpose. The opening length must be measured below the top fitting line, eg measure the length of a neck opening below the neck fitting line, the length of a skirt waist opening below the waist fitting line, etc. If the opening comes in a seam, make the seam first, leaving the opening length unstitched.

Some openings meet edge to edge when they are fastened eg a wrong side faced opening (258, page 155). These always tend to part slightly in use and show the body or underwear, so they should be used with discrimination. A more inconspicuous way to form an opening is to prepare a neatened or faced edge on the upper (ie the outer side of the opening) and set it over a wrap which forms an underlay to the opening, eg continuous straight strip openings (page 157), and a wrap and facing opening (page 164).

Plan openings to fasten right over left on women's and girls' clothes, and left over right on men's and boys' clothes.

Press openings during construction so that they are flat when finished. As openings undergo a certain amount of strain in wear, they should be strengthened at the closed ends if necessary, eg at the lower end of a skirt opening, at the upper end of a wrist opening, etc. Extra stitching cannot be added to a neck opening as it would be conspicuous. In this case the opening must be cut long enough to pass very easily over the head, and so avoid any strain in use.

Great care must be taken to see that each side of an opening is equal in length, and that any band into which it is set meets level across the opening, eg a cuff must meet level across the wrist opening. Similarly, a waistband must be level across a skirt opening. When making an opening which crosses the waist line, the waist seam must be level across the opening.

When press studs, hooks etc are used to fasten an opening, they must be strongly sewn, but no stitching should show through to the right side of the upper half of the opening. Therefore in planning the opening, choose one which provides double or reinforced fabric on the upper half if fastenings will be needed down the length of the opening.

A wrong side faced opening
This opening may be used as a wrist opening above a cuff (258). It has a very flat and neat finish. It may also be used as a short neck opening. In this case, it is usually fastened with buttons and worked or rouleau loops (259).

258 *A wrong side faced opening used above a cuff*

259 *A wrong side faced opening used at a neck line and fastened with buttons and loops*

Preparation of garment
Tack the line of the opening, which should be straight, with a thread of fabric (260).

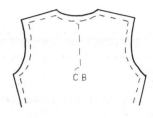

260 *The line of the opening tacked at the centre back neck line*

Preparation of facing
Cut a strip of fabric to the following size:
Length   = length of opening
(cut warpway)
              + 35 mm for a wrist opening
              + 60 mm for a neck opening
Width   = 75 mm
The extra 35 mm or 60 mm on the length are allowed for neatening the outer edges of the facing and for trimming the facing to the shape of the wrist or neckline. They also provide an extension beyond the opening length for final strengthening and neatening.   Turn and tack a turning 5 mm wide round three sides, leaving one width edge raw. Machine close to the folded edge. Crease lengthways along the centre of the prepared facing (261).

261 *The prepared facing*

Making the opening
Place the right side of the facing to the right side of the garment, with the creased line over the tacked line. Tack them together along the opening line and trim the raw edge of the facing to match the wrist or neck line. The remainder of the facing length projects beyond the opening length.

Machine round the tacking so that the stitching is evenly spaced apart, with 6 mm width at the base and 3 mm width at the top of the opening (262a). Cut up the line of the opening, snipping into each corner at the top (262b).

Fold the facing through to the wrong side of the garment and crease back along the machine stitching. Press the facing flat on the wrong side and machine round the opening, close to the edge, to secure the narrow turnings (262c).

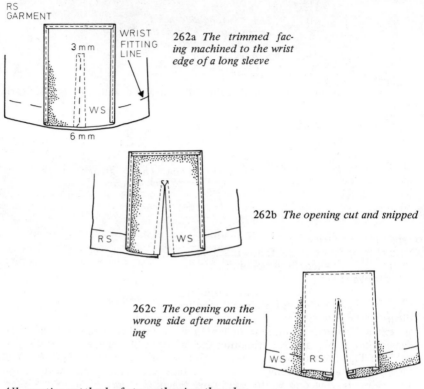

262a *The trimmed facing machined to the wrist edge of a long sleeve*

262b *The opening cut and snipped*

262c *The opening on the wrong side after machining*

Alternative method of strengthening the edge
The weakest part of the opening is obviously at the point where the turnings have to be narrow. This point may be reinforced by buttonhole stitch if a less conspicuous strengthening is required. Work the buttonhole stitch for about 25 mm in a continuous line on the right side of the garment. This protects the weak point for about 12 mm either side (263).

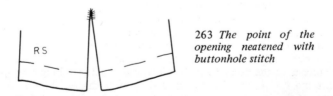

263 *The point of the opening neatened with buttonhole stitch*

Fixing the facing on the wrong side
When the opening is at a neck line, there is no need to fix the free end of the facing as it will hang downwards in place. At a wrist line the free end of the facing lies upwards and needs fixing in position. Slip-hem the facing edge to the sleeve, spacing the stitches about 10 mm apart (figure 264).

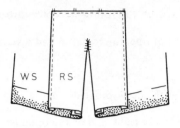

264 *The finished wrong side faced opening, on the wrong side, showing buttonhole stitch strengthening*

Continuous straight strip openings

These openings are made, as the name suggests, by applying a straight strip of fabric to an opening. The opening can be either a straight slit, or a space left at the top of a seam. The strip should be cut with the warp grain running along the length, so that the opening is firmly supported. They can be used as wrist openings, as side openings in children's summer skirts or as the centre back opening in a child's dress either from the neck line, or in a yoked dress, for the skirt section of the opening below the yoke.

A straight strip opening can be adapted to a wrap and facing opening but, in this case, a line of hemming shows through to the right side on the upper part of the opening. However, it makes a firm, flat opening, and is sometimes useful for children's clothes.

Preparing the garment and strip for both types of opening
(a) Length of openings
(i) Wrist opening above a cuff — 60 mm or 75 mm above the wrist fitting line
(ii) Neck opening — long enough to allow the head to pass through very easily. For a child's dress — approximately 220 mm — 250 mm down the centre back.
(iii) Waist opening — half the difference between waist and hip measurement + 25 mm for ease.
(b) Preparing the garment
For an opening in a slit, measure correct length of slit and mark the position with pins.

If the opening is coming in a seam, fasten off the seam stitching securely at the base of the opening.
(c) Cutting the strips
Cut a warpway strip of the garment fabric.
Length = 2 length of opening + 12 mm
Width = 2 finished width + 2 turnings of 6 mm
The finished width is usually 12 mm, but it can be more or less according to the amount of overwrap required.
Example For an opening 180 mm long, with a 12 mm overwrap, cut the strip as follows:
Length = 2 x length of opening + 12 mm
Width = 2 x finished width + 2 turnings of 6 mm

A continuous straight strip opening in a slit

This opening is weak at the point and is, therefore, not much used on modern, fraying fabrics. It does, however, show the basic method of making a continuous straight strip opening, and all the following adaptations are based on it.

Cut a straight warp slit for length of opening required and a warpway strip to fit

Setting the strip

1 Open out the slit and hold it with the wrong side of the garment facing the worker.

2 Place the right side of the strip to the right side of the opening.

3 Pin the strip in position with the garment turning tapering almost to nothing at the base of the slit (265a).

To place this accurately, pin the strip level with the garment at each end of the opening. Gradually let the garment edge fall below the edge of the strip until it is about 5 mm below at the centre. Pin carefully here so that the warp-line, continuing from the base of the slit, is at right angles to the edge of the strip.

4 Stitch the strip and the garment together parallel to the edge of the strip and using 6 mm turnings. The stitching needs great care at the base of the slit where the garment turning is very narrow, as it must be smooth and unpuckered here. Fine running stitches are suitable for setting the strip with back-stitching for about 25 mm across the centre to give extra strength (265b).

If machine stitching is used, the fabric must be carefully manipulated through the machine across the base of the opening to make it strong and flat, so that it will close smoothly.

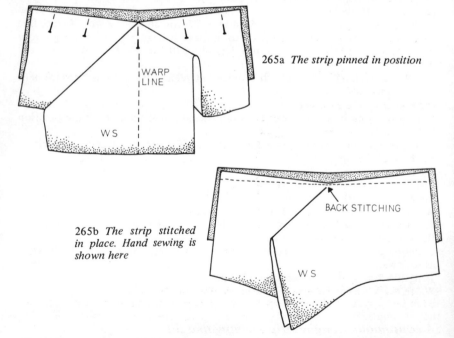

265a *The strip pinned in position*

265b *The strip stitched in place. Hand sewing is shown here*

5 Remove the tacking and press the strip and turnings away from the garment.

Crease a 6 mm turning along the free raw edge of the strip. Fold over the strip, pin and tack in place, so that the first stitching just shows below the edge of the strip (265c).

6   Hem down the edge of the strip, taking care that no hemming stitches show through to the right side (265d).

7   When the opening is closed the strip folds back on the upper part of the opening to form a facing. On the under part it is outstanding, forming a wrap (265e).

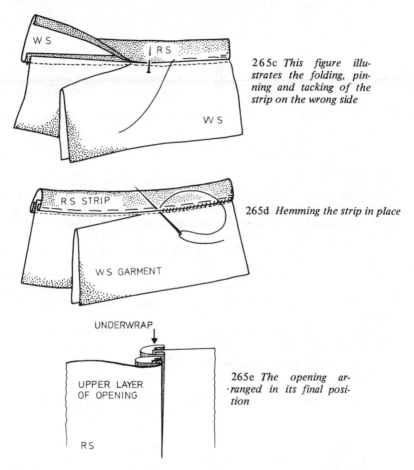

265c *This figure illustrates the folding, pinning and tacking of the strip on the wrong side*

265d *Hemming the strip in place*

265e *The opening arranged in its final position*

The use of a dart to strengthen fraying fabric

If the fabric frays badly the very narrow turning of the garment at the base of the opening is too weak to withstand wear and laundering. It is wise to make an adjustment in the method and stitch a small dart to provide a wider turning allowance. Prepare the slit and strip for the opening as previously explained.

Making the dart
Fold the garment along the line of the opening so that the edges of the slit come together with a straight fold below. Stitch a small dart, about 3 mm wide and 25 mm long, just below the base of the slit (266). When the slit is opened out, a 3 mm turning is provided along the full length of the opening.

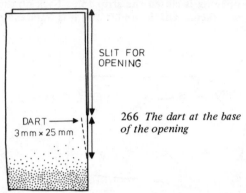

SLIT FOR
OPENING

DART
3 mm × 25 mm

266 *The dart at the base of the opening*

Making the opening
The width of turning used for sewing on the strip must equal the width of the dart. Stitch at this distance below the raw edges on the wrong side from the right-hand end as far as the dart. Stab the needle through the top of the dart from the right-hand to the left-hand side. Continue stitching up the left-hand side of the opening (267a). If machine stitching is used for setting the strip, it must be done in two steps. Work with the garment uppermost and machine down the opening from top to dart. Fasten off the machine thread ends. Reset the work in the machine, bringing the needle down at the top of the dart on the opposite side, and stitch the second side of the opening. Fasten off the machine thread ends at the top of the dart to ensure a firm base to the opening.

Flatten the dart with its fold pressed open over the stitching line (267b). Tack and hem the strip in position (267c).

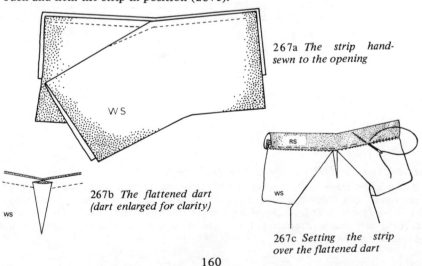

267a *The strip hand-sewn to the opening*

W S

267b *The flattened dart (dart enlarged for clarity)*

ws

RS

ws

267c *Setting the strip over the flattened dart*

The continuous straight strip adapted to a wrap and facing opening in a slit

Prepare the garment and strip, and work as far as point 5 according to the instructions for a continuous straight strip opening. The neatening strip is tacked in place from the base to the top of the opening on the under section. On the upper half, part of the strip is cut away, leaving 6 mm turnings beyond the base of the slit, and along the outer edge of the strip (268a).

Fold the strip flat to the wrong side of the garment on the upper edge of the opening and tack to form a facing. Hem the facing on to the garment very neatly as these stitches will show through to the right side. Refer to figure 268b and caption for guidance.

To close the opening, lap the facing over the underwrap (268c).

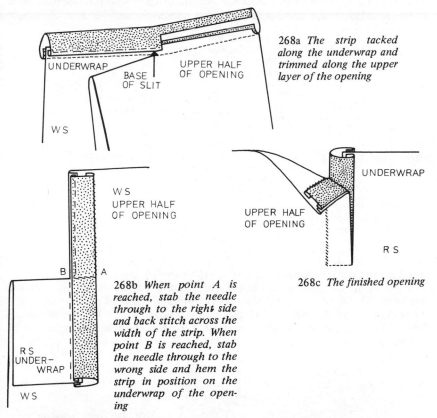

268a *The strip tacked along the underwrap and trimmed along the upper layer of the opening*

268b *When point A is reached, stab the needle through to the right side and back stitch across the width of the strip. When point B is reached, stab the needle through to the wrong side and hem the strip in position on the underwrap of the opening*

268c *The finished opening*

A continuous straight strip adapted to a wrap and facing opening may also be worked above a dart. Prepare and set the strip in the same way, trimming it as previously shown.

Setting a continuous straight strip opening or the wrap and facing adaptation into seams

Either opening is easily set into a seam if the seam and the opening turning are prepared first, and the width of the turning used for setting on the strip is carefully planned.

161

Setting a continuous straight strip opening into a french seam
Complete the french seam as far as the base of the opening. Fasten off the machine stitching strongly at this point. The fitting line of the opening is a continuation of the fitting line of the seam. At the base of the opening, snip across and release the inner turnings of the french seam. Trim the openings turnings level with the outer edge of the seam (269a). This leaves a 6 mm turning for setting the strip.

Snip across the width of the seam at the base of the opening, and loop-stitch across the seam to strengthen the cut edge (269b).

A seam turning of equal width all along the opening has now been provided for setting on the strip. The strip is sewn in place onto the right side of the opening (269c), and folded over for final hemming onto the wrong side. Catch a hemming stitch into the end loop-stitch to strengthen the base of the opening.

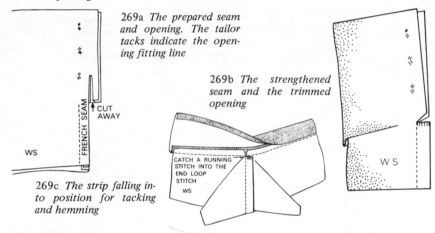

269a *The prepared seam and opening. The tailor tacks indicate the opening fitting line*

269b *The strengthened seam and the trimmed opening*

269c *The strip falling into position for tacking and hemming*

Setting the wrap and facing adaptation into a french seam
For the wrap and facing adaptation the seam is turned to the back of the garment. The strip is trimmed away as previously described, leaving 6 mm turnings beyond the seam and along the outer edge (270a). Flatten the facing onto the front of the garment and fix the strip with hemming and back stitching as before (270b).

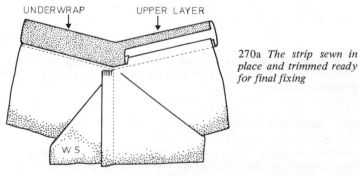

270a *The strip sewn in place and trimmed ready for final fixing*

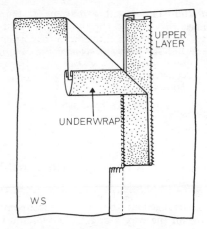

UPPER LAYER

UNDERWRAP

W S

270b *The finished opening*

Setting the openings into a plain seam

Complete the seam to the base of the opening and fasten off strongly. Round off the top of the seam turning and strengthen the raw edges with loop-stitching. Trim the opening turning to 6 mm (271).

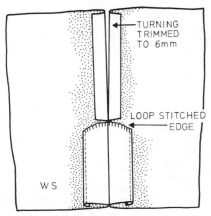

TURNING TRIMMED TO 6mm

LOOP STITCHED EDGE

W S

271 *The seam and opening prepared for adding the strip*

Stitch the strip to the opening using the 6 mm turning allowance. Care must be taken to ensure the strength at the base of the opening, and special attention must be given to the stitching at this point for both hand and machine setting. Finish the opening as required.

A bound opening

A bound opening is also made with a continuous strip, but this time a crossway strip is used, and the opening is visible on the right side (272). It may be used for back or front neck openings on blouses, frocks, lingerie and children's clothes. The binding should be narrow, ie 5 mm or less when finished. It is not, therefore, a suitable opening to use on fraying fabric where narrow turnings would be weak. The opening comes in too conspicuous a position to take a dart below the base of the slit as shown for a continuous

163

straight strip opening in figure 266. The opening may be fastened with buttons and loops or with tie strings.

272 *A bound opening used with a Peter Pan collar and fastened with a button and loop*

Preparing and making a bound opening
Cut a crossway strip to the following size:
    Length=2 x length of opening + 25 mm
    Width=4 x finished binding + 3 mm for loss in width.
The opening is made following the rules for a continuous straight strip opening and the setting of crossway binding.

The right side of the strip is placed to the right side of the garment. A very narrow turning of the garment is arranged at the base of the opening. The width of the strip turning is 5 mm all the way along. Fold over and tack the strip ready for hemming on the wrong side (273a). No hemming stitches must show through to the right side.

To shape the base of the opening, oversew the outer edges of the binding together for 6 mm or 7 mm on the wrong side (273b).

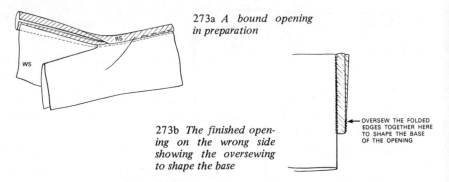

273a *A bound opening in preparation*

273b *The finished opening on the wrong side showing the oversewing to shape the base*

OVERSEW THE FOLDED EDGES TOGETHER HERE TO SHAPE THE BASE OF THE OPENING

A wrap and facing opening

This opening is always made in a seam. It is made with two separate strips of fabric. One is sewn as a facing to the upper edge, and the other is sewn as a wrap to the under edge of the opening.

A wrap and facing opening may be used as a waist opening for lingerie with fitted waist lines, eg a waist slip, or as an inexpensive opening on children's summer skirts.

Cutting the strips
If the line of the opening is straight, which is rare, straight warp strips may be used. The line of the opening is usually shaped to some degree to fit and then crossway strips, or strips cut to shape from the garment pattern must be used so that the opening sets flatly to the shape of the side seam line.
Length of strips   Cut each strip to equal the length of the opening + 35 mm
Width of strips   The finished width = 12 mm for lingerie and 25 mm for summer skirts.

Cut the facing to equal 2 x the finished width + 12 mm (two turnings of 6 mm).
Cut the wrap to equal 2 x the finished width 12 mm (two turnings of 6 mm).

Setting a wrap and facing opening
(a) In a french seam
Trim and prepare the seam and opening as shown for a continuous straight strip (269a and 269b).
Setting the Facing to the front of the opening
    Use the narrow strip.
1 Place the right side of the strip to the right side of the garment with the raw edges level at the top and down the edge of the opening.
2 Stitch in place with 6 mm turnings — this places the stitching in line with the wrong-side stitching of the french seam, and leaves a short length of fabric as a flap at the base of the opening.
3 Fold the facing over to the wrong side and tack close to the edge of the opening (274a).
4 Trim the facing to the width required, fold under the turning and tack in position.
5 Hem neatly from the top to the base of the opening.
Setting the wrap to the back of the opening
    Stitch the right side of the wide strip to the right side of the back of the garment as for facing method, stages 1, 2 and 3.
4 Press the two turnings on to the strip and press a 6 mm turning along the raw edge of the strip.
5 Lay the folded edge of the strip just above the first row of stitching to form a wrap.
6 Tack and hem in place.
7 Back stitch across the width of the opening on the right side just above the top of the seam. Neaten the raw edges of the flaps by back stitching and then loop stitching them together (274b).

274a *The facing tacked to the upper side of the opening*

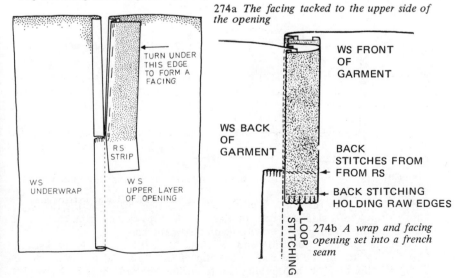

274b *A wrap and facing opening set into a french seam*

165

(b) In a plain seam

Cut across the seam turnings on the side of the underwrap section of the opening. Strengthen the raw edges with loop stitching. Set on the strips and strengthen the base of the opening as before (275).

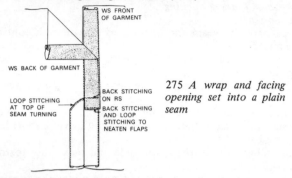

275 *A wrap and facing opening set into a plain seam*

(c) In a double machine-stitched seam

To place a wrap and facing opening in a double machine-stitched seam, the preparation and fixing has to be slightly altered.

1 Make the opening 6 mm longer than the required finished length.

2 Cut the strips this same length and the width required + turnings.

3 Snip across the inner turnings of the seam to free the seam turning allowance on both sides of the opening.

4 Leave the full seam turning allowance on the upper layer of the opening. Trim away the turning of the underlay to leave a 6 mm turning outside the fitting line (276).

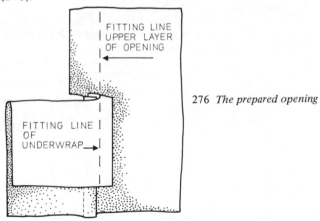

276 *The prepared opening*

5 Sew the facing onto the front, 6 mm outside the fitting line. Turn to the wrong side and hem in place.

6 Sew the wrap to the back, 6 mm inside the fitting line. Trim the turnings. Turn to the wrong side and hem in place. Both strips extend from the top to the base of the opening with no extension below the base.

7 Press the opening in position and, working from the right side, backstitch across the width of the opening at the top of the seam and 6 mm above to strengthen the base of the opening and to enclose the raw edges of the strips.

8 Loop-stitch across the raw edges on the wrong side.

15 Fastenings

The following fastenings are the ones most commonly used:
1 Zip fasteners – used on dresses, blouses, jackets, housecoats, pockets, bags, etc.
2 Buttons and (a) buttonholes (i) worked by hand, (ii) worked by machine
                (b) loops (i) worked, (ii) rouleau
Button fastenings are widely used for clothing and household articles.
3 Press studs – used to hold an opening where there is very little strain.
4 Hooks, (a) with either metal or worked bars. Used on overlapping edges.
           (b) with eyes. Used where two edges meet without overlapping.
Hooks are used when there is some strain on the opening and a flat, inconspicuous fastening is required. A worked bar is flatter and less visible than a metal bar. Hooks and bars are useful to hold the end of a belt or waistband, to fasten the corner of a neck opening under a collar, at the back neck above a zip set by the concealed method etc. Hooks and eyes are useful to fasten petersham at a skirt waist, and at the back neck above a zip set by the semi-concealed method, etc.
5 Eyelet holes and lacing. Sometimes used on smocks and children's garments. Their use is dependable on fashion.
    Hems and casings with slotted ribbon forming tie strings are closely related to the reduction of fullness and are included in that section.
    Fastenings are usually set after the opening has been made. Rouleau loops, however, are set during the making of the opening. Except for the method of setting on page 168, the setting of a zip fastener makes the opening at the same time. A zip fastener, therefore is sometimes classed as an opening, but its name seems to demand its inclusion in this section.

Zip fasteners

Zips are sold in a range of sizes. If the exact length required is not available, choose the nearest longer length so that there is no fear of strain on the base of the opening while dressing, as this weakens the end stop.
    The length of a zip is measured from the top of the slider to the end of the teeth. The opening, therefore, must be marked and measured before the zip is bought.
    Buy a zip which matches the colour of the garment if possible. Failing that, choose either the nearest colour or a neutral colour.
    Zips are made in varying weights and should be selected according to the fabric and type of garment. Never attempt to use a light-weight zip in heavy fabric or a heavy-weight zip in thin fabric, as the wear will be unsatisfactory. Curved zips can be bought for trousers, and open-ended zips for jackets.
    Zips may be concealed or conspicuous in the finished garment according to the method of setting.
    A turning allowance of 25 mm for a zip seam will facilitate the setting and

give a better finish. A turning of this width can be pressed more satisfactorily than a narrower one. Remember to protect the garment fabric by slipping a strip of paper or muslin under the turnings while pressing.

When a zip is set into a seam, the stitching of the seam must be fastened off strongly at the base of the opening.

The edges of the opening, when prepared for the zip, should be pressed to give a smart appearance to the finished setting. Once the zip is stitched in place, it is impossible to press these folded edges again.

A piping or cording foot used on the machine gives a neater setting. This is a single foot, and allows the needle to stitch close to the raised teeth of the zip. The two lines of stitching should be parallel, and only far enough apart to allow the zip to run easily.

There are many ways of setting zip fasteners. The following methods give a reasonable choice of setting and can be adapted as desired. Zips are usually set by machine, but can be stitched by hand if preferred.

Setting zip fasteners

A conspicuous setting as used when a zip is set into a slit, eg to form a centre front neck opening on sports wear (277), or a short centre back neck opening on a dress which has no centre back seam. It is also used on knitwear, but in this case three stitches must be cast off at the centre back in the right position, and the opening knitted into the garment.

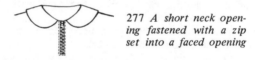

277 A short neck open-
ing fastened with a zip
set into a faced opening

Setting a zip into a faced opening

To calculate the length of zip required, measure round the head and round the neck fitting line of the garment. Halve the difference of these two measurements and add 20 mm for ease. This gives the length of zip required. Example:

Head measurement 555 mm
Neck fitting line measurement 405 mm
555 - 405 = 150
$\frac{150}{2}$ + 20 = 95

Therefore the length of zip required is 95 mm. If this length zip is not obtainable, choose the nearest length above this measurement.

A wrong side faced opening must be made at the neck, equal in length to the zip plus the neck turning allowance + 3 mm for ease. The opening is squared at the base to equal the width of the closed zip teeth, and the machine stitching is parallel to the centre line up each side of the opening (278a). Otherwise the method is similar to the faced opening on page 154.

The opening is cut along the centre line and a snip taken diagonally into each corner at the base. Fold the facing through to the wrong side, tack and press it into position.

Tack the zip firmly into the opening. The top of the slider must come 3 mm below the neck fitting line, to give scope for finishing the neck edge. The zip teeth should fit between the neatened edges of the opening. Machine as close to the edge of the opening as possible, turning neat, square corners (278b).

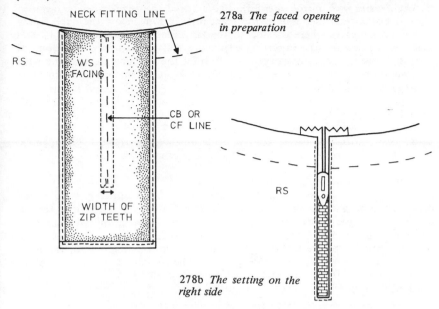

278a *The faced opening in preparation*

278b *The setting on the right side*

To neaten the wrong side, fold back the tape ends diagonally each side at the top, and hem them in place. Join the zip tape to the facing by hemming down the long sides of the tape. Slip-hem the lower edge of the facing to the garment with widely spaced stitches.

There are several inconspicuous ways of setting zips so that the teeth are partly or wholly covered by fabric. In each case the zip must be set carefully in relation to the fitting line at the top, ie the waist fitting line for skirts and trousers, and the neck fitting line for dresses and blouses with a centre front or back opening. It is essential that these fitting lines are clearly defined before planning the position of the zip at the top and marking the length of the opening.

Marking the position for a zip

(a) For skirts and trousers
On each side of the seam, below the waist fitting line, mark a point to indicate where the top of the zip slider must be set. The distance below the waist fitting line varies according to the final waist finish.

(i) For a waist-band finish:
Set the top of the zip slider 3 mm below the waist fitting line. This small space eases the setting of the waist band after the zip is stitched in place.

(ii) For a facing or petersham finish:
Set the top of the zip slider 12 mm below the waist fitting line. This space allows room for sewing on a hook fastening to hold the top of the opening together and to prevent the zip slider from slipping down in wear.

Below the marked points, measure the length of the opening required, making sure that it is a buyable zip length. Mark the position for the end of the opening. The seam can now be machined from this point.

(b) For dresses with a neck opening
Mark a point on either side of the seam line 12 mm below the neck fitting line. This indicates where the top of the zip slider must be set. The 12 mm space is to allow for ease in setting a facing or collar, and to provide room for a small hook and eye or worked bar to hold the opening close at the neck line. Measure the opening length from the tack-marks, and machine the seam as previously described.

Semi-concealed setting
Uses For skirts, trousers, centre back and centre front neck openings (both long and short) and for fitted long sleeve openings.

(a) Preparing the opening and setting the zip
Join the edges together along the fitting lines of the opening, using either coarse running stitches or machine tacking and a contrasting colour thread. Strong stitching is necessary as there is strain on it during the setting of the zip. Press open the turnings on the wrong side, and tack them to the garment, stitching parallel to the tacked fitting line. Use contrasting colour cotton to make an easy guide for machining later. The width between the tacking stitches will be 10 mm, 12 mm or 14 mm, according to the width of the zip teeth (279a).

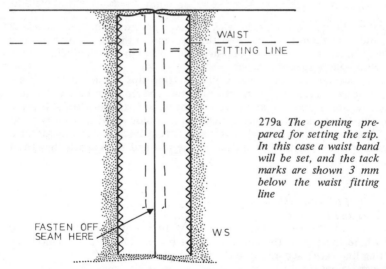

WAIST

FITTING LINE

279a *The opening prepared for setting the zip. In this case a waist band will be set, and the tack marks are shown 3 mm below the waist fitting line*

FASTEN OFF
SEAM HERE

W S

Place the right side of the zip to the wrong side of the opening, setting the top of the slider to the marked position. The centre of the zip must come exactly over the opening fitting line. Pin and tack the zip in position, taking the stitches through to the right side. Machine on the right side along the tacked line, using a piping foot on the machine. Stitch the left-hand side first, turn a right angle just below the base of the zip teeth, and machine across to the second guide line. Turn again at a right angle and machine the second side. Remove the tacking, including the stitches down the seam fitting line. This frees the zip for use (279b).

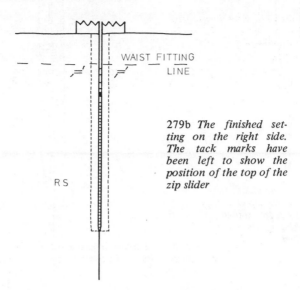

WAIST FITTING LINE

R S

279b *The finished setting on the right side. The tack marks have been left to show the position of the top of the zip slider*

On an unlined skirt, the zip tape may be hemmed down the sides and loop-stitched across the bottom to attach it to the seam turnings. On a lined skirt, the lining will be set over the tape and hemmed along the machine stitches.

(b) To set a lining at the back of a zip with a semi-concealed setting
The zip must be machined in place and the bottom of the tape catch-stitched across the seam turnings.

Machine and neaten the lining seam to within 25 mm-30 mm of the base of the zip. On each side of the opening, at the waist edge, fold back and pin the turning 5 mm inside the seam fitting line (280a). Continue pinning back the opening turnings 5 mm inside the seam fitting line for the length of the zip teeth, then taper the turnings to the top of the seam stitching. Tack the opening turnings (280b).

The prepared opening should fit neatly behind the zip on the wrong side, leaving the teeth clear with a margin of tape on either side. Hem the lining round the zip (280c).

SEAM FITTING LINES

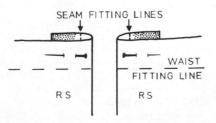

WAIST FITTING LINE

R S   R S

280a *The seam fitting line folded back to the wrong side and pinned at the waist edge of the opening*

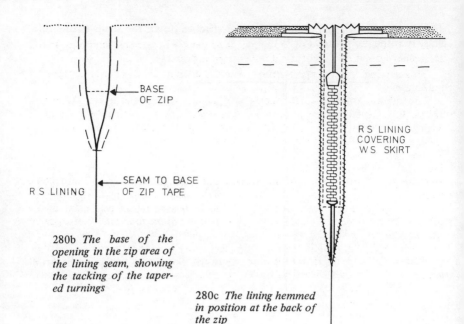

BASE
OF ZIP

SEAM TO BASE
OF ZIP TAPE

R S LINING

R S LINING
COVERING
W S SKIRT

280b *The base of the opening in the zip area of the lining seam, showing the tacking of the tapered turnings*

280c *The lining hemmed in position at the back of the zip*

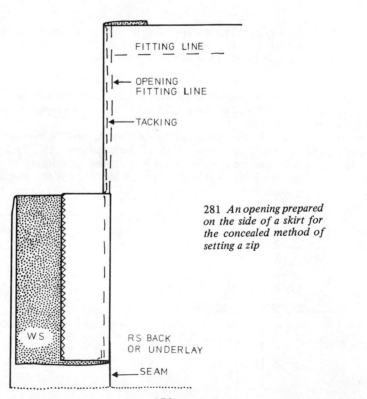

FITTING LINE

OPENING
FITTING LINE

TACKING

281 *An opening prepared on the side of a skirt for the concealed method of setting a zip*

W S

R S BACK
OR UNDERLAY

SEAM

Concealed setting

Uses For skirt and trouser openings, long centre back neck openings, fitted long sleeve openings, and for side openings in dresses.

This setting is neater than the previous setting, as the zip is completely hidden.

The turning on the front edge of side openings, and the left-hand side of centre back openings must be at least 15 mm wide, preferably 25 mm. A wrong side facing of thin fabric, in a matching colour, may be put on, if necessary, to make this turning of adequate width.

Preparing the opening and setting the zip
Method A — This is for use on straight openings (281, 282, 283 and 284). Each side of the opening is prepared differently (281). One edge is folded back 3 mm outside the fitting line and tacked, making a small pleat in the turning below the opening. This preparation comes along the back edge of side and sleeve openings. and to the right-hand side of centre back openings. The other edge is folded back along the fitting line and tacked. This edge, therefore, falls to the front of side openings, and to the left-hand side of centre back openings. Press the edges of the opening, allowing the small pleat to flatten out into a seam a short way below the base of the opening.

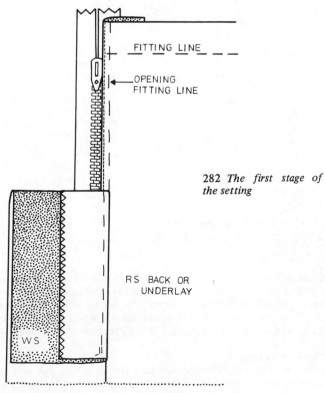

FITTING LINE

OPENING
FITTING LINE

282 *The first stage of the setting*

RS BACK OR
UNDERLAY

W S

(a) First stage of setting

According to the opening position on the garment, tack either the back, or the right-hand opening edge, over the zip tape about 1 mm away from the zip teeth. Using a zipper foot, machine close to the folded edge (282). Fasten off the machine thread ends firmly at the base of the opening.

(b) Alternative method for the first stage of the setting

Lay the zip onto the required side of the opening with right sides touching, and the left-hand side of the zip teeth about 1 mm outside the opening fitting line. Pin and tack the left-hand side of the zip tape to the opening turning. Using a zipper foot, machine close to the left-hand side of the zip teeth (283).

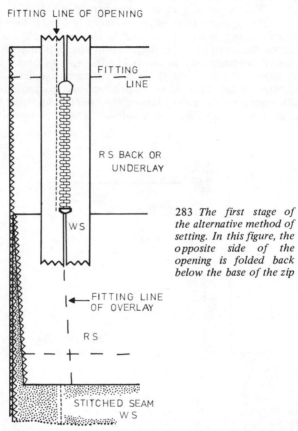

283 *The first stage of the alternative method of setting. In this figure, the opposite side of the opening is folded back below the base of the zip*

Remove the tacking and fold the opening turning to the wrong side along the fitting line. The zip is carried back with the turnings and the teeth and one side tape are left outstanding from the fitting line. The appearance resembles that in figure 282, but no machining is visible. Press the seam turnings on the wrong side, being careful not to press over the zip teeth.

(c) Second stage of setting

Fold back the second side of the opening to cover the zip and tack the opening fitting lines together firmly. Tack the garment to the zip tape 12 mm

174

inside the fitting line, along the length of the opening. Machine the second side of the zip, stitching parallel to the tacking, and fairly close to the zip teeth. Bring the machine stitching across to the fitting line with a squared or sloping line (284). Fasten off the machine thread ends at the base of the opening. When the tacking stitches are removed, the zip is set inside a long, narrow pocket.

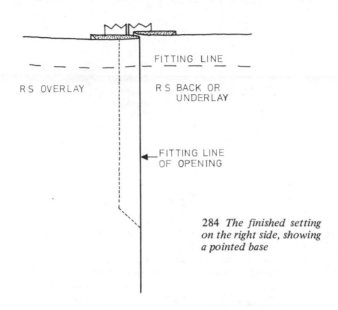

FITTING LINE

R S OVERLAY

R S BACK OR UNDERLAY

FITTING LINE OF OPENING

284 *The finished setting on the right side, showing a pointed base*

Neaten the wrong side of an unlined skirt as suggested in the previous method.

(d) To set a lining at the back of a zip with a concealed setting
Make and neaten the lining seam from a point 5 mm below the base of the opening.

On the under side of the opening, ie the back edge of a side opening, or the right-hand edge of a centre back opening, fold the turning to the wrong side, along the fitting line, and tack it in place.

Measure the width between the two lines of machine stitching holding the zip. On the upper side of the lining opening, mark this distance with a tacked line parallel to, and inside, the fitting line. Square across the seam 5 mm below the base of the opening.

Trim away the surplus fabric, leaving a turning of about 15 mm outside the tacked guide. Snip into the right-angled corner of the turning, fold back the turnings along the tacked guide line, press and tack them in place.

The prepared lining sets behind the zip, and can be hemmed in position along the machine stitching (285).

175

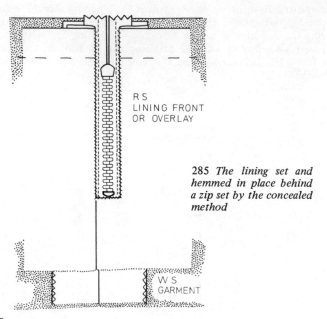

R S
LINING FRONT
OR OVERLAY

285 *The lining set and
hemmed in place behind
a zip set by the concealed
method*

W S
GARMENT

Method B

This is a safer method to use when a zip is set into a curving line, eg the shaped side seam of a skirt, where the fabric may be inclined to stretch. Machine the seam as far as the base of the opening. Join the fitting lines of the opening together with small tacking stitches, and press open the turnings.

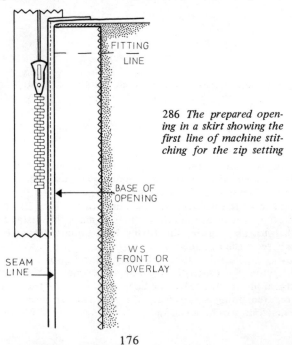

FITTING
LINE

286 *The prepared open-
ing in a skirt showing the
first line of machine stitching for the zip setting*

BASE OF
OPENING

SEAM
LINE

W S
FRONT OR
OVERLAY

Fold back the turnings 3 mm outside the fitting line and tack it in place. Lay the zip right side uppermost under this 3 mm fold. Tack and machine close to the folded edge along the full length of the tape (286).

Fold back the front of the opening to cover the zip and, with the right side uppermost, tack and machine on the right side as shown in the previous method. Remove all tacking.

The treatment of the little pleat on the wrong side below the opening, and the wrong side finish of the opening, are both dealt with as described in Method A.

Method C (287 and 288).
This is a good method to choose for heavy fabric where the pleat on the wrong side, at the base of the opening, would provide unwanted bulk.

On each side of the opening, fold back the turnings along the fitting lines, and tack them to the wrong side (287). The zip is set in two stages.

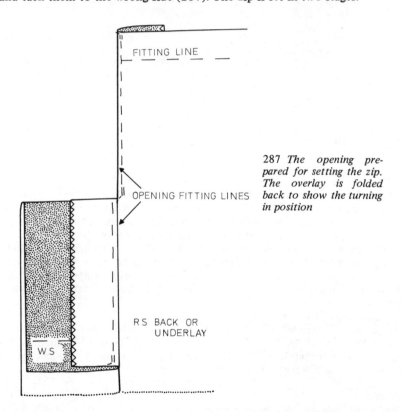

FITTING LINE

OPENING FITTING LINES

RS BACK OR UNDERLAY

WS

287 *The opening pre-pared for setting the zip. The overlay is folded back to show the turning in position*

(a) First stage of setting
Place the back edge of a side opening, or the right-hand edge of a centre back opening, over the zip tape, bringing the wrong side of the opening to the right side of the tape, with the fitting line alongside the zip teeth. Tack and machine this edge to the zip tape from bottom to top (288). The machine thread ends must be securely fastened off at the bottom.

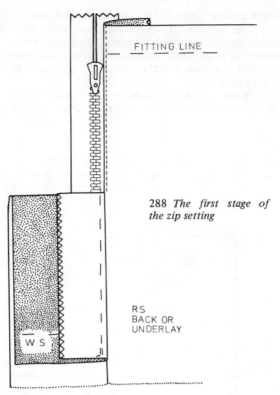

288 *The first stage of the zip setting*

FITTING LINE

R S
BACK OR
UNDERLAY

W S

(b) Alternative first stage of setting
Refer to the alternative method for the first stage of setting given on page 176. A similar method may be used here, so that no machining is visible on the right side of the zip. There is one difference in the preparation: fold back and tack to the wrong side the turnings on the front or left-hand side of the opening (according to position). The turning on the back, or right-hand side, should be left free and tacked in place before the second stage of the setting is done. The first stage of the setting can then be carried out as previously described.

(c) Second stage of setting
Place the second side of the opening over the zip, setting the fitting line just to cover the machining. Tack this edge firmly. Then tack the garment to the zip tape about 10 mm inside the fitting line. Finish setting the zip and neaten the wrong side as directed for Method A.

Method D
Setting a zip fastener with an underwrap
The addition of an underwrap behind a zip, prevents the zip teeth from rubbing against the skin or underwear.

(a) Preparing the underwrap
Trim across the lower end of the zip tape. Cut a strip of garment or lining fabric 90 mm wide and the full length of the zip tape. Fold the strip in half lengthways, right side out, tack and press.

(b) Attaching the zip to the underwrap
Tack the zip to the underwrap, right side uppermost, with the right-hand side of the zip 3 mm from the long raw edges of the underwrap. Machine close to the edge of the zip tape along the right-hand side only. Zigzag (or overcast) over the two long raw edges of the underwrap and across the lower edge, including the trimmed edges of the zip tape (289).

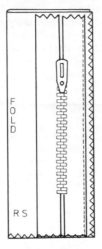

289 *The zip atached to the neatened underwrap*

(c) Setting the zip
Prepare the garment and stitch the back edge of a side opening, or the right-hand side of a centre back opening, as directed for Method A, B or C according to choice. Stitch right through the zip tape and the underwrap. Fold the underwrap out of the way, and tack the other side of the opening to the zip tape 12 mm from the opening fitting line. Tack from the top for the length of the zip teeth, then tack in a sloping line to meet the seam. Keep the underwrap folded back out of the way, and stitch to the right side, parallel to the straight line of tacking, from top to bottom. Fasten off the machine thread ends on the wrong side. Replace the underwrap to its normal position and stitch at the bottom of the opening to join garment, zip tape and underwrap together (290a and 290b).

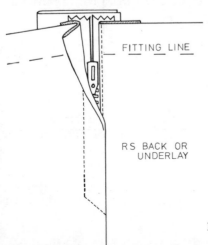

290a *The final position of the shield when the zip is finished*

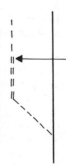

290b *Begin the final machine stitching where indicated by the arrow. Overlap the previous machining for 15 mm before sloping off to the seam line. This machining passes through garment, zip tape and underwrap (machine stitching magnified)*

179

Setting a zip in the side or central back waist opening of a dress

Occasionally a zip is required just across the waist line in the side or centre back seam of a dress. A usual length for a waist opening zip is 225 mm. Plan for two fifths of the zip length to come above the waist line and three fifths below.

Either the semi-concealed or the concealed method of setting can be used in either position. The pattern of setting is almost the same as already described for neck and skirt waist openings. The only difference lies in the machining at the top of the zip, which must be planned to enclose the slider. As the slider is broader than the teeth, a slight shaping is necessary when machining round this area. Figures 291 and 292 show the arrangement at the top of the zip. The lower end of the setting is the same as previously described.

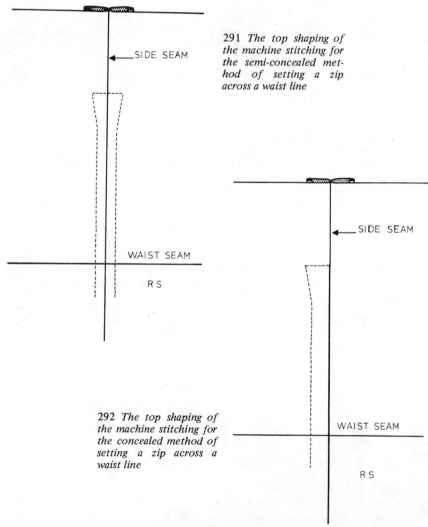

SIDE SEAM

291 *The top shaping of the machine stitching for the semi-concealed method of setting a zip across a waist line*

WAIST SEAM

R S

SIDE SEAM

WAIST SEAM

R S

292 *The top shaping of the machine stitching for the concealed method of setting a zip across a waist line*

Buttonholes
General information for all types of buttonhole

Buttons must always be bought before buttonholes are made, so that the correct buttonhole length can be ascertained both for cutting handworked buttonholes and for stitching machine-made and bound buttonholes.

The length of a buttonhole equals the width of the button plus a small amount of ease to accommodate the thickness of the button in use, and to prevent strain on the buttonhole. Allow 2 mm ease for thin buttons : heavier buttons need up to 6 mm ease according to thickness. The buttons, however, must be sewn on after the buttonholes are made, so that they can be placed to fit accurately into the finished buttonhole.

Buttonholes must always be made on double fabric, and are cut straight with the fabric grain. This gives the cut straight, firm edges which prevent it from stretching and weakening with use. If a garment style happens to place buttonholes off the straight grain, they must be reinforced with a straight strip of fabric on the wrong side before marking, to support the fabric when cutting and making the buttonholes. Interfacing fabric or lining fabric could be used for this purpose.

On girls' and women's garments, buttonholes are made so that the garments fasten right over left. When making clothes for boys and men, the openings are arranged to fasten left over right.

Hand-worked buttonholes

Hand-worked buttonholes are made in one of two possible shapes:
(a) Horizontal buttonholes (293)

FITTING LINE
OF OPENING

293 *An enlarged figure to show the shaping of a horizontal buttonhole which always has one round and one square end*

The round end is specially shaped to hold the shank of the button, and is strongly made to support any strain in use. The square end is shaped to hold the edges of the buttonhole together so that it retains a good shape after use, and presents a neat finish when the buttonhole is closed over the button. This type of buttonhole is used on cuffs, belts and bands, on full length back openings on blouses when fashionable, and on the front of blouses, shirts and dresses without panel openings (294a and b).

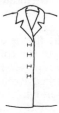

294a and b *Horizontal buttonholes on a shirt and belt. The round ends come at the ends where the buttons will fit in wear*

A horizontal buttonhole is never made with two round ends. In use the button can pull into only one end of the buttonhole, and this is the end which needs the round shaping. A buttonholed slot, for threading ribbon or elastic, has two round ends to accommodate the ribbon etc, but this is not a buttonhole, and requires the two round ends to allow the width of the ribbon to slip through easily.

(b) Vertical buttonholes (295)

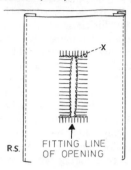

295 *An enlarged figure to show the shaping of a vertical buttonhole which always has two square ends. X indicates the starting point for working the buttonhole*

The button shank rests in the centre of a vertical buttonhole when it is closed. The square ends provide a firm finish and keep the buttonhole a good shape. When a buttonhole is closed the square ends give a neat appearance, as they show either side of the button.

Vertical buttonholes are far less frequently used than horizontal ones. They are useless when there is any pull imposed on the opening in wear, as any strain causes the button to slip undone. This makes vertical buttonholes quite unsuitable for back openings, and they should not be used in this position. Their most common use is in a front panel opening (296).

296 *A panel opening with vertical buttonholes*

Marking the position of horizontal buttonholes
These buttonholes are always cut in relation to the centre front or back of a garment or the fitting line of an opening.

The fitting line of the opening must come at least half the width of the button inside the outer edge of the opening, so that the button does not project beyond the opening edge when the buttonhole is closed. The space between the fitting line and the edge of the opening may be more than half the width of the button, but it must never be less.

The rounded end of the buttonhole must come at the fitting point on the fitting line of the opening. The button can then be sewn to the corresponding fitting point on the fitting line of the opening underwrap (see figure 299). The position of the buttonhole, therefore, must be marked from the fitting point inwards. When the round end stitches are worked, they will fan outwards beyond the fitting point. The facing, or hem, of the opening must be wide enough to provide the double fabric required for working the buttonhole and for sewing on the button.

Measure the length required from the fitting point on the opening fitting line and mark the position with pins (297).

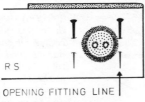

Sometimes a line of buttonholes is needed down the length of an opening, eg the front of a shirt. In this case the centre lines should be tacked down each side of the opening, and the fitting points marked to show the position for each buttonhole and button. Measure the positions of the top and bottom buttonholes, and join the two inner points with a line of tacking parallel to the centre line. The buttonholes will fit between these two guide lines. To mark the buttonhole positions, tack from each fitting point, straight with the fabric grain, between the two guide lines.(299). Check that the distance between the buttonholes is equal.

Marking the position of vertical buttonholes

A vertical buttonhole is cut along the fitting line of the opening and is measured so that the fitting point comes in the centre of the length. This brings the button in a central position when the opening is closed. Mark the length of the buttonhole with two pins, remembering to add ease to the width of the button (298).

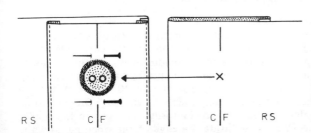

298 *This figure shows a section of a centre front panel opening of a shirt. A button position is indicated at X on the left-hand side, and the arrow points to the corresponding buttonhole position on the right-hand side*

Check the spacing when all the buttonhole positions are pinned out, and tack across the centre of the panel to mark the top and bottom of each buttonhole.

The buttonholes are now ready for cutting and working unless the fabric is either fraying or slippery, when some further preparation is helpful.

Preparing difficult fabric for hand-worked buttonholes

When working the buttonhole, the under layer of fabric may tend to slip aside and, therefore, not get caught firmly by the buttonhole stitches. There are two ways of dealing with this problem:
(a) On each side of the buttonhole guide line, work either fine running or fine machine stitching, making the two lines about 3 mm apart (299). The buttonhole can then be cut between these lines of stitching. The buttonhole stitching will cover them and, incidentally, they will act as a guide for keeping the buttonhole stitches equal in length.

183

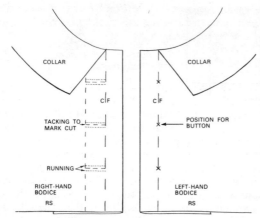

299 *This figure shows the centre front lines of a bodice. On the right-hand side a tacked line, parallel to the centre front, marks the width of the buttonholes, and the cutting guide lines are tacked across between them. The addition of fine running stitches for use with difficult fabric is also shown. On the left-hand side, the button positions are indicated*

(b) A type of machine buttonhole can be made with fine machine embroidery cotton, and then the hand stitches worked over it. To do this, use the machine-made buttonhole mechanism, but set the machine for a small sized zigzag stitch instead of using the satin stitch setting. At each end, work only two double width stitches. Cut the buttonhole in the usual way and proceed to work by hand, covering the zigzag stitches. This provides a light-weight reinforcement which is useful for fine, fraying fabric which would not stand the firmness of an ordinary machine-made buttonhole. The preparation should be tried out before working on the garment.

Cutting hand-worked buttonholes
Special buttonhole scissors can be bought for cutting buttonholes, but they have a limited use. The blades have a gap at the top, and the cutting length is adaptable by means of a screw which sets the blades to the required length. However the blades are not very long in their full cutting length, and can only be used for cutting buttonholes up to approximately 20 mm - 25 mm in length. Vertical buttonholes are almost impossible to cut with these scissors, but horizontal buttonholes can be cut satisfactorily. The gap in the blades allows the scissors to begin cutting inside the edge of the opening, and the buttonhole is cut from the round end along the tacked guide line.

Small, pointed scissors are the more practical type to use. When cutting vertical buttonholes, insert the point at the lower end of the buttonhole and cut straight with the fabric grain along the tacked guide line. Horizontal buttonholes can be cut in this way, beginning at the fitting line, ie the round end of the buttonhole.

There is an alternative way of cutting horizontal buttonholes. Fold the tacked guide line in half and make a very small snip into the fold, just over the tacking (300). Open out the fabric and cut to each end of the tacked line. The cut must be perfectly straight with the fabric grain and exactly the length required.

300 *The arrow indicates where to make the initial snip for cutting the buttonhole*

184

Coarse fabric which frays easily can present a difficulty even if reinforced stitching has been used. For guidance in handling this problem, refer to figure 301.

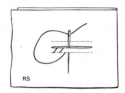

301 *If the fabric is loosely woven and frays easily, it is helpful to overcast the cut edges to the depth of the reinforcing stitches. The final buttonhole stitches must cover all the preparatory stitching*

Stitching hand-worked buttonholes

On most fabrics use sewing thread for stitching the buttonholes, but on heavy fabric use buttonhole twist if possible. It is difficult to join on a new length of thread while working a buttonhole, therefore it is advisable to begin with a thread long enough for the whole process. As an approximate guide, allow 40 cm thread for working a 12 mm buttonhole, and 60 cm thread for a 20 mm buttonhole.

Refer to page 17 for information about working buttonhole stitch. The stitches should be very close together, with knots touching, to form a hard, firm covering for the raw edge. They should be as short as the fabric will allow, but they must cover any preliminary reinforcement which has been worked.

Working horizontal buttonholes

The following figures, 302a–302h, with their captions, give directions for working a horizontal buttonhole. The fitting line of the opening, and some reinforcing stitches are shown in figures 302a and b, but thereafter they have been omitted to ensure clarity of the working method.

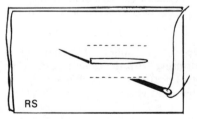

302a *Pass the needle between the double fabric. Bring it out just to the left of the cut and in line with it. Pull it through so that the end of the thread is trapped between the fabric*

302b *Begin working at the inner left-hand corner along the lower cut edge. Take the first stitch so that the knot lies on the raw edge and right up in the corner. Continue working the stitch until the whole of the lower raw edge is covered*

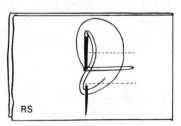

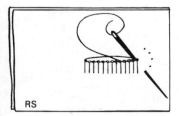

302c *The round end should be made of overcasting stitches worked closely together, and pulled firmly, to make a strong end for withstanding the pull of the button in wear. These over-casting stitches should equal the knotted stitches in length. Running stitches omitted here and in subsequent figures to reduce detail.*

185

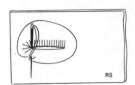

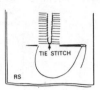

302d *Work the last stitch of the round end as a knotted stitch, thus forming the first stitch of the second side at the same time. The cotton is now in position for working the second side. Continue along this side with equal length buttonhole stitches until it is entirely filled in*

302e *To make the square end take the needle through the knot of the first stitch worked and bring it out at the end of the last stitch worked. This forms a tie-stitch which holds together the edges of the buttonhole by uniting the first and the last knots worked*

302f *Take a long bar-stitch across the full width of the worked buttonhole. This forms a guide for the square end knotted stitches*

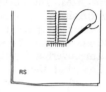

302g *Putting the needle just behind the bar-stitch each time, fill in the width of the worked buttonhole with short knotted stitches*

302h *Put the needle through to the back beside the knot of the last stitch, to tie it down firmly*

To fasten off, pass the needle under the backs of the first side stitches, on the wrong side, and cut off the cotton.

Working vertical buttonholes
The order of work is different for this type of buttonhole. The first side is worked as previously described, then, continuing with the same thread, cross to the second side (303a) and fill that with knotted stitches. Work a square end as previously shown. Pass the needle behind the stitches of the first side, on the wrong side. Bring it through to the right side at the point X (303b). It is now ready to work a second square end, beginning with the bar-stitch.

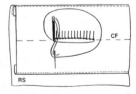

303a *The first stitch of the second side is in position. This figure shows a buttonhole being worked on the centre front line of a shirt with a panel opening*

303b *A completed vertical buttonhole showing the order of work*

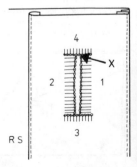

Machine-made buttonholes

These are quickly made on modern domestic sewing machines, and should be used whenever possible. The method of working varies according to the make and type of machine. The buttonhole instruction section of the machine manual should be studied, and some trial buttonholes made, before stitching on the garment. Refer to the general information for all buttonholes on page 181. It will also be helpful to read the section on marking the position of buttonholes beginning on page 182.

It is wise to reinforce the buttonhole area by putting a layer of organdie, or a similar thin, firm fabric between the two layers of garment fabric. This supports machine-made buttonholes and prevents the edges from stretching.

Use the type of sewing thread recommended in the machine manual to ensure a good result. Too thick a thread makes a clumsy buttonhole which will pull away from the fabric.

On medium and heavy-weight fabrics, the introduction of a cord into the buttonhole gives a firm, strong finish which looks attractive. Directions for making corded buttonholes will be found in the machine manual.

Great care must be taken when cutting machine-made buttonholes, as this is done after they are stitched. Careless cutting will slice through the machine stitching and into the garment fabric. A 'quick unpick', if used, must be handled with extreme caution. If scissors are used, choose a pair with fine, sharp, pointed blades.

Bound buttonholes

Bound buttonholes are not satisfactory on washing garments as the corners are, of necessity, weak in construction and tend to fray out if washed frequently. Small squares of garment fabric are required for bound buttonholes, which are made early in the construction of the garment, before the front facing is fixed by a collar or seam. The finished width of the binding should be as narrow as the fabric will allow.

The buttonholes are worked on the outer layer of the fabric, which is usually interfaced, and neatened on the wrong side by the garment facing.

The use of interfacing gives a better result, but it must always be set behind the outer fabric. In this position it masks the binding square and prevents it from showing through to the right side of the garment. An interfacing would give a clumsy finish to the wrong side of the buttonhole.

Preparing for the buttonholes

Plan the position, spacing and width of the buttonholes as already described for hand-worked buttonholes. Thread mark along the buttonhole lines through garment, interfacing and facing (304). Snip the thread marks to separate the layers.

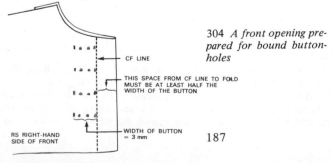

CF LINE

THIS SPACE FROM CF LINE TO FOLD MUST BE AT LEAST HALF THE WIDTH OF THE BUTTON

RS RIGHT-HAND SIDE OF FRONT

WIDTH OF BUTTON = 3 mm

304 *A front opening prepared for bound buttonholes*

187

Cut a binding strip for each buttonhole to the size required, ie cut length warpway for length of buttonhole plus 25 mm, and 50 mm wide.

Making the buttonholes
The following figures, 305a - 305g, with their captions, give directions for making bound buttonholes.

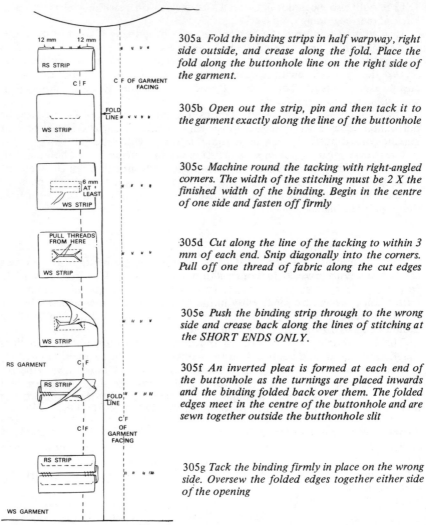

305a *Fold the binding strips in half warpway, right side outside, and crease along the fold. Place the fold along the buttonhole line on the right side of the garment.*

305b *Open out the strip, pin and then tack it to the garment exactly along the line of the buttonhole*

305c *Machine round the tacking with right-angled corners. The width of the stitching must be 2 X the finished width of the binding. Begin in the centre of one side and fasten off firmly*

305d *Cut along the line of the tacking to within 3 mm of each end. Snip diagonally into the corners. Pull off one thread of fabric along the cut edges*

305e *Push the binding strip through to the wrong side and crease back along the lines of stitching at the SHORT ENDS ONLY.*

305f *An inverted pleat is formed at each end of the buttonhole as the turnings are placed inwards and the binding folded back over them. The folded edges meet in the centre of the buttonhole and are sewn together outside the butthonhole slit*

305g *Tack the binding firmly in place on the wrong side. Oversew the folded edges together either side of the opening*

The wrong side finish
Fold back the garment facing to cover the wrong side of the buttonhole. Pin it in place and test the length and line of the thread marking against the bound buttonhole. Adjust if necessary. Cut a straight slit in the facing to correspond to the length of the button plus a bare 2 mm extra at each end of the cut. Using a needle, turn a narrow turning inside the edges of the slit, and

hem round to join it to the back of the binding. The hemming stitches must not show through to the right side (306).

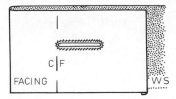

306 *The wrong side finish of a bound buttonhole*

Alternative method of finishing the back of a bound buttonhole

Cut the facing carefully in the centre of the buttonhole line, leaving about 3 mm of the line uncut at each end. Make even length diagonal snips from each end of the cut (307, top illustration). Turn under the two small triangles at each end, and the turnings along each long side. Hem the slot to the join of the bound buttonhole, leaving the binding showing on the wrong side (307 lower illustration).

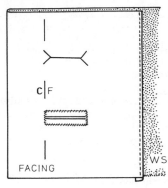

307 *This figure shows the cutting plan for the slot, and a finished buttonhole on the wrong side of the facing*

Buttons

Buttons must always be sewn on to double fabric. If the fabric is single it must be reinforced with a stay of fabric, tape, ribbon or Paris binding. This stay may be hemmed to the back of the fabric (308) or held only by the button stitching (309). In either case any raw edges on the stay must be neatened.

308 *Stay hemmed to fabric*

309 *Detached stay with neatened raw edges being fixed with the button stitching*

The button should rest entirely on fabric, and not protrude beyond the edge of the opening. Buttons are sewn on to the centre or fitting lines of openings. To find the exact position of a button for a buttonhole, pin the opening together and stab a pin through the round end of a horizontal buttonhole (310), and through the middle of a vertical buttonhole (311).

189

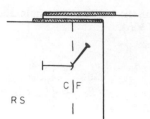

310 *Checking the button position for a horizontal buttonhole*

R S   C | F

When the buttons are to be fastened with loops, they should be spaced as desired along the opening and lie just within its edges (312).

311 *Checking the button position for a vertical buttonhole*

RS

RS BACK OF GARMENT

312 *Spacing buttons for a loop fastening*

Sewing the buttons

Buttons are sewn AFTER buttonholes and rouleau loops are made, but BEFORE worked loops are made. Sew the buttons with a single thread of a suitable colour and thickness. Fasten on with a double back stitch on the right side at the button position.

A shank is necessary between the button and the fabric to allow the fabric to remain unpuckered when the thickness of the buttonhole is fastened in place. If a shank is not moulded on to the button, one must be made when sewing it on. The thicker the fabric, the longer the shank needs to be.

(a) Sewing on two-holed buttons

Arrange the holes to run in line with the buttonhole. Pass the needle and thread six to eight times through the holes in the button, taking care to sew in the same position through the fabric each time, so that a neat bar of stitches is formed on the wrong side. When the first stitch has been made, insert two or three pins between the thread and the button. This lengthens the stitches and gives depth for the shank later (313a).

When the stitching is done pass the needle through the button, but not through the fabric, and remove the pins. Wind the thread firmly round the 'stem' between the button and the fabric to form the shank, finally passing the needle through to the wrong side for fastening off (313b).

313a *The first stage in sewing on a button*

313b *The finished shank*

A small, flat two-holed button is sometimes used as a wrong side stay under buttons sewn on heavy garments, eg coats, raincoats etc. It is attached to the wrong side of the garment and is sewn on at the same time as the top button by stabbing the needle to and fro through the top button, garment fabric and stay button. After the shank has been made under the top button, pass the needle to the wrong side and wind the cotton a few times between the stay button and the garment. Fasten off by stitching to and fro under the stay button two or three times. Cut off the cotton.

(b) Sewing on four-holed buttons
The stitches are usually arranged to form two bars (314a) or a cross (314b). Sew over pins as before and arrange the stitches to go through the fabric at two points only, thus forming a bar on the wrong side. The diagonal stitches forming a cross should be worked alternately.

314a and b *Two stitch arrangements for four-holed buttons*

(c) Sewing on buttons with moulded shanks
Sew on each button with six or eight stitches through the shank, forming a bar on the wrong side (315).

315 *A section of fabric has been cut away to show the moulded shank and the sewing stitches as they pass through the fabric*

If the moulded shank is not deep enough to accommodate the thickness of the buttonhole, the button should be sewn on loosely, so that a thread shank can be made between the moulded shank and the fabric.

The wrong side finish for all buttons
There should always be a bar of stitches on the wrong side if the button has been sewn on carefully. Pass the needle to the wrong side at one end of this bar, when the shank has been completed, and loop stitch over it (316). Fasten off with a double back-stitch at the end of the fabric beside the bar. Alternatively, whip over the bar of stitches as for a tailor's bar tack on page 86.

316 *Loop-stitching the bar at the back of a button*

Making worked loops
The edges of the opening must be pressed and the buttons sewn on first. Use strong, matching thread for the loops. Set the top button in a suitable position below the top edge fitting line, and then space them as required.

(a) Preparing the edge
On the loop edge, put a tack mark opposite the centre of each button. These tacks mark the centre of each loop. Tack the wrong side of this edge to stiff paper to support it while working the loops (317a). At each side of each tack mark, set evenly spaced pins to measure the button width. These pins mark the width of a loop (317b). Half the width of a button away from the edge of the opening, and opposite the tack mark, insert a pin into the paper. This pin is a guide for the size of loop (317c).

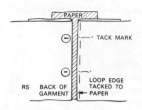

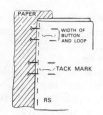

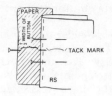

317a *The prepared loop edge*

317b *The marked loop positions*

317c *The final preparation for working the loop*

(b) Working the loop

The edge of the opening must be held towards the worker. Pass the needle through the fold of the fabric and bring it out at the left-hand pin. The needle enters the fabric again at the right-hand pin and the thread loops round the central pin.

Pass the needle through the fold and bring it out at the left-hand position again. Continue doing this to form a foundation of the right thickness for the loop. Prepare three or four strands for fine fabric, more for heavier fabric (318a). Loop stitch closely and firmly over the strands, using the eye end of the needle. The first and last stitches should be taken through the fabric (328b). Fasten off with a double back-stitch on the wrong side.

318a *Stranding the loop*

318b *Securing the loops,*

Making rouleau loops

These loops can only be set where there is a join along the edge of the opening. They cannot be set into a fold of fabric.

Narrow crossway strips of the garment fabric are required for making the loops. The turnings must be very narrow, therefore fabric which frays badly on a cross-cut edge does not make satisfactory rouleau loops.

Small buttons give the most attractive finish and are usually sewn on after the loops are made and set.

(a) Preparing and making the loops

Cut the crossway strips 15 mm-20 mm wide. Fold them in half lengthways, wrong side out, and tack along the centre. As only short lengths are required there is no need to join the strips (319).

Hand sewing gives the best result as it is flexible. Fasten on and off very firmly. If machine stitching is used, a loose tension is necessary. Stitch about 3 mm-4 mm away from the fold. Trim the turning a little narrower than the width of the rouleau.

Slip a tapestry needle, which has a blunt point, inside the tube and sew it to the fabric through the eye (320). Turn the rouleau right side out by means of the needle, removing it when the rouleau is formed. Press the rouleau with the join along one edge.

319 *A rouleau strip pre-pared for machining*

320 *A tapestry needle slipped inside the trim-med rouleau*

(b) Setting the loops

Press the edge of the garment and mark the fitting line. Measure out the required position of the loops as previously shown for worked loops, remembering to place the top loop in a suitable position below the top edge fitting line. Place the rouleau strip as shown in figure 321, so that the loops lie on the garment inside the fitting line, and project within it for the width of the button. Several lengths of rouleau may be used to provide the loops for one opening if necessary. Pin, and then tack the loops firmly in place.

If the loops are required to touch along the opening, it is better to cut the rouleau into even, short lengths, so that each loop is formed separately, thus reducing bulk within the turning (332).

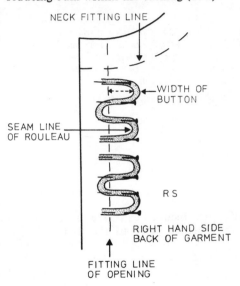

321 *The setting of spaced rouleau loops on a back neck opening*

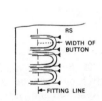

322 *The setting of close rouleau loops*

(c) Preparing and setting the facing

Join the facing along the fitting line, leaving the seam open for the length of the opening. Iron the turnings open flat, leaving the edges raw. Fold and machine a single turning down each long side of the facing and across the seamed edge.

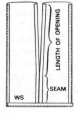

323 *The prepared facing for a rouleau loop open-ing*

193

Place the right side of the facing to the right side of the garment, with fitting lines over each other and tack in position. The loops are sandwiched between the garment and the facing. Machine on the fitting line along each side of the opening, making sure that the machining appears to be a continuation of the machining of the garment seam, so that the base of the opening is strong. Trim the turnings and the enclosed ends of the rouleau.

Fold the facing through to the wrong side, pulling out the rouleau from the fitting line of the opening. Tack close to the edge to hold the opening in position for pressing. Press lightly, remove the tacking stitches and press more firmly.

Mark the positions for the buttons and sew them in place (324).

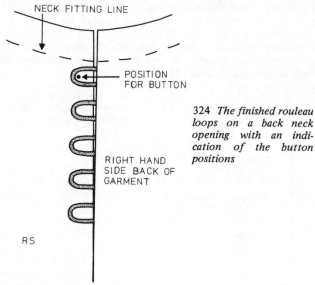

NECK FITTING LINE

POSITION FOR BUTTON

RIGHT HAND SIDE BACK OF GARMENT

RS

324 *The finished rouleau loops on a back neck opening with an indication of the button positions*

If the fabric does not press easily, or is inclined to fray, a line of machine stitching may be worked round the opening close to the fitting line, to strengthen and flatten the edges.

Press studs

These form a quick and easy method of fastening. They are not very satisfactory if strain is imposed on the opening as they tend to burst open. Laundering also weakens press studs. They are more often used on frocks and blouses than on underwear, for these reasons, and then only as subsidiary fastenings. They should never be used as the main method of fastening, eg down the centre front of a blouse, as they give no style to a conspicuous opening, and often cannot be sewn firmly without the stitching coming through to the right side of the garment.

The knobbed half (325a) which has a flat back, must be sewn to the overlap of the opening so that, if the garment is ironed on the right side, the fabric will not be worn away behind the stud.

The socket half (325b) which is not flat at the back, would wear through the fabric if it were frequently ironed from behind. For this reason it should be sewn to the underlay of the opening.

194

325a *The knobbed half of a press stud*

 325b *The socket half of a press stud*

Sewing on press studs

Three or four stitches should be made into each hole according to the size of the stud. Oversewing stitches may be used, but buttonhole stitch gives a much firmer and stronger setting. Fasten on with a double back stitch which will be covered by the stud. When working the buttonhole stitch, the knots must lie on the outer edge, or the stud will not close securely (326a). Pass from one hole to the next by slipping the needle between the double fabric (326b).

 326a *Forming a buttonhole stitch in one of the holes*

 326b *Passing the needle from one hole to the next*

Fasten off with a back stitch beside the last hole sewn and pass the cotton between the double fabric. The stitches should not show on the outer side of the opening. If it is impossible to prevent this, a different type of fastening should be chosen for use.

Placing the studs (327)

Mark the positions of the studs on the wrong side of the overlap. They should be fairly close together, ie no more than 25 mm apart, and are usually placed 3 mm inside the edge of the opening, or in the centre of a hem or facing. Sew on all the knobbed parts first. Chalk all the knobs, close the opening and pin it in position, pressing the studs into the underlap. Open the opening and put a pin into each chalk mark. When the fabric is white, or too pale in colour for the chalk to show, the opening must be closed and pins inserted into the underlap under the knobs, but this method is not as accurate. Sew on the socket parts to match the knobbed parts. The opening should close flat with the fitting lines over each other, and the studs should be invisible.

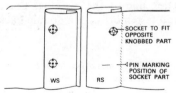

327 *Placing press studs*

Hooks eyes and bars

These must be placed and set so that they are invisible from the outside of the garment.

Hooks and eyes are only used on openings which have no wrap. Hooks and bars are only used on openings which have a wrap.

Check the positions of the hook and its closure, marking with pins.

(a) Sewing the hook for either type of opening

Fasten on with a double back stitch which will be covered by the hook. Place the bend of the hook 3 mm in from the edge of the opening, and sew it in place with four or five overcasting stitches, pushing the needle through the

195

fabric under the bend of the hook and stranding the cotton over the hook inside the bend (328a). Pass the needle to the eyelet end of the hook and work buttonhole stitches (or overcasting) round the two rings of the eyelet (328b). Overcasting gives a weaker setting. Finish by stranding across the centre of the eyelets two or three times, and fasten off with a double back stitch (328c). The stitches should not show through to the right side of the garment.

328a *The first step in attaching a hook*

328b *Sewing the eyelets with buttonhole stitching*

328c *The final appearance of the hook*

(b) Sewing an eye (329)

The bend of the eye should project 3 mm beyond the edge of the opening, so that it fits into the hook set 3 mm within the edge on the opposite side of the opening. The edges of the opening therefore meet. Fix the eye with three overcasting stitches each side near the edge of the opening. Buttonhole (or overcast) round the two eyelets, finishing with two or three overcasting stitches between the eyelets. Fasten off with a double back stitch beside the eye. The stitches should not show through to the right side.

329 *An eye sewn to the edge of an opening*

(c) Sewing a bar (330)

Place the bar 3 mm inside the fitting line of the opening. Buttonhole (or overcast) round the eyelets. Begin and fasten off with a double back stitch.

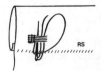

330 *A metal bar sewn to the edge of an opening*

(d) Making a worked bar

Worked bars are neater and flatter than metal ones, but should be used only if little strain is imposed on the opening.

Strand the bar flat on to the fabric and inside the fitting line of the opening. Loop stitch over the strands firmly and closely, forming the purled edge towards the fitting line so that it will take the rub of the hook in use.

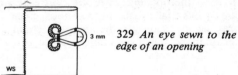

331 *Loop-stitching a worked bar. The size of the bar and the loop stitching are magnified for clarity*

Laced eyelet holes

Eyelets on outer garments may be laced with ribbon, rouleau or cord. An eyelet and lacing fastening may be used only on an opening which meets edge to edge and which provides double fabric. They are, therefore, generally used with a faced opening (332 and 333).

332 *A laced fastening used with a wrong side faced opening*

333 *A laced fastening used with a right side faced opening*

To work an eyelet

Mark the desired position with a pencil dot and press the end of a small circular object, eg a pencil, to imprint an outline for the eyelet.
(a) Work running stitches finely round the circular imprint.
(b) Pierce the fabric with a stiletto, working it well through the fabric to open the hole.
(c) Overcast finely round the hole covering the running stitches. Pull the stitches tight to keep the hole open.
(d) Loop stitching may be used to make a stronger eyelet, but the thickness of the purled edge tends to make the hole a little smaller.

334a, b, c and d *The three stages in working an eyelet, showing both overcasting and loop stitching at the final stage. The working diagrams are magnified for clarity*

For the lacing use fine rouleau made from the garment fabric, or a round cord. Hand-made cord is more attractive than a bought one, and the colouring can be mixed if desired. Make it from single, not stranded, embroidery cotton.

Making a looped cord with the fingers

This cord takes four times its finished length of thread to make, and two lengths are required, eg a metre of cord requires two lengths of thread each of four metres. Try a practice length first, using two different colours for clarity. When experienced, the cord is easy enough to make in one colour if preferred.

197

1 Knot the two different coloured threads together and keep the colours separate. Hold the knot with the right middle finger and thumb, and twist the black thread over the first finger, keeping that finger upright (335a)

2. Hold the white thread with the three end left fingers and pick up the white thread with the left first finger through the loop of the black thread (335b)

335a, b and c *The development of a looped finger cord*

3 As the left first finger becomes upright, change the grip on the knot to the left middle finger and thumb and pull the black thread tight (335c)

4 Working from the other side, lift up the black thread through the white loop, change the knot grip to the right middle finger and thumb, and pull the white thread tight. The black end always keeps to the right side and the white end to the left. It is only the cord that changes sides.

16 Collars

Many garments are fitted at the neck edge with some type of collar. This should be chosen to suit not only the style of the garment, but also the face and neck of the wearer, eg a tight-fitting stand collar does not suit a person with a short, thick neck. She would look more attractive with a cross-cut, turn-over collar styled to stand away from the neck at each side, which would make her neck appear narrower. Alternatively, a shirt collar worn with the neck open would help to give the effect of a longer, narrower neck.

A collar is a very conspicuous feature of a garment and, as well as being chosen with thought, must be given care in making and setting.

The following illustrated information gives a coverage of basic collar shapes. More elaborate collar styles, if studied and analysed carefully, will prove to have been developed from these basic shapes. This point is illustrated later by the analysis of a shirt collar. Where necessary, the shape of the collar pattern is shown beside the illustration of the collar. These pattern shapes do not contain turning allowances, but the straight grain lines are indicated by arrows. Unless otherwise stated, the centre back line of the collar pattern is placed to a fold of fabric when the garment has a front opening. When the garment has a back opening, the collar pattern is divided at the back, the front usually being left in its original shaping. Sometimes, however, the collar is styled without front shaping, and is cut with the centre front line to a fold of fabric.

1 Flat collars

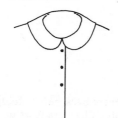

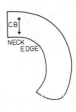

336a *The Peter Pan style of flat collar*

336b *The shape of a Peter Pan collar pattern*

Flat collars turn away from the neck-line and lie flat on the shoulders, eg a Peter Pan collar, figure 336a. These collars are rounded in shape, with the neck line a similar shape to the neck line of the garment. The centre back line of the collar is always cut parallel to the warp grain. The neck fitting line of the collar should equal the neck fitting line of the bodice in length.

Figure 336a shows a typical flat collar with rounded edges at the centre front. The centre fronts may be squared or pointed if preferred. Sometimes a flat collar is made in two sections to allow for a back opening. In this case it is shaped at the centre back to correspond to the centre front.

When cutting out, the pattern must be placed so that the warp grain runs parallel to the original centre back line (337). The edges of the collar are left loose at the back and fall away each side of the opening.

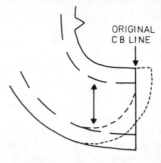

ORIGINAL
C B LINE

337 *The broken line shows a curved centre back line drawn onto a one-piece collar pattern. The arrowed grain line has been drawn parallel to the original centre back line. The fine dotted line indicates the additional turning allowance required for a two-piece collar*

2 Roll collars

Roll collars stand up above the neck line at the centre back for half or less than half their width, and then fold over. The fold rolls down to the centre front, where the full width of the collar falls back from the neck line when it is fastened. Roll collars are found in two basic styles, the half-roll collar (338a and b), and the full roll collar (339a and b).

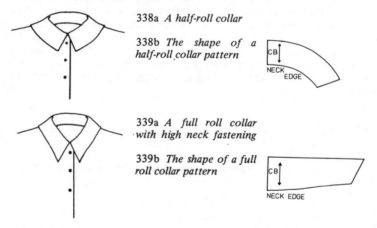

338a *A half-roll collar*

338b *The shape of a half-roll collar pattern*

CB

NECK EDGE

339a *A full roll collar with high neck fastening*

339b *The shape of a full roll collar pattern*

CB

NECK EDGE

The half-roll collar rises $\frac{1}{4}$ to $\frac{1}{3}$ its width at the centre back before folding over, and is always set to a high neck line. The full roll collar rises $\frac{1}{2}$ its width at the centre back before folding over. This collar can be set to a high neck line (339a), or it may be pressed flat as a collar and rever to form an open neck line.

As previously mentioned, the flat collar has a neck fitting line equal in length to the garment neck fitting line, and curved to correspond in shape. This collar, therefore, lies flat round the neck area of the garment when set and fastened in position. In order to achieve the characteristic rise at the centre back of roll collars, the roll collar neck fitting line equals the garment neck fitting line in length, but is much straighter than a flat collar in shape. This straighter neck line will not allow the collar to lie flat when set to the much more curved line of the bodice neck, and when fastened in position it is forced to rise at the back. The straighter the neck line, the higher the rise of the collar at the back, therefore the full roll collar has a neck line which is only very slightly curved. The half-roll collar has a more curved neck line, hence the slighter rise at the centre back, but it is not nearly as rounded as the neck line of the flat collar.

The centre back line of all roll collars is set to the warp grain, the strength of which helps to support the raised line.

Both types of roll collar can be divided at the centre back to set above a back opening. For methods of fastening the collar see figure 371.

3 Stand collars

Stand collars are upright in line, setting from the neck line upwards, towards the chin. This style of collar should always be interfaced if it is to retain the smart appearance of its upright line.

(a) Stand collars cut with the warp grain

These collars measure 25 mm or more in width according to style and fashion. They are often narrow and close fitting, with a front opening (340a and b). In this case the centre back is cut parallel to the warp grain.

340a *A stand collar with a front opening. This style is often called a Manderin collar*

340b *The shape of a stand collar pattern*

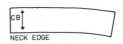

Sometimes a stand collar is made in two sections, and styled with either a front or back opening. All two-section stand collars are cut with the warp grain parallel to the centre back, on the same principle as the flat collar (336a).

A one-piece stand collar can be styled to open at the back instead of at the front. In this case the centre front is cut parallel to the warp grain. A narrow stand collar does not need fastening together at the back above the opening. A wider one is fastened edge to edge with two or three hooks and loops.

The neck fitting line of a narrow stand collar curves only very slightly, which causes the collar to stand up neatly round the neck when set in place. If the collar fits closely to the neck, the length of the collar neck fitting line should be about 5 mm shorter than the length of the bodice neck fitting line. This necessitates the collar being stretched very slightly in setting and aids the neat, upright line of the collar, causing it to fit closely to the neck. If the collar is styled to stand away from the neck, the neck fitting line of the collar and bodice should be equal in length.

(b) Stand collars cut on the cross

A stand collar can be cut on the cross and made wide enough to fold over on itself, making a style known as a cross-cut turn-over collar. When styled this way, the opening always comes at the back if the collar is set on a high neck line (341a and b). For the method of fastening the collar at the back above the garment opening, refer to figure 371.

For a lower neck line which does not require an opening, the collar can be

201

joined in a circle before setting.

341a *A cross-cut turn-over collar with a back opening*

341b *The shape of a cross-cut turn-over collar pattern. The pattern is laid on single fabric*

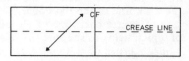

In making, the collar is first folded along the crease line, bringing the two outer edges together for the neck edge. After setting, the collar folds over to half its depth, having four thicknesses in its final position.

A shirt collar

A shirt collar is an example of a style founded on basic shapes, as it is a combination of two collars, ie a stand collar with a roll collar set along the top edge of the stand, or under section, of the shirt collar, and folding down over it.

342 *A shirt collar with a high neck fastening*

A shirt collar is styled for a front opening and is usually worn closed, either with or without a tie. A more casual appearance can be achieved by wearing the collar unfastened. If a tie is worn, it fits neatly round the stand of the shirt collar, and is overlapped by the top section, which is spaced at the centre front to accommodate the knot.

A shirt collar is usually given a crisp finish with machine edge stitching, and is often set above a machine-stitched shirt opening. Flat buttons should always be used with this collar and opening.

Shaping and supporting collar and neck fitting lines

Accuracy is most important when making collars to ensure a perfect shape at the outer edge, and when setting them to ensure their correct placing at the centre back and at the centre front of the neck-line.

As the fitting lines of the neck, and often of the collar, are curved, they tend to stretch a little out of shape unless the fabric is very firmly woven. This may be prevented by stitching a line of small tacking stitches along the collar and garment neck fitting lines when the tailor tacking is finished. This tacking is known as stay stitching, and should be pulled fairly tightly to support the fabric along the curved line. Some dressmaking directions recommend machining the line of stay stitching, but hand sewing is safer, as the machining, unless expertly worked, can tend to stretch the fabric.

The aim in all collar setting is to achieve a perfectly flat line round the neck with a setting which is as inconspicuous as possible from the right side.

Machining should never show round the neck-line on the right side.

The following directions for making and setting collars, attempt to give comprehensive guidance for handling basic collar styles in general, so that the topic may be studied as a whole. However, it is possible to pick out directions for making any one particular style if desired.

Making collars

1 Plain collars without interfacing

Unless otherwise stated in the directions for setting, the machine-stitching, when making the collar, should be worked right up to the raw edge at the neck as shown in figure 343a. The neck edge of all collars should be left open, but the neck fitting-line should be marked.

(a) Flat collars

Place the two collar sections with right sides touching and tack round the fitting line on the outer edge. The neck edge must be left free. The collar may be machined, using a short stitch length, as this gives a smooth, flexible line on the curve. Fine running stitches give a more flexible line for stitching the much curved line of a flat collar, and are recommended for the small, flat collars often used on babies' clothes.

On firmly woven fabric, trim the under collar turning to 3 mm, and the upper collar turning to 5 mm: on loosely woven fraying fabric, trim the under collar turning to 5 mm, and the upper collar turning to 8 mm.

Snip V-shaped notches out of the turnings, being careful not to cut the stitches (343a). Adjust the closeness of the notches according to the curve of the outer edge: The sharper the curve, the closer the notches.

Fold the collar right side out, getting a smooth edge pushed out along the line of stitching. Tack round the edge, and cross-tack across the width of the collar to keep it flat (343b).

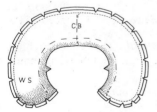

343a A flat collar, Peter Pan style, stitched, layered and notched

343b A flat collar, Peter Pan style, tacked and cross-tacked on the right side

Press the collar lightly on the underside to set the edge, remove the straight tacking stitches and press more firmly to sharpen the edge. Take care not to mark the fabric by pressing over the cross-tacking, which must be left in place until the collar is set.

(b) Roll Collars

A straight collar which is cut in one piece with a fold line through the centre (344a) is very easy to make. It is folded in half along its length, then tacked and machine-stitched at the two side edges (344b)

Sometimes a roll collar is cut in two sections, ie an upper and an under collar (345a). This type is made with a seam along the outer edge (345b). It is not a suitable choice for thin or transparent fabric, as the seam turnings would show through and spoil the appearance of the outer edge.

203

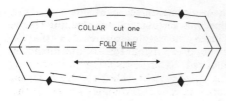

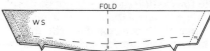

344a *A one-piece collar pattern, showing the centre fold line and the turning allowance on neck and side edges*

344b *A one-piece collar folded and machined at the two side edges*

345a *A two-piece collar pattern, showing the turnings on all edges*

345b *A two-piece collar machined at outer and side edges*

Trim away the corners of the turnings to remove bulk at the front points, and layer the side turnings (346a and b), making the upper collar turnings slightly wider. There is no need to snip or notch the turnings unless the collar is styled to curve along the outer edge. This styling usually produces more accentuated front points which require careful trimming (347).

346a *A section of a one-piece collar with layered side edges and trimmed front corner*

346b *A section of a two-piece collar with layered turnings and trimmed front corner*

347 *A section of a collar showing the curved outer edge notched and the prominent front point trimmed away*

Press the collar all over and then, using the finger and thumb, press the collar turnings apart along the machine stitching. This helps to ensure a sharply creased edge when the collar is finished.

Turn the collar right side out, and push out the points carefully. A button gauge, which can be bought in a haberdashery department, has one end specially shaped to assist with easing out collar points. Tack round the outer edge of the collar, and across the width, as for a flat collar.

Interfaced collars

An interfacing gives a crisper finish and helps to prevent a collar from becoming crumpled when worn under a coat.

In most cases it is wiser to use a woven interfacing, as it gives a smoother line along the fold of the collar where it rolls over. A bonded interfacing tends to crease at the roll-line and break the smoothness of the roll. For open-weave, semi-transparent fabrics, choose a light-weight interfacing, eg organdie, and set it to the upper side of the collar as its secondary use is to mask the turnings when the collar is turned right side out. Medium and heavy-weigth fabrics can have the interfacing set to the under collar, so that the finished appearance is not too hard.

Setting the interfacing   Method 1
This method can be used for collars of any style when the upper and the under collars are cut separately. It is always used for collars where the interfacing is set to the upper collar. It also provides the quickest and simplest setting of an interfacing for collars where the interfacing is set to the under collar.

Cut the interfacing from the collar pattern if a special one is not provided. Match the grain of a woven interfacing with the grain of the collar, so that they pair accurately and will not twist after washing or cleaning. Pin the interfacing to the wrong side of the chosen collar section, keeping it perfectly flat. Tack the collar and interfacing together across the centre of the width, tacking with the straight grain of the fabric (348).

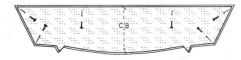

348 *A full roll collar with the interfacing tacked across the centre and pinned to the collar section*

Many collars, with a seam along the outer edge, have pointed or angled ends at either the centre front or the centre back or, sometimes, in both positions when there is a centre back opening. The interfacing can present a problem at the point or angle, by giving unwanted bulk when the collar is finally turned right side out. To prevent this, the interfacing can be trimmed away at the point or angle before the collar is machined. Figure 349 indicates, in an enlarged diagram, how this is done.

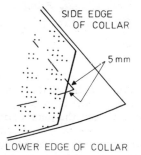

349 *Mark points 5 mm along the fitting line either side of the point, and trim away the interfacing diagonally, cutting through these two points. This removes a small triangle of interfacing at the point*

Tack together the interfacing and the chosen side of the collar all round the collar shape on the fitting line, smoothing and tacking from the centre, first to one side and then the other. This section of the collar is henceforth handled as a single layer of fabric (350).

205

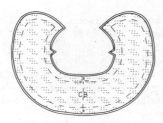

350 *A flat collar, Peter Pan style, with the interfacing tacked to the collar section across the centre and round the neck and outer edge fitting lines*

With right sides touching, pin and tack the two collar sections together along the outer edge fitting lines. Leave the neck edge open.

Machine the outer edges of the collar, using a medium length stitch, as there are three layers to penetrate. Stitch carefully, following the shape of the collar, ie keeping a smooth curve, or straight lines with neatly angled corners according to style.

Trim the interfacing close to the machine stitching and layer the two outer turnings. On curved or rounded collars, snip V-shaped notches out of the turnings (refer figure 343a). On pointed collars, trim away the turnings at the points (refer figure 351). On squared collars, trim away the corner turnings and notch the corner area (352). For detail of corner refer to figure 349.

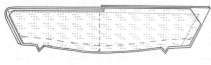

351 *A two-piece full roll collar. The interfaced collar has been machined on the outer fitting line. Half the collar is fully prepared to show the interfacing cut close to the machine stitching, the turnings layered and the point trimmed to reduce bulk*

352 *A narrow stand collar. Half the collar is fully prepared as in figure 351 but, in this case, the corner has been notched as well as trimmed. The two side edges are machined only as far as the neck fitting line*

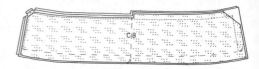

Remove the short line of tacking which holds the interfacing across the centre of the collar, but leave the tacking round the neck edge.

Press open the turnings and turn the collar right side out as directed for the collar on page 203.

Setting the interfacing   Method 2

This method is used for a collar and under collar that is cut in one, eg a full roll collar or a cross-cut, turn-over collar. Cut the interfacing half the width of the whole collar shape, so that it fits between the neck edge and the centre line.

Trim off a narrow strip, eg 2 mm, along the long, straight edge of the interfacing. Decide which half is to be the upper collar, ie the section to show when the collar is being worn. Tack the interfacing to the under collar section, with the long, trimmed edge just clear of the fold line.

Catch-stitch the interfacing to the collar, setting the stitches just clear of the fold line, so that they will not show along the edge of the collar (353).

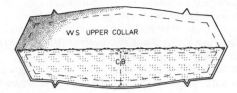

353 *A one-piece full roll collar, with the interfacing tacked and catch stitched. The fold line of the collar runs between the two outer angles*

For guidance on catch stitching, refer to figure 246a, b and c, page 146, and the information on placing interfacing to a fold line.

Fold the collar in half along the fold line, with the wrong side outside. Pin, tack and machine stitch along the fitting line of the two short edges. The neck edge must be left open. Layer the turnings and trim away the corners. Refer to figure 346a.

Press open the collar turnings and turn the collar right side out, as directed for the collar on page 203.

Setting the Interfacing Method 3

This method is suitable only for medium and heavy-weight fabrics, as the interfacing is set to the under collar and, therefore, cannot mask the turnings as is desirable for thinner fabrics. It is more difficult to handle, as it requires care and accuracy in placing, trimming and setting. It does however, give a very satisfactory finish on heavier fabric, as it is possible to press a finer, sharper edge to the collar.

Paying attention to the matching of the grain, cut the interfacing to the size of the under collar. Pin it to the wrong side of the under collar and, with the collar fabric uppermost, tack together along the centre back and then along all edges, stitching 5 mm inside the fitting lines.

Turn the under collar to bring the interfacing uppermost. Trim away the interfacing just inside the fitting-lines on all edges (354a).

Catch stitch the interfacing to the under collar, stitching just inside the fitting lines (354b).

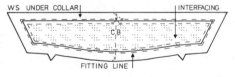

354a *The interfacing tacked to the under collar and trimmed*

354b *The interfacing catch stitched to the under collar, and the tacking stitches removed*

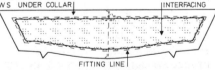

Remove the tackings and press the interfaced under collar. It is now handled as single fabric, and the collar is made as previously directed on page 203.

Setting collars

The neck opening and any seams running into the neck line of the bodice must be finished and pressed before the collar is set.

Tack the collar ready for machine stitching, and check that the neck fitting lines of collar and bodice are balanced in measurement. Adjust the collar if necessary, as a collar should be set smoothly and be neither eased nor stretched excepting in the case of a narrow stand collar, which is sometimes stretched slightly in setting. When adjusting a collar length at the centre front edges, take care not to spoil the outline shape of the collar edge.

Interfacing is not shown in any of the following collar setting figures to prevent overloading the figures with detail. When it is used, remember to trim away the interfacing turnings close to the machine stitching to remove bulk from the setting. Refer to figure 351.

Setting flat collars
(a) Setting a flat collar to a bodice with a buttoned overwrap
A buttoned opening with an overwrap is often used with a flat collar as this style of collar is often worn with a high neck line. Prepare the bodice facing in readiness for setting the collar. Refer either to the section on shaped facings, page 135 for a plain setting, or to the section on interfacings, page 145 for an interfaced facing. A shaped back neck facing is not required for setting a flat collar.

Pin the collar round the neck between the centre front lines, matching the collar and bodice neck fitting lines, and balancing the centre back lines and any neck balance notches. Tack the collar to the bodice along the neck fitting line (355).

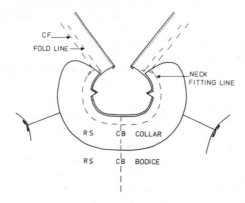

355 *A flat collar tacked to the neck fitting line of a bodice*

Fold the bodice facings back to the right side, along the fold lines, so that the front sections of the collar are sandwiched between the bodice and the bodice facings.

Prepare a crossway strip of the bodice fabric 25 mm wide and long enough to fit round the neck-line. Lap the crossway strip 10 mm over the right-hand facing and, using a 5 mm turning, pin it round the neck line on top of the collar. Arrange the left-hand side of the setting to match.

Tack from the outer fold of the right-hand facing, along the neck fitting-line, to hold the bodice facings and the crossway strip to the collar and bodice neck lines (356).

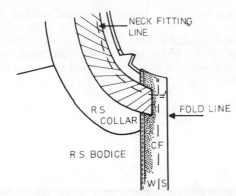

NECK FITTING LINE

R S COLLAR

FOLD LINE

R S BODICE

CF

W S

356 *A section of the neck, showing the collar, with the front facing folded to the right side, and the crossway strip, all tacked together along the neck fitting line*

Machine along the neck fitting lines from the left-hand to the right-hand fold line. Trim the neck turnings to 5 mm and snip towards the fitting line so that the turning will open out and lie flat when it is folded back to the wrong side of the bodice. Turn the bodice facing to the wrong side and lift the collar away from the bodice. Flatten the turnings onto the bodice and away from the collar. Fold the crossway strip onto the bodice to cover the turnings, and crease it back sharply along the neck line. Check that the bodice is also creased back sharply along the neck line. Tack close to the neck line to hold the bodice facings, the crossway strip and the neck turnings to the bodice.

Arrange the crossway strip to form a facing no wider than 10 mm to cover the neck turnings, and tack it in place. Hem the bodice facings to the crossway facing, and then slip hem the crossway facing onto the bodice (357).

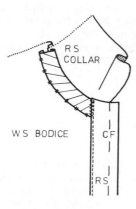

R S COLLAR

W S BODICE

CF

R S

357 *This figure shows the bodice facing hemmed and the crossway facing slip-hemmed in positions*

Press the collar and the facings, and turn back the collar to the right side along the neck fitting line. It will roll back very slightly from the neck fitting line, and set flat over the shoulders as seen in figure 336a.

A flat collar is often set with an edge-to-edge opening, eg a wrong-side faced opening (page 155), a bound opening (page 164) or a zip fastener. Complete the opening according to the appropriate instructions before setting the collar.

(b) Setting a flat collar to a bodice with a wrong-side faced opening or a bound opening

Both these openings have an edge-to-edge closure along the centre front line, therefore the neck fitting line of the collar must be set accurately at the opening edges (358), so that the collar meets neatly together at the centre front when the opening is closed.

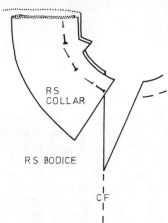

358 *The neck fitting line of the collar set accurately at one edge of the centre front opening. In this case it is a wrong side faced opening. Note that the neck turning of the collar protrudes beyond the edge of the opening*

Pin the collar to the right side of the bodice neck line at the two centre front points (one side shown in figure 358). Then pin it at the centre back point and at any neck balance points. Finish pinning the collar in place, keeping the two neck fitting lines over each other. Tack the collar to the bodice along the neck fitting line.

Prepare a crossway strip of the bodice fabric, cutting it 25 mm wide and the full length of the neck fitting line + 20 mm for turnings. Pin and tack the crossway strip along the neck fitting-line, allowing 10 mm to project beyond the two centre front edges, and using a 5 mm turning along the neck line (359).

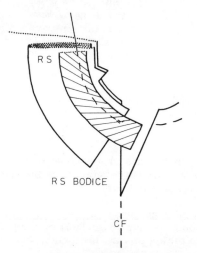

359 *The crossway strip, collar and bodice tacked together along the neck fitting line. A wrong side opening is shown here*

Machine along the neck line between the two centre front edges. Fasten off the machine thread ends very neatly and strongly at the centre front points. Trim the 10 mm projections to 5 mm, and fold them back to the right side in line with the centre front, taking care not to stretch the folded edges. Fasten them down by hand along the neck fitting line (360a). Trim the neck turnings to 5 mm and snip at intervals, taking care not to cut the machine stitching.

Place the eye of a fairly coarse needle into the seam at the edge of the collar projection above the neck fitting line. Push the collar seam inwards and down to the neck fitting line, following the line of the dotted arrow in figure 360b, and press it in place.

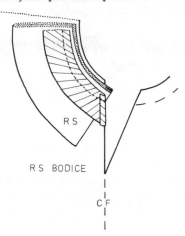

360a *The stitched and trimmed neck edge, showing the neatened crossway strip*

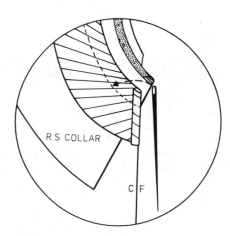

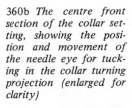

360b *The centre front section of the collar setting, showing the position and movement of the needle eye for tucking in the collar turning projection (enlarged for clarity)*

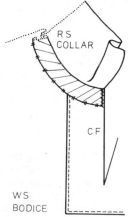

361 *A wrong side faced opening is shown at the centre front. The crossway facing has been hemmed at the centre front edge and slip-hemmed along its lower edge*

211

Manipulate the collar and the crossway facing as outlined for the previous setting, but at the centre front the crossway facing, in this case, will lap over the wrong side facing (or the binding of a bound opening), and the folded edge of the crossway strip will lie just clear of the centre front edge of the opening on the wrong side (361).

Press the collar and its facing. Fold the collar over to the right side of the bodice and make a button and loop fastening.

(c) Setting a flat collar to a zipped opening
The semi-concealed method of setting the zip is the most usual for this style of collar and fastening. A shaped neck facing is used to set the collar and neaten the top of the zip tape on the wrong side. Set the zip according to the directions on page 170.

Pin and then tack the collar to the neck line as shown in figure 358, remembering that, in this case, the centre front line of the bodice comes along the folds of fabric over the centre of the zip teeth.

Prepare the shaped facing for the neck as described on page 129, but allowing a 20 mm turning at the centre front. An interfacing is not necessary in this case as it would add unwanted bulk and firmness.

Place the right side of the shaped facing over the right side of the collar, and pin the facing round the neck line, matching the centre front points, the centre back points and the shoulder seams, and setting the facing smoothly between these positions. Check that the 20 mm turning allowed beyond the centre front lines of the shaped facing, project evenly either side of the zip opening. Tack the facing round the neck fitting line. Machine stitch through all thicknesses, stitching along the neck fitting line between the centre front points (362).

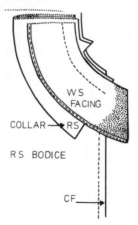

WS FACING

COLLAR → RS

RS BODICE

CF

362 *The shaped facing and collar machined along the neck fitting line from the centre front edge. The zip had been previously set*

Layer the neck turnings and snip at intervals round the neck, snipping nearly to the neck fitting line. Treat the projection points of the collar at the centre front as shown in figure 360.

Lift up the shaped facing and turn it back sharply along the neck fitting line. Understitch the neck turnings to the facing in a similar way to that shown in figures 221a and b on page 131 of the shaped facing section. In this case, however, the collar turnings are included.

Trim the shaped facing projections at the centre front to 10 mm. Fold them back to the wrong side, bringing the fold in line with the centre front. Press the folds and stitch the turnings by hand along the neck fitting line.

Fold the shaped facing to the wrong side of the bodice, pulling it back sharply along the neck fitting line, so that the collar springs slightly as it folds over on the right side, and shows a fraction on the wrong side above the filling line.

Tack the shaped facing to the bodice about 10 mm below the neck fitting line, keeping it smooth and flat. Hem the facing edge to the shoulder seam of the bodice. Back stitch the facing to the zip tape, taking care not to let the stitches come through to the right side. This forms a pocket into which the zip can run as it closes up the neck line (363).

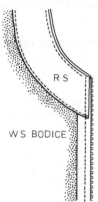

RS

WS BODICE

363 *The completed setting on the wrong side, showing one centre front edge*

Setting a roll collar   Method A

This method of setting a roll collar is suitable only for fabrics which do not fray, eg poplin, as a weak point occurs at the centre fronts where the neck turning has to be snipped.

(a) Preparation of collar
For this method of setting, the neck turning of the collar must be left free at either end (364).

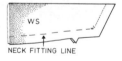

WS

NECK FITTING LINE

364 *One side of the collar joined as far as the neck fitting line*

(b) Preparation of bodice
Roll collars are frequently used in conjunction with a buttoned opening. In this case the collar is set to the centre front points, and there is an extension beyond the centre front edge of the collar which forms either the overwrap for the closing of a high neck line, or the 'step' of the rever for an open neck line.

A shaped front facing must be used with an open neck line, but a back neck facing is not required. For a closed neck line, either a shaped or a straight front facing may be used. Refer to the facing and interfacing sections for guidance on preparing and setting bodice facings and interfacings.

213

The shoulder edges of a shaped facing must be neatened before the collar is set. After the long outer edge turning has been prepared for machine stitch neatening, trim the shoulder turning and prepare it to match, making a neat corner. The two edges can now be machine neatened and pressed.

(c) Preparation of the extension
(i) For a bodice with a shaped facing cut separately
Place the right side of the facing to the right side of the bodice. Tack and machine from the centre front, ie the collar fitting point, along the neck line as far as the fold line. Turn a right-angled corner and stitch down the fold line to join the facing to the bodice. Snip the neck turnings at the centre front, that is at the collar fitting point, trim the corner and layer the turnings (365a).

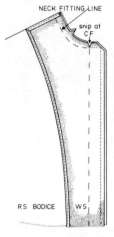

365a *The machine stitching along the extension and the centre front, the snip at the centre front neck edge, the trimmed corner and the layered front turnings*

Turn the facing to the wrong side and tack close to the outer edge, tacking from the collar fitting point to the lower edge of the facing. Cross tack the facing to the wrong side of the bodice to hold it firmly in place when attaching the collar (365b).

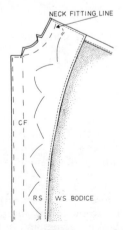

365b *The prepared facing on the wrong side*

(ii) For a bodice with a straight facing cut separately
Neaten the long, free edge of the facing. Tack it to the bodice with the right sides together and machine from the collar fitting-point to the fold line, and then down the fold line to the lower edge of the facing. Snip the neck turnings, trim the corner and layer the turnings (366a).

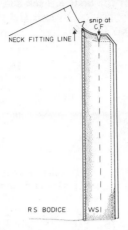

366a *The machine stitching along the extension and the centre front, the snip at the centre front neck edge, the trimmed corner and the layered front turnings*

Turn the facing to the wrong side of the bodice. Tack from the collar fitting point to the lower edge of the facing, and through all thicknesses along the centre front line (366b).

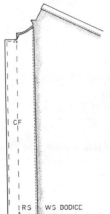

366b *The prepared facing on the wrong side of the bodice*

(iii) For a bodice cut with a facing attached
The following information applies to either a shaped or a straight facing: Neaten the facing edges as previously described. Fold back the facing section onto the right side of the bodice and machine along the neck fitting line from the collar fitting point to the outer fold. Snip the neck turnings at the collar fitting point, trim the corner and layer the turning above the machine stitching.

Turn the facing to the wrong side and tack it as shown in either figure 365b or figure 366b according to the type of facing.

215

(d) Attaching the collar
(i) For an open neck-line
Pin the upper collar to the WRONG SIDE of the bodice, along the neck fitting line, matching the centre back lines and the balance notches. The centre front edges of the collar must fit exactly at the two collar fitting points above the centre front line of the bodice. Tack and machine along the neck fitting line between these two points, to join the upper collar to the bodice. Fasten off the cottons securely (367a).

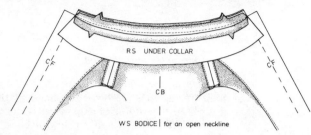

367a *The upper collar machined to the bodice neck line. In this case the collar is being attached to the wrong side of the bodice first for an open neck line*

Trim and snip the turnings of the upper collar and bodice neck line, and fold them upwards inside the collar.

Trim the under collar turning to 5 mm and fold it back inside the collar. Pin it along the neck fitting line (367b). Tack and hem the collar along the fitting line, sewing neatly into the machine stitching.

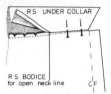

367b *The under collar being pinned in position on the right side for an open neck line*

If a shaped facing has been used, the neatened shoulder line of the facing should be hemmed to the shoulder seam.

Remove all tacking stitches and press the collar.

(ii) For a closed neck line
Pin the upper collar to the RIGHT SIDE of the bodice along the neck fitting line and proceed as already described in section (d) (i).

Setting a roll collar   Method B
For this method of setting a roll collar a whole neck facing is used. It is a particularly good method to use with fabrics which fray badly, as there are no weak points in the setting. However, it can be used satisfactorily with any fabric, providing it is not very heavy in weight.

If facing patterns have to be made, refer to the shaped facing section for guidance in making the back neck and centre front facing patterns.

(a) Preparing the facing
Tack the back neck facing to the front facings at the shoulder lines. Test the fitting with the bodice neck-line, and adjust if necessary.

Machine the shoulder seams, trim the turnings to 5 mm and press them open flat.

Round the outer edge of the whole facing, fold and tack a 5 mm turning to the wrong side. Machine close to the folded edge and trim away the surplus turning (368).

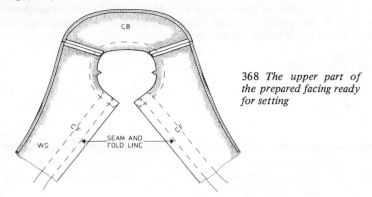

368 *The upper part of the prepared facing ready for setting*

(b) *Attaching the collar*

Arrange the collar with the under side touching the right side of the bodice, and set the neck fitting line of the double collar along the neck fitting line of the bodice. Pin first at the centre back points, the balance points and the centre front points. Then pin between these points. Tack along the neck fitting line (369a).

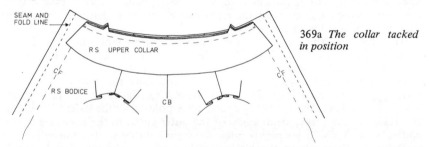

369a *The collar tacked in position*

Pin and tack the prepared facing along the fitting lines of the neck and front edges, so that the collar is sandwiched between the bodice and the facing. Machine along the neck and the front edge fitting lines. Layer the turnings, trim the corners and snip the neck turnings (369b).

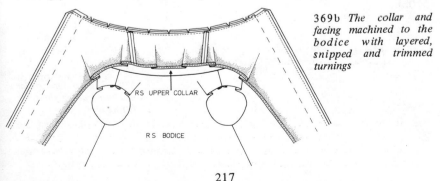

369b *The collar and facing machined to the bodice with layered, snipped and trimmed turnings*

217

Fold the facing to the wrong side of the bodice, pulling out the collar and easing back the front edges along the machine stitching. Tack close to the front edges and along the bodice neck line. Press the collar and facing lightly to set the outline, remove the tacking and press more firmly. Hem the outer edge of the facing to the shoulder seam turnings of the bodice, and also to any darts which run into the back neck line.

Setting stand collars

(a) Attaching stand collars cut with the warp grain

The collar may be set in conjunction with either a buttoned or a zipped opening. In either case the neck turning of the collar is not stitched across in making. Refer to figure 352 for guidance in making the collar.

As the collar is almost straight, care is needed when setting it to the bodice neck line, which is so much more curved. The fitting lines must be pinned together, and the bodice neck line kept smooth. Watch that it does not fold back into little pleats under the collar, as these would get caught in with the tacking and machine stitching.

(i) Attaching in conjunction with a buttoned opening

If the garment is styled with a buttoned opening, the collar is set as shown in figures 367a and b.

(ii) Attaching in conjunction with a zip

The neck fitting line of the collar must be clearly marked. The outer side of the collar, which will show on the right side when the collar is set, should be chosen and marked with a tack mark.

Trim the neck turning of the inner collar to 5 mm-6 mm. Fold and pin the trimmed turning to the inside of the collar. Tack it in place to hold the fitting line along the folded edge, and press to sharpen the fold.

Arrange the collar with the outer side touching the right side of the bodice, and set the neck fitting line of the outer collar along the neck fitting line of the bodice. Pin first at the centre back points and the balance notches, and then pin the centre front edges of the outer collar to the zip edges of the bodice neck. These front points must be accurately set so that the collar will meet edge to edge when the setting is finished and the zip closed. Finish pinning together the outer collar and bodice neck fitting lines. Tack and machine along the neck fitting line, keeping the centre front edges accurately placed. This joins the outer collar to the bodice neck, and leaves the inner collar free (370a). Layer and snip the neck turnings of bodice and outer collar (370b).

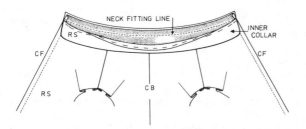

370a *The outer collar machined along the neck fitting line*

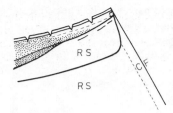

370b *The prepared neck turnings. Figure enlarged for clarity*

Press the machined neck edge to flatten the fitting line, and fold the collar upwards, slipping the prepared neck turnings inside the collar. Tack the outer collar to the neck turnings to hold it up sharply along the neck fitting line (370c).

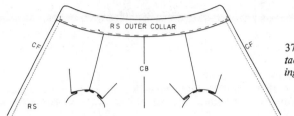

370c *The outer collar tacked to the neck turnings*

Press the collar lightly, remove the tackings and press more firmly to give a good line round the neck, as this will be very conspicuous when the collar is finished.

On the inside of the bodice, the inner collar will be falling into place. Pin and tack the prepared edge along the neck fitting line. Hem the folded edge to the machine stitching.

A small hook and a worked bar, or a metal eye, should be stitched at the base of the collar, on the neck fitting line, to hold the centre front edges together above the zip. Refer to pages 195 and 196 for guidance in setting this fastening.

(b) Attaching a stand collar cut on the cross ie a cross-cut turn-over collar
The collar is made following the directions given on page 206, making interfaced collars, Method 2. The neck turning of the collar is not stitched across in making. Refer to figure 364.

(i) Attaching to a high neck line
For this style of collar the garment is usually fastened with a zip set at the centre back. Although the collar is wider than a stand collar, it is attached in the same way as for a stand collar cut with the warp grain at the centre back, and attached in conjunction with a zip. In this case, however, the centre front points of collar and bodice are set together, and the centre back points of the collar are set above the zip. Otherwise the handling of the collar and neck line is the same.

As the collar meets edge to edge at the centre back, and is deeper than a stand collar, it needs a more secure fastening. Three hooks and worked bars are required to hold it firmly when it is folded in its final position (371). Attach two hooks to the inside of the collar, placing them as shown. Make two worked bars to pair with them for holding the collar in its upright position. The lower, outer corners must now be held together by attaching a third hook, and making a worked bar to pair with it. These fastenings must be invisible from the outside of the finished collar.

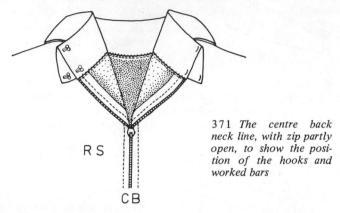

371 *The centre back neck line, with zip partly open, to show the position of the hooks and worked bars*

(ii) Attaching to a low neck line
No opening is required with a low neck line as it will slip easily over the head. The collar can be narrow in finished width, or cut wide enough to form a cross-cut, turn-over collar. Whatever width is desired, the collar is interlined as already described on page 206, but is then joined into a circle before setting. Cut away the interfacing turnings close to the seam machine stitching, trim the seam turnings to 5 mm - 6 mm and press them open flat (372).

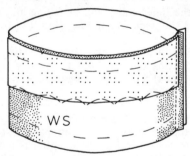

372 *The interfaced collar joined into a circle. The interfacing and turnings have been trimmed ready for pressing*

Fold the collar in half to bring the right side on the outside. Cross tack it together to prevent it slipping out of alignment in handling.

The collar can be set in one of two ways. The seam should be set to the centre back for either method.

Method 1   The collar can be machined to the neck fitting line on the right side of the bodice, and hemmed onto the wrong side. This is very similar to the method shown for use with a zipped opening on page 212.

Method 2   A shaped facing can be made to fit the neck and joined into a circle. The collar is then set between the right side of the bodice and the right side of the shaped facing. For guidance in using a shaped facing, refer to the facing section, and also to setting a flat collar to a zipped opening on page 212, but in this case, of course, there will be no opening to consider.

If there is a zipped opening at the centre back, the centre back edges of the collar must be handled and fastened as described in section (a) (ii) on page 218.

A shirt collar
Making and setting a shirt collar with a two-piece pattern
For the finished style of this collar refer to figure 342 on page 202.

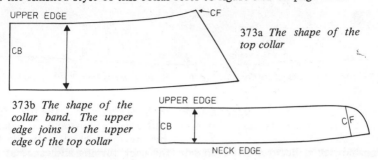

373a *The shape of the top collar*

373b *The shape of the collar band. The upper edge joins to the upper edge of the top collar*

(a) Making the top collar
Make the top collar section as for a roll collar with interfacing. Study figures 344a and b, 345a and b, 346a and b, 347 and 348. Select from these figures the ones which relate to your collar, follow the text concerned, and proceed accordingly. When the top collar has been pressed and cross-tacked, it is usual to machine edge stitch or to top stitch the three outer edges, stitching with the upper collar side uppermost.

(b) Making the collar band
This must also be interfaced to provide a firm stand for the collar. Use the collar band pattern and cut an interfacing for the outer section of the band. Pin and tack the interfacing to the outer band, following the principles indicated in figures 348 and 350.

Trim the neck turning of the inner band to 5 mm and fold the trimmed turning to the wrong side, along the neck fitting line (347). Tack the turning in place.

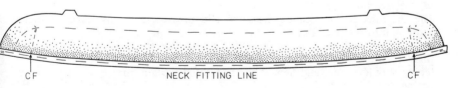

374 *The prepared inner section of the band*

(c) Joining the collar together
Work in the following order:

1   Lay the interfaced outer band, right side up, on the table with the neck edge towards you.

2   Place the top collar with the under side touching the outer band, and the raw edges away from you. Match the centre back points and the balance notches, and place the centre front edges to the centre front positions on the outer band. Pin and tack the top collar to the outer band along the seam fitting line (375).

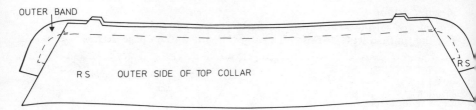

OUTER BAND

R S   OUTER SIDE OF TOP COLLAR

R S

375 *The top collar tacked to the outer section of the band which is interfaced on the wrong side*

3   With the turning side uppermost, pin the inner band over the top collar, placing the raw edges together. Match the centre back points and the balance notches. The outer band is now covered by the inner band, with the top collar sandwiched between. At each side, the neck turning allowance of the outer band shows below the folded neck edge of the inner band. Tack and machine through all thicknesses from the neck fitting line one side to the neck fitting line the other side. Fasten off securely at each end (376).

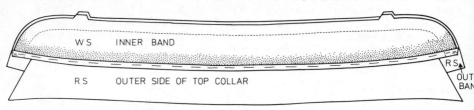

W S   INNER BAND

R S

OUT
BAN

R S   OUTER SIDE OF TOP COLLAR

376 *The top collar machined between the inner and outer sections of the collar band*

4   Trim away the interfacing close to the machine stitching on the outer band. Layer and snip the collar turnings.
5   Turn the collar band downwards, away from the top collar, and press.

(d) Preparation of shirt
The shoulder seam must be neatened and pressed, also any darts or tucks running into the neck line.
    Interface and neaten the front facings of the shirt. Fold and crosstack them to the wrong side in their final position. Turn under the raw edge of the facing shoulder line, and hem it to the shoulder seam turning along the seam fitting line.

(e) Setting the collar
With right sides together, pin the fitting line of the outer, interfaced section of the collar band to the shirt neck fitting line, matching the centre back, the balance notches, the centre front points and the front edges. Tack and machine along the neck fitting line (377).
    Trim away the interfacing close to the machine stitching, layer and snip the turnings. Fold the turnings upwards inside the collar band and press carefully. Tack the folded edge of the inner section of the band along the machine stitching on the neck fitting line. This can be hemmed in place and the band left plain, but it is usual to machine-stitch all round the band (378). Remove the tacking and give a final press.

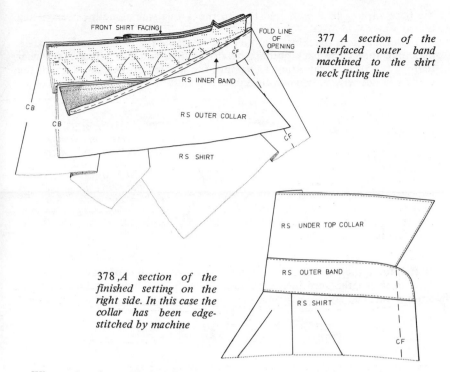

377 *A section of the interfaced outer band machined to the shirt neck fitting line*

378 *A section of the finished setting on the right side. In this case the collar has been edge-stitched by machine*

When the fastenings are worked on the shirt front, a button and buttonhole will be required to fasten the collar band at the neckline. If the band is inclined to swing on the neck-band button, a very small hook and worked bar can be sewn invisibly at the neck fitting line.

Making and setting a shirt collar with a one-piece pattern

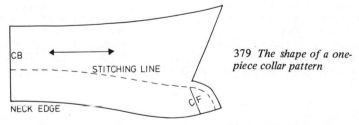

379 *The shape of a one-piece collar pattern*

This is a further example of styling a collar from basic collar shapes, and is a development of the two-piece shirt collar. In this case the stand and roll collar are not prepared separately and joined together in making, but are combined in the pattern itself.

This shaping of the pattern gives a collar which is quicker to make and which closely resembles the two-piece shirt collar in appearance. It is not as firm as the two-piece style as the grain line of the 'band' section is altered, and the lack of the central seam causes a loss of firmness. It is adequate in cut for the more casual, open-necked shirt style.

Attach interfacing to one section of the collar. On the second section, trim

223

the neck turning to 5 mm, fold this to the wrong side along the neck fitting line and tack it in place.

With right sides touching, pin, tack and machine the two sections together, matching the centre back points, the fitting lines and the points and corner shaping (380). It is important to balance the shaping of the side edges, or the collar will not set evenly when finished.

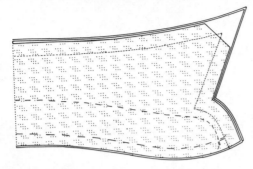

380 *A section of the collar after machining. Cross-tacking of interfacing is omitted, but both the stitching line and the neck fitting line tacking are shown. For detail of corner, refer to figure 349*

Reinforce the corners at either side with a second line of machining about 25 mm in length. Snip into each corner of the machine stitching trim the outer points and layer the turnings (381).

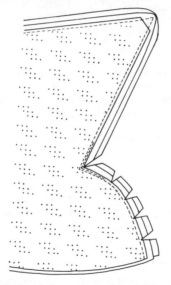

381 *An enlarged section of one side edge of the collar, showing the snipped corner and prepared turnings. All tackings are omitted*

Turn the collar right side out and press carefully. Cross-tack the upper section of the collar above the stitching line, and tack through the collar stitching line.

The collar is attached to the neck line of the shirt as for a two-piece collar (page 223) as far as the tacking of the folded edge along the neck fitting line.

The final machine stitching now has to be done. Work as follows:

1 On the right side machine from the centre back, along the neck fitting line as far as the beginning of the stitching line, turn the work on the machine needle and machine smoothly along the stitching line to the opposite front

point. Turn the work again and machine along the neck fitting line to the centre back. Fasten off the machine thread ends on the wrong side of the shirt.

2 Turn the shirt wrong side upwards. This brings the collar in the right position for top stitching the overlap section on its right side. Top stitch the three outer edges of the collar overlap at a width of 5 mm (382).

3 Remove all tacking and press the collar.

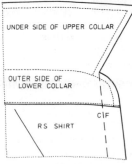

382 *A section of the finished one-piece shirt collar. In this case the upper section of the collar has been top-stitched*

The upper part of the collar is now folded back, along the stitching line, to cover the lower part, which takes the place of the band in the collar previously described.

Setting a flat collar into a lined yoke

Make and press the collar parts according to previous instructions. Machine the shoulder seams of the yoke and lining on the fitting lines. Trim the turnings to 6 mm and press them open flat.

Lay the yoke right side upwards on the table. Place the collar to the yoke neck line, matching the centre back, the centre front and the neck fitting lines. Tack the collar and yoke together along the neck fitting line (383a).

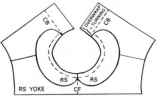

383a *The collar tacked to the yoke*

Lay the yoke lining wrong side upwards over the prepared yoke and collar. Pin and tack through all the layers, stitching along the back and neck fitting lines. Machine along the tacking. Layer the turnings, trim away the back neck corners and snip the neck turnings (383b).

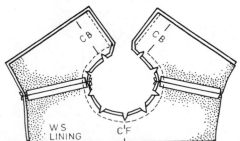

383b *The machined and prepared back neck edges of the yoke with the collar sandwiched between*

Turn the yoke right side out and ease out the collar and centre back neck corners. Press the back edges and the collar setting to give a flat finish. Tack through the yoke and neck turnings, under the collar, to hold the setting firmly in place. Tack the yoke and lining together through the centre of their width (383c).

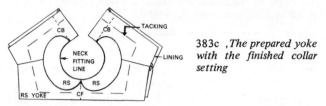

383c ,*The prepared yoke with the finished collar setting*

The yoke is now ready for setting to the lower part of the garment.

A detachable collar

This type of collar is useful as it may be removed easily for washing.

Make the collar to the size and shape required, leaving the neck edge unfinished. Prepare a crossway strip 30 mm wide, and 50 mm longer than the neck line of the collar.

Tack the strip round the neck edge of the collar, leaving 25 mm projecting at each end, and tacking 3 mm outside the neck fitting line. The width of the neck turning allowance is thus reduced by 3 mm (384a).

Stitch along the line of the tacking and trim the neck turning to 6 mm. Finish the crossway strip to form a binding (see page 118), hemmed to the underside of the collar. Neaten the ends so that they finally project 20 mm. Press the binding to the underside of the collar so that the fitting line comes to the final neck edge (384b).

In order to place the collar accurately to the neck edge each time it is re-set, it is helpful to sew a small press-stud to the centre back of the bodice and collar neck line. It can then be pinned and tacked evenly either side of the centre back without having to measure. It is not wise to use press-studs all the way round the neck, as they are not as flat and strong as tacking.

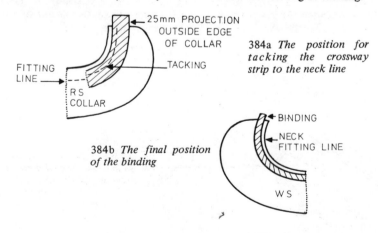

384a *The position for tacking the crossway strip to the neck line*

384b *The final position of the binding*

17 Pockets

Pockets usually have a utilitarian purpose, although they are used sometimes purely decoratively. In many cases both purposes are combined.

There appears to be a wide variety of pocket styles but, when analysed, they will be found to belong to one of the following types:
(a) A patch pocket, which is applied to the outside of a garment,
(b) a set-in pocket which is really a bag set behind a prepared slot, or
(c) a pocket set into a seam.

The position of a pocket is important. From the strictly utilitarian point of view, a pocket should be set in a convenient place for inserting the hand. However, to achieve a balanced line and/or to create a desired decorative effect, the purely convenient position may have to be altered slightly.

Thread mark the pocket position from the pattern to the garment, and study the position carefully when fitting. Adjust the position to suit your own needs if necessary. This is especially important if you have had to adjust the pattern in size and/or make alterations to the garment in fitting. If a pocket is being added to a garment, the position should be decided during a fitting.

A reinforcing strip is usually required to support the top of the pocket to withstand strain in use, but this does not make a pocket strong enough to carry heavy articles.

Patch pockets
Shaping patch pockets
The basic shape of a patch pocket is square (385a), but it may be pointed (385b) or rounded (385c) at the base, according to taste. Dirt is apt to collect in pocket corners, therefore a round base is easier to keep clean.

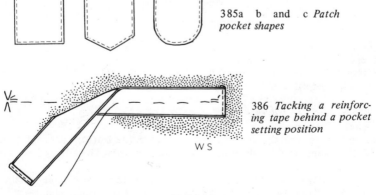

385a b and c *Patch pocket shapes*

386 *Tacking a reinforcing tape behind a pocket setting position*

W S

227

Reinforcing the garment
Cut a strip of ribbon seam binding, ribbon or tape 30 mm wider than the top edge of the pocket. Stitch a turning about 3 mm wide across each cut edge. Tack the prepared tape to the wrong side of the garment, just to cover the top setting line of the pocket (386).

A single patch pocket
(a) Cutting the pocket
It is usual to cut a patch pocket with the weft grain straight along the top edge. This brings the warp grain downwards, and balances the garment grains. A pocket of patterned fabric should be cut to fit exactly over the design in the pocket area of the garment, so that the pocket does not disturb the effect of the pattern as a whole. Remember this when cutting out, and do not cut out the pockets until the setting positions have been checked in fitting.

At the top edge allow a first turning of 3 mm-5 mm, plus a second turning of 15 mm-40 mm according to the size of the pocket. Allow 10 mm-15 mm turnings on the other edges.

(b) The top hem
Fold the first turning of 5 mm to the wrong side and edge stitch by machine. Fold and tack the second turning to the right side. Machine (or back stitch) across the hem at each side, along the fitting line. Trim the turning to 5 mm as shown in figure 387. Snip the turning corner diagonally.

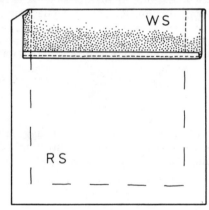

WS

RS

387 *The top hem in preparation with one side turning trimmed and layered*

Turn the prepared hem finish to the wrong side, pushing out the two corners to a good shape and press the fold. If the fabric presses sharply, leave the hem unstitched, but if the fabric is springy, loosely slip hem the hem with stitches spaced 10 mm-15 mm apart.

(c) The lower edge treatment
(i) Square Corners
Fold and press first the side turnings and then the bottom turnings to clarify the fitting lines. If the fabric does not press sharply, the fitting lines must be thread marked.

Open out the turnings. Fold and then trim the two corners as shown in figure 388a. Reset the turnings so that the corner is formed as a mitre (388b).

Trim and tack the turnings all round the pocket. Slip stitch together the folded lines of the mitre.

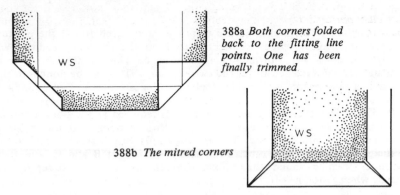

388a *Both corners folded back to the fitting line points. One has been finally trimmed*

388b *The mitred corners*

(ii) A pointed base

Check the angle of the point to discover whether it is a right or obtuse angle. Fold and press the side turnings and then the turnings either side of the point. Thread mark the fitting lines if necessary. A right angle must be mitred as described for a square corner. For an obtuse angle, fold back the turning on each side of the angle, and a neat corner will result. Trim, tack and press the turnings.

(iii) A rounded base

Run a fairly fine gathering thread in the curved areas, setting it in the turning allowance 3 mm-5 mm outside the fitting line. Fold back the full turning allowance to the wrong side, and ease up the fabric on the gathering threads to give a smooth curve to the fitting line and to flatten the turning. Snip out notches in the fullest parts of the turning. Tack the turning to the wrong side and trim (389). Press the pocket along the outer edges.

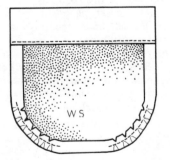

389 *The preparation of a rounded pocket*

(d) Top stitching

Top stitching is often used on a patch pocket. On medium and heavier weight fabric it is better to work the top stitching before attaching the pocket, as it is easier to keep a good line. Trim away the pocket turnings to within 3 mm-4 mm of the top stitching on the wrong side.

(e) Stitching the pocket

Tack the pocket in place on the right side of the garment, setting it fairly easily, otherwise it will cause the garment to pucker. The warp grain of the pocket is usually set parallel to the centre front of the garment.

(i) A plain pocket
Begin machining the pocket at the top edge, and stitch round the pocket, keeping close to the edge. Remember to keep the machine needle down through the fabric when turning corners or angles. The machine thread ends must be securely fastened off at the two top edges. This can be done into the reinforcing tape on the wrong side. A plain setting is shown in figures 385a, b and c.

If you feel that an extra reinforcement is required at the pocket top to take strain in wear, eg on children's play clothes, a triangle can be machined when beginning and finishing the stitching (390). Stitch from A to B to C, making BC 3 mm-5 mm long. Turn sharp corners at B and C, and then continue stitching round the pocket. Reverse the stitching order of the triangle when fastening off.

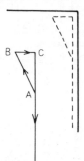

390 *A magnified figure to show the arrangement of the stitching for a triangular reinforcement at the top corner of a pocket*

(ii) A top stitched pocket
(a) *On thin fabric*   Machine the pocket at the required distance in from the edge, so that the top stitching and the setting of the pocket are done together. Fasten off the machine thread ends securely, as a triangle reinforcement looks out of place with top-stitching.
(b) *On medium and heavier weight fabrics*   Attach the pocket from the wrong side, back stitching through the garment and the pocket. Stitch as finely as the fabric will allow, and make sure that the stitching does not penetrate through to the right side of the garment, but only picks up the back of the garment fabric along the line of the top stitching.

A double patch pocket
A double patch pocket has a firm appearance and gives a neat, easy top finish. A single pocket pattern can be adapted easily. Fold back the whole of the top edge turning allowance, and place this folded edge to a weft fold of fabric. Cut the usual turning allowance on the remaining edges.

Keep the pocket folded in half across the width and tack and machine along the fitting lines on the wrong side. Leave a gap in the centre of the base (unless it is pointed, when a gap must be left in the centre of a straight side, where it will come on the straight grain). Layer the turnings and trim any corners or angles (391).

230

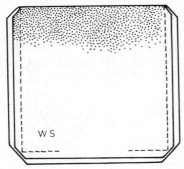

391 *A prepared double patch pocket*

Turn the pocket right side out through the gap, pushing out the edges along the machining. Turn in the turnings across the gap, tack and slip stitch invisibly. Press the pocket.

Follow the directions for top stitching and setting as given for a single patch pocket.

A lined patch pocket

A lined pocket is used on medium and heavy-weight fabrics, and is lined with lining fabric to prevent it from being too bulky. An interfacing is usually set along the top edge.

(a) Cutting the pocket

Cut the pocket section as directed for a single patch pocket on page 228.

Measure the finished depth of the pocket, and cut the lining that depth minus the width of the turning allowance at the top edge, eg for a pocket with a finished depth of 120 mm and a turning allowance of 20 mm, cut the lining 100 mm deep. It is necessary, however, to allow a 5 mm turning at the top edge when cutting the lining.

(b) Interfacing the pocket facing

If the fabric is loosely woven, or inclined to curl over along a folded edge, a strip of interfacing will give a better line to the top of the pocket. Cut the interfacing the pocket width X the facing depth. If using woven interfacing, match the grain to the pocket grain.

Tack the interfacing to the wrong side of the pocket from the top edge line downwards, and catch stitch it lightly across the two long edges. This stitching must not come through to the right side (392).

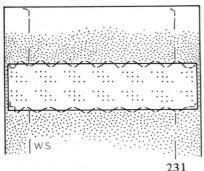

392 *The interfacing catch-stitched to the top of the pocket*

(c) Making the pocket

With right sides together, tack and machine the lining to the top raw edge of the pocket, making the seam 5 mm wide. Press the seam turning onto the lining.

Ignoring the pocket facing section, and the lining, fold and tack the pocket turnings to the wrong side, dealing with the shaping at the lower edge as previously described on page 228.

At the seam line, move the fitting line at each side of the pocket facing 3 mm inwards. Crease back the facing turnings from these points to the original fitting line at the top edge of the pocket. Fold the lining turnings to the wrong side in line with the slightly reduced width. This will make the lining a little narrower than the pocket. Shape the lower edge of the lining as for the pocket, and tack the turnings in place.

Trim the turnings so that they are no wider than 10 mm on the pocket and 5 mm - 6 mm on the lining. Press the pocket and lining (393).

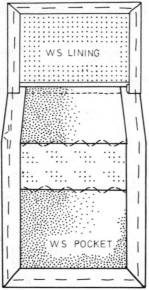

393 *The prepared pocket and lining*

Turning back along the top edge line of the pocket, fold the lining and the pocket facing to cover the wrong side of the pocket, and tack in place. This should fit just within the outer edges of the pocket (394). Slip stitch the facing and lining to the back of the pocket, taking care not to stitch through to the right side. Press the pocket.

394 *The facing and lining tacked to the wrong side of the pocket*

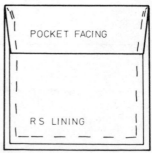

(d) Setting the pocket

For a machined setting, follow the directions for setting a single patch pocket.

For a classic finish, the pocket is set by hand, either back stitching finely from the wrong side, or slip stitching on the right side. The hand setting stitches must not show on the right side.

A patch pocket with a flap

(a) The pocket

This style of pocket is generally used on sports or casual wear. Therefore a machined finish is suitable.

A double patch pocket is the best choice, as it balances the flap in weight. Follow the instructions on page 230.

For added strength, the pocket can be set with a double line of machine stitching. Stitch close to the edge and continue round for a second time 5 mm inside the first line (395).

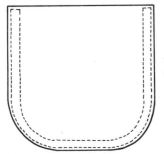

395 *A pocket with double machine-stitched setting*

(b) The flap

Cut the flap on double fabric, with the weft grain across the width. Allow 10 mm - 15 mm turnings on all edges. If a firm finish is required, cut a strip of interfacing the same size. Tack the interfacing to the wrong side of one flap section, and make this the underside of the flap, so that the final appearance is not too hard.

Machine together the two flap sections, leaving the long straight edge open. Trim and layer the turnings (396a). Turn the flap right side out, push out the edge, tack and press. Machine a double line round the edge of the flap to match the double setting of the pocket.

If the flap is to be fastened with a button and buttonhole, make a vertical buttonhole at this stage (refer to page 186).

Place the flap above the pocket with its outer side touching the right side of the garment. The open edge fitting line should be 20 mm above the pocket top. Tack and machine along the fitting line and fasten off securely.

Trim the turnings to a bare 5 mm (396b).

Fold the flap downwards, creasing sharply along the line of machining. Press and tack to hold the position. On the pocket, measure the distance between the outer edge and the inner line of machining. Machine across the flap at this distance below the top (396c).

If a button is required, check its position through the flap buttonhole, and sew it to the pocket.

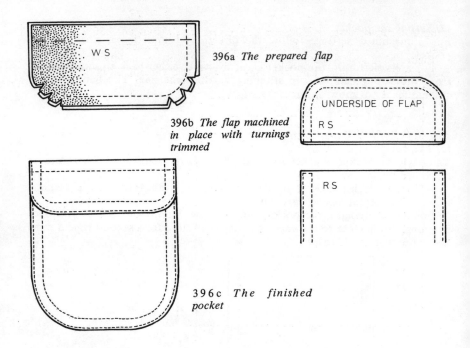

396a *The prepared flap*

396b *The flap machined in place with turnings trimmed*

UNDERSIDE OF FLAP

R S

R S

396c *The finished pocket*

Bound slot pockets

A straight bound slot pocket

On the right side this type of pocket appears like a long bound buttonhole. The making of a bound buttonhole should be understood and practised before attempting to make a bound pocket (refer to page 188).

The width of the pocket binding should be as narrow as possible eg 3 mm on thin fabrics and 5 mm on heavier ones (397).

397 *A bound slot pocket on the right side*

Mark the pocket position on the garment with a line of tacking.

It is easier to manipulate a bound pocket if it is cut straight with the grain of the garment fabric. Sometimes, for reasons of style, they are made on a diagonal line. In this case great care must be taken to keep the edges flat and unstretched.

(a) Preparing the pocket

The pocket is made in the same way as a bound buttonhole (refer to page 188), but in this case the binding strip provides the fabric for making the entire pocket, so it has to be cut large enough to do this. To make a pocket with a right side slot of 90 mm, bound with a 5 mm binding, and a pocket bag 100 mm deep on the wrong side, cut the strip as follows:

Width — cut weftway = 90 mm + 20 mm for pocket + 2 x 10 mm for turnings = 130 mm

Length — cut warpway = 100 mm + 110 mm for the two sides of the pocket bag + 4 x 5 mm for the binding + 2 x 10 mm for turnings = 245 mm.

Figure 398 is a plan of the pocket. It indicates how the above measurements are arranged, and shows the 10 mm turning allowance on all edges.

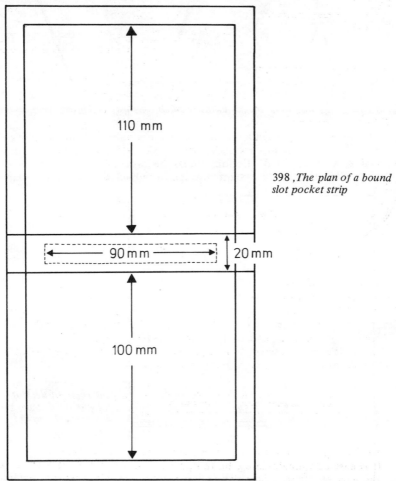

398 , *The plan of a bound slot pocket strip*

Tack a line on the binding strip straight with the weft grain, and equal in length to the pocket width. Set the tacking across the centre of the width and 120 mm up from one end. The 120 mm comprises the depth of pocket (100 mm) + 2 x width of binding (10 mm) + a turning of 10 mm. The tacking marks the cutting line of the slot which comes through the centre of the machined rectangle shown in figure 398.

(b) Setting the pocket
Place the right side of the strip to the right side of the garment, with the tacked lines matching, and with the longer length of the strip *above* the pocket line. Tack the strip and the garment together along the pocket line.

Make the opening following the directions given for a bound buttonhole. Press the bound slot on the wrong side. Close the folded edges of the binding together with fishbone stitch (399a, b and c).

399a, b and c *Working fishbone stitch*

On the right side machine round the outer rectangle of the binding to hold the pocket strip in place on the wrong side. If a machined finish is not desirable, invisible stab stitching must be worked into the seam of the binding. Stab the needle straight through from back to front in the seam line,

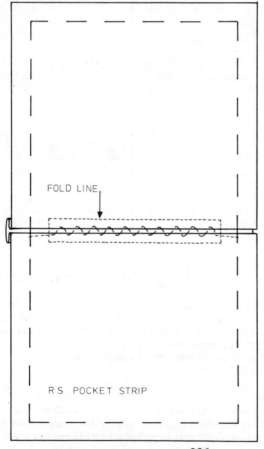

FOLD LINE

R S POCKET STRIP

400a *The finished slot on the wrong side. In practice the fishbone stitch should be closing the edges of the slot. The 10 mm turning allowance is marked round the edges*

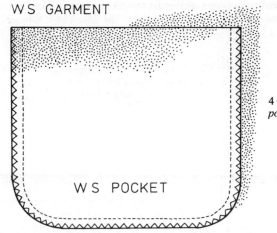

WS GARMENT

WS POCKET

400b *The finished pocket on the wrong side*

and back again from front to back, forming a minute stitch on the right side which sinks invisibly into the seam line. Pass over about 5 mm - 6 mm on the wrong side and repeat the stabbing.

The pocket is now finished on the right side, and the strip is now ready for folding over and forming the pocket on the wrong side (400a).

The pocket bag is made by folding the upper flap of the strip downwards over the lower flap along the top of the machining or stab stitching. Machining is shown in figure 400a. Pin the pocket bag together and tack along the 10 mm turning allowance line, rounding off the two lower corners. Machine on the tacked line, trim the edges and neaten with machine zigzagging or by overcasting (400b).

If the garment fabric is thick and would make a bulky pocket, lining fabric can be used at each end of the strip. Measuring across the cutting line of the slot, use garment fabric for half the 110 mm section (398) and for 30 mm of the 100 mm section ie about 95 mm in all plus seam turnings. Join the garment and lining sections and press the seam turnings onto the lining fabric. Note that the seams are arranged so that they do not overlap, and a wider area of garment fabric is planned to fall at the back of the pocket, where it might show through the slot.

A diagonal bound slot pocket
This is a more difficult pocket to make, as a diagonal line requires more careful handling than a straight line.

A strip of thin lining fabric or lawn should be used to support the line of a diagonal slot pocket. Cut it on the straight grain, about 25 mm wide and about 30 mm longer than the pocket width, and tack it to the wrong side, with the pocket line coming through the centre of the strip.

(a) Cutting the pocket
Use the pattern given for a diagonal welt pocket on page 243. Place the diagonal line of the pattern to a crossway fold of fabric, so that the pocket shape is cut out double. Allow a wide turning allowance of 20 mm on all edges, as the pocket has to be trimmed to shape during the construction. To cut a pocket for the left-hand side of a garment, fold the fabric wrong side

out, and lay the pattern with the diagonal line from left to right (401a).

Figure 401b shows the pocket shape tacked to the left-hand side of a garment along the cutting line for the slot, with the machined rectangle for forming the binding.

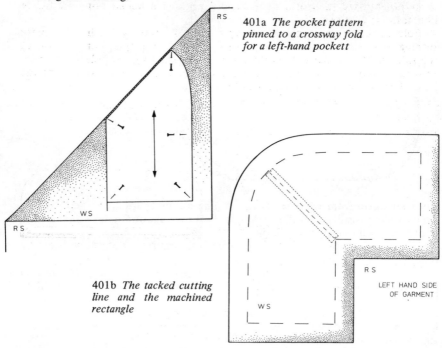

401a *The pocket pattern pinned to a crossway fold for a left-hand pockett*

RS

WS

RS

401b *The tacked cutting line and the machined rectangle*

RS

LEFT HAND SIDE OF GARMENT

WS

(b) Making the pocket

The pocket is made on the same principle as the straight bound pocket, but special care must be taken not to stretch the binding in this case, as it is being made on the crossway of the fabric.

When the pocket is folded into position on the wrong side, the raw edges do not fall exactly over each other. Trim away the outstanding single fabric on the three raw edges before joining and neatening the pocket bag.

A flap for a bound slot pocket

A flap is sometimes set over a bound slot pocket for decorative purposes. A button and buttonhole fastening is not used with this style of pocket, and it is usually left plain without a machine-stitched finish.

(a) Cutting and making the flap

Make the flap 5 mm wider than the bound slot, and 35 mm deep for use with a 90 mm slot. The flap can be squared or rounded at the corners. Cut a 15 mm turning allowance on the upper edge, and 10 mm turnings elsewhere. If the corners are squared, the flap can be cut with a fold along the lower edge. If used, interfacing should be catch-stitched to the under side of the flap.

When making the flap, do not machine beyond the fitting line of the setting edge (402a). Apart from this, the making of the flap is similar to the method given on page 233.

238

(b) Attaching the flap

Place the right side of the flap to the right side of the garment, with the fitting line of the open end 10 mm - 15 mm (according to fabric thickness) above the top edge of the bound slot. The flap, being 5 mm wider, should come just beyond the slot at either end. Tack and machine along the fitting line, fastening off securely.

Fold back the upper seam turning out of the way, and trim the under turning to 3 mm. Snip the side edges diagonally. On the upper turning, fold in the side edges diagonally, trim the raw edge if necessary, and fold the turning to make a hem over the trimmed under turning (402b). Tack and stitch the hem. It can be machined or hemmed (402c).

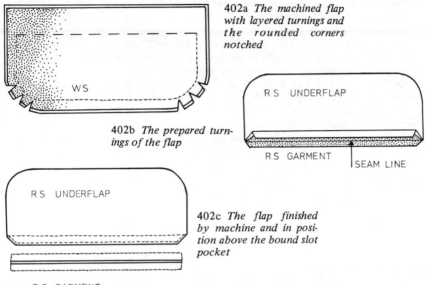

402a *The machined flap with layered turnings and the rounded corners notched*

402b *The prepared turnings of the flap*

402c *The flap finished by machine and in position above the bound slot pocket*

Fold down the flap in position and press. Slip a strip of clean paper under the flap while pressing to protect the garment fabric, and use a pressing cloth over the flap to prevent shining.

Hold the flap in place with 3 or 4 slip stitches either side at the top on light-weight fabrics. A fine bar tack (refer to page 86) can be used at the top edges on heavier fabric.

Welt pockets

A welt pocket has a rectangular slot on the right side which is covered by the welt. The welt is an inserted band of fabric with a fold along the top edge. A welt pocket is more difficult to make than a bound slot pocket, and should be practised before embarking on the garment. It is essential to prepare the pocket accurately and to take trouble to work with the grain of the fabric.

The pocket requires three pieces of fabric. The welt strip and one pocket section must be made from the garment fabric. The second pocket section can be made from lining fabric if it is necessary to reduce bulk.

The line of the pocket must be clearly marked on the garment. The pocket

239

can be either straight or diagonal. If straight, the line must run with a weft thread: if diagonal, the line must be straight in itself. Correct the line if it has become uneven in marking it from the pattern.

The directions given in the following instructions are for a pocket with a finished width of 100 mm and a welt 30 mm deep, which is a usual size. These measurements can be adapted as desired so long as they are kept in a suitable proportion.

A straight welt pocket
(a) The welt
The turning allowance should be 5 mm all round on thin fabric, and 10 mm on heavier fabric. Cut the welt the following size:

Weftway 100 mm + 2 turnings

Warpway 60 mm + 2 turnings

On medium and heavy-weight fabric, the welt can be interfaced with a strip of interfacing cut 100 mm plus 2 turnings weftway, and 30 mm warpway. Catch stitch it lightly to the wrong side of half the welt strip.

Fold the welt in half weftway with the wrong side outside, and machine the two side edges using the full turning allowance. Trim away the turnings of the interfacing if used. Trim and layer the welt seam turnings (403a). Turn the welt right side out and press.

Working on the right side of the garment, place the open edge of the welt along the lower side of the pocket line, and tack along the welt fitting line (403b). If the welt is interfaced, place the interfaced side uppermost.

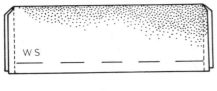

W S

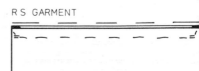

403a *The prepared welt*

R S GARMENT

R S

403b *The welt tacked in place*

(b) The pocket sections
The turning allowance should be 10 mm on all edges except for fraying fabrics, when it is wiser to use a 15 mm allowance. Cut the pocket sections to the following size:

Weftway 130 mm + 2 turnings

Warpway 140 mm + 2 turnings

Take one pocket section (the lining fabric if being used), and place it over the welt with the wrong side uppermost. Set the top weft edge 25 mm plus a turning allowance above the pocket line, and check that the welt is centrally placed within the width of the pocket section. Tack the pocket section to the garment along the pocket line, keeping the weft grain of both pocket and garment aligned.

Tack a rectangle round the pocket line, making it the following size:

Length = 100 mm ie the exact width of the welt

Width = 2 X turning allowance of welt, ie either 10 mm or 20 mm according to fabric.

The tacked rectangle must be aligned with the grain on all four sides, as it is the guide for the machining (404a).

Machine the pocket slot, following the tacking, and turning accurate corners. Slit the rectangle through the centre and diagonally into the corners (404b). When slitting the lower corners of the rectangle, do not cut into the welt turning, but snip pocket and garment separately.

R S GARMENT

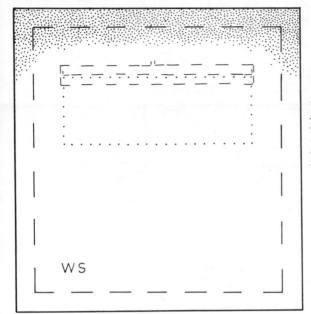

404a *The slot prepared for machining. The fine dotted outline indicates the position of the welt underneath the pocket sections,*

R S GARMENT

404b *The slot machined and cut*

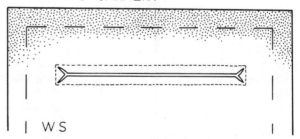

Turn the pocket section through the slot to the wrong side of the garment, easing it gently back along the line of the machine stitching. The welt automatically folds upwards, but is free at the sides.

Tack round the slot on the wrong side, tacking through pocket and garment at the sides and top, and through the welt turnings as well at the bottom (405a). The underside of the welt shows through the slot on the wrong side of the garment. The seam at the base of the welt must be flat on the right side. Press the slot and the welt seam, taking precautions not to mark the fabric.

Tack the top of the slot to the welt to keep the slot in shape during the remainder of the pocket construction.

Lay the second pocket section, wrong side uppermost, to cover the first one, setting the raw edges together at the top to align the grain. Smooth it over the whole of the pocket area, then pin and tack the two pocket sections together round all four sides, evenly rounding the two bottom corners. Trim the edges as required. Machine all round the pocket fitting line, and neaten with zigzagging or hand overcasting (405b). Press the pocket.

Slip-stitch the side edges of the welt to the garment, making small stitches of an even tension so that the joining is invisible and unpuckered (405c). Press from the wrong side.

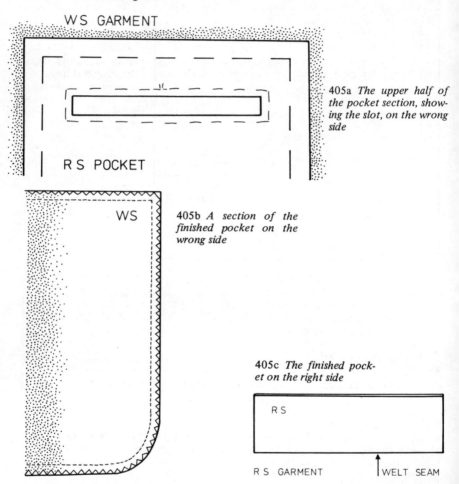

405a *The upper half of the pocket section, showing the slot, on the wrong side*

405b *A section of the finished pocket on the wrong side*

405c *The finished pocket on the right side*

A diagonal welt pocket
The method of making this pocket closely resembles the method given for the straight welt pocket. There is, however, an added precaution, and also an alteration to the pocket shape.

(a) Reinforcing the pocket line
Tack-mark the diagonal line on the garment, and reinforce it on the wrong side with a strip of interfacing fabric. The strip should be cut 120 mm long warpway, and 30 mm - 40 mm wide according to the thickness of the garment fabric. Tack the strip to the garment with the diagonal pocket line centrally placed.

(b) Shaping the pocket sections.
The square shape used for the straight pocket does not give a satisfactory result in this case, as it could not hang downwards in wear without dropping sideways. A pocket shape with a raised diagonal line at the top must be built up from the square (406).

Use squared paper, and draw a diagonal line for the width of slot and welt required. From its lower point, drop a perpendicular for the depth of the pocket, and square across for the pocket width. Square again up to the lower level of the diagonal, and curve from there to the top of the diagonal line.

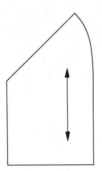

406 *The pattern shape for a diagonal welt pocket. Allow 15 mm turnings on all edges*

Cut out two pocket sections from the pattern, leaving turnings and arranging the use of fabric as suggested for a straight welt pocket. When using fabric with a right and wrong side, check before cutting that the diagonal slope of the pocket will fit with the tacked pocket line on the garment, to bring the right side of each pocket section in the desired position.

(c) Making the pocket
The welt is cut on the straight grain, and the setting and construction of the pocket follow the directions already given for the previous pocket.

Side seam pockets
A side-seam pocket can be set into an opening in the side seam of any garment. If the garment has a waist band or seam, the pocket is set into the top of the skirt side seam, and the top of the pocket is joined in with the waist band or seam.

Making the pocket pattern
(a) For a one-piece dress (407)
Select the position of the pocket and mark this on the side seam of the garment pattern, making the marks 130 mm apart.

Look for the straight grain line on the pattern and rule a parallel grain line, drawing it opposite the pocket markings, and a short distance away from the seam line.

Draw the top line of the pocket from the upper pocket mark at right angles to the grain line, extending from the edge of the pattern to 50 mm beyond the side seam fitting line.

Rule a line parallel to the top line, drawing it from the edge of the pattern, through the lower pocket mark, and extending it as a guide line for 120 mm beyond the side seam line.

As a further guide for drawing the pocket bag, drop a perpendicular of 45 mm from the centre of the previous guide line. Draw the pocket bag as shown by the solid line in figure 407.

Trace the pocket shape and grain line onto spare paper, and cut out the pocket pattern.

A larger or smaller pocket can be drawn on the same principles. The measurements given here produce a pocket of average size.

(b) For a dress with a waist seam or a skirt with a waist band
The pocket position is marked on the side seam of the pattern from the waist fitting line downwards. The top line of the pocket is drawn along the waist fitting line, and is made 70 mm in length. This makes the outer edge of the pocket less curved. The extended size is required to make the pocket easier to use in this position. The difference in shaping is indicated by dotted lines in figure 407. Otherwise the shaping is the same as for the previous pocket.

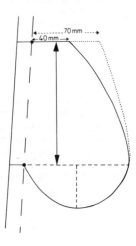

407 *The pocket pattern for a side-seam pocket in a one-piece dress (solid lines). The dotted lines indicate the extended shape required when the pocket is set partly into the waist line. In this case the 70 mm line is drawn along the waist fitting line*

Making a side seam pocket in a one-piece dress
(a) Preparing the side seam
Machine the side seam on the fitting line either side of the pocket opening. Fasten off the machine thread ends securely. Check that the seam fitting line is tack marked on both sides of the pocket opening. Press the seam open flat.

(b) Cutting and preparing the pocket
Cut two pocket shapes, leaving a turning of 15 mm all round, but sloping out to meet the seam line, where the turning is already provided. Mark the fitting lines with tacking or chalk (408).

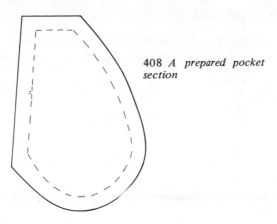

408 *A prepared pocket section*

(c) Setting the pocket

Work on the wrong side of the skirt. Take one pocket section and, with the wrong side uppermost, place the side seam edge to the pocket opening, aligning it exactly across, but setting the pocket seam fitting line 3 mm inside the skirt side seam fitting line. Tack and machine along the pocket fitting line. Figure 409 shows the finished machining from the underside of the skirt seam turning, where it can be illustrated more clearly.

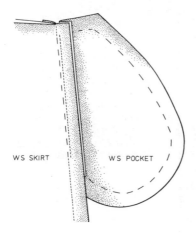

WS SKIRT   WS POCKET

409 *A pocket section machined in place. In this figure the top of the skirt has been cut away to show the position of pocket and skirt*

Set the second pocket section to the opposite side of the pocket opening in a similar way.

Place the two pocket sections together and fold back the skirt away from them. Tack and machine the pocket sections together, beginning and finishing 3 mm away from the machining on the seam turning.

Trim the turnings round the pocket bag to 10 mm, but leave the turning intact along the seam edge. Machine zigzag or hand overcast the curved edge of the bag as far round as possible (410).

Trim the pocket turnings level with the skirt seam turnings. Neaten the skirt seams, including the pocket turnings, with machine zigzagging or whatever suitable method is desired.

245

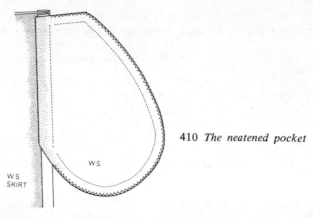

410 *The neatened pocket*

Fold the pocket onto the front of the skirt and press, ensuring that the pocket opening is pressed along the skirt seam fitting line on either side, with the pocket seams lying 3 mm inside.

A short length of ribbon seam binding can be sewn diagonally across from the seam to the outer top corner of the pocket, to hold it permanently in position (411). A tailor's bar tack (page 86) should be worked across each end of the pocket opening on the right side.

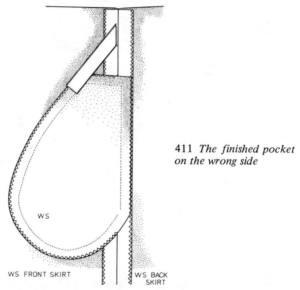

411 *The finished pocket on the wrong side*

Making a pocket set into the side and waist seams
(a) Preparing the side seam
Machine the side seam on the fitting line as far as the pocket opening. Proceed as for the side seam of the previous pocket.

(b) Cutting and preparing the pocket
Cut two pocket shapes, leaving a turning at the waist edge equal to that on

246

the skirt. The side-seam turning is already provided. Leave a 15 mm seam turning round the curved edge. Mark the fitting lines with tacking or tailor's chalk.

(c) Setting the pocket
The method resembles the setting of the previous pocket in relation to the side seam fitting lines and the lower edge. At the top, the fitting line of the pocket lies along the waist fitting line of the skirt.

When the pocket is finished and folded to the front of the skirt, tack the two top edges of the pocket to the waist fitting line of the front skirt, bringing the fitting lines of the skirt side seam edges together, with the pocket seams inset by 3 mm. Work a tailor's bar tack across the base of the pocket opening.

Lining fabric can be used for part of each side of the pocket if it is desirable to reduce bulk. Make the seam straight with the warp grain and placed in the position of the grain line in figure 407. The right sides of the seams should face each other on the inside of the pocket. Press the seam turnings onto the lining fabric.

18 Sleeves and cuffs

Sleeves must be accurately cut, fitted and set if they are to be attractive in appearance and comfortable in wear. Due attention must be paid to the position of the fabric grain throughout, and care must be taken to fit the sleeves so that the arm can move easily. If these precautions are followed by smooth, even setting, the results will be satisfactory and pleasing in all respects.

Sleeves can be divided into the three following basic types, from which all styles are developed:

(a) The inset (or set-in) sleeve. This fits into a circular armhole with the crown of the sleeve fitting to the armhole end of the shoulder seam, and the sleeve seam joining the side-seam of the bodice at the underarm (412). In dressmaking one-piece sleeves and puff sleeves fall into this category.

(b) The raglan sleeve. This joins the bodice with a slightly curved seam running diagonally into the neck line (413). The shoulder line is shaped by means of a dart. This shape of sleeve often provides an easy, comfortable setting for people who have difficult shoulders for fitting with an inset sleeve.

(c) The kimono sleeve. This is cut in one with the bodice (414). When it is short, it usually requires reinforcement at the undeearm, but when long, a gusset is required for comfort in movement.

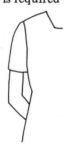  

412 *A short inset sleeve*   413 *A three-quarter raglan sleeve*   414 *A full length kimono sleeve*

Handling inset sleeves

See figure 412 for the finished appearance of an inset sleeve, and page 33 figure 36 for the pattern shape.

Both sleeves should be made and fitted into the armholes before the wrist line, or lower edge, is finished, so that this fitting line may be finally tested for position on the arm before the opening is made or the cuff is set.

Inspect the garment armholes and the sleeve crowns to make sure that the fitting lines are in order and that all the required balance points are clearly indicated. If any are missing, replace them from the pattern. It is important that these are accurate if the sleeve is to set and hang correctly.

Checking the sleeve crown and the bodice armhole fitting-lines
If any alteration was made to the upper part of the bodice pattern, the armhole fitting line should have been tested for size and compared with the sleeve crown fitting line, and any necessary adjustments made to the sleeve crown (refer to page 42). However, it is necessary to test the measurements again before setting the sleeve, especially if any alterations have been made to the shoulder and/or underarm lines in fitting the bodice.

Measure round the right armhole and the right sleeve crown and compare the measurements. The sleeve crown should measure 25 mm - 40 mm more than the armhole, so that it may be eased into the armhole and fit smoothly over the rounded shape of the top of the arm.

Preparing the bodice armhole
The side and shoulder seams must be finished. The neck finish should be complete,but if this is not possible tack it in preparation, as it is important to be able to check the finished shoulder length when fitting the sleeve.

Try on the bodice, closing any openings, and examine both armholes. It is wise to fit each armhole independently as there is often slight irregularities between the left and right shoulders. A right-handed person tends to be more developed on the right side and vice versa.

Study the shoulder lines from the neck along to the armhole end, and set a pin where you think the sleeve crown balance point should be set. This should be at the end of the shoulder and the top of the arm. Lift the arm, and look at the underarm fitting line. Decide whether it is right, too high or too low. Mark a new line if necessary. The underarm point should be far enough below the arm-pit to be comfortable in wear, ie approximately 25 mm - 35 mm according to the bust size.

Having settled the upper and lower points, study the front and back lines. They should be smooth from shoulder to underarm and provide adequate width across the chest and shoulder blades.

Remove the bodice and study any alterations, adjust slightly if necessary so that the fitting line follows a smooth line round the armhole. Examine the altered lines and refit the bodice if there is any doubt.

Tack mark any alterations to the armhole lines in a colour which will be clearly distinguishable when setting the sleeve.

Pairing sleeves and relating them to the bodice armhole
When working on fabric with no apparent right side, ascertain that the sleeves are correctly paired before pinning and tacking. Fold the sleeves in half lengthways, and place them on a table with the seam edges facing. If they are correctly paired, identical balance notches should appear on the two upper layers, and also on the two under layers (415). These balance notches pair with those on the bodice armhole. The crown setting point on a printed pattern is usually marked with a large, solid spot. This should have been transferred to the sleeve with a tailor tack (415), so that it can be fitted accurately to the shoulder line. This is usually a seam (416), but not necessarily, eg in a saddle yoke, which provides a back and front shoulder

yoke in one piece without a seam. Where there is no shoulder seam, the shoulder line should be marked with a tailor tack from a mark on the pattern.

The position of the crown setting point is very important in fitting. A warp line of fabric should fall from the crown setting point down the length of the sleeve. If, for reasons of style, the sleeve is cross cut, the crossway line should fall from the crown setting point.

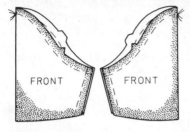

415 *Two sleeves correctly paired, showing the corresponding balance notches and the crown setting-point marked with a tailor tack*

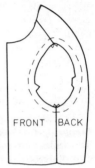

416 *The right armhole of a bodice showing the balance notches which pair with those of the right sleeve in figure 415*

Preparing sleeves for fitting

If the sleeve is to be shaped with darts or is puffed with gathered fullness, the darts and gathering should be worked before making the seam, as the sleeve is easier to handle when open flat. The positions of the darts should be tailor tacked from the pattern. Two rows of gathers should be used for a puffed sleeve. Work them between the points marked on the pattern, stitching one row on the fitting line and the second 6 mm outside the fitting line on the turning.

The elbow shaping of long, fitted sleeves must be prepared. Either tack the darts or run in a gathering thread according to style. Tack the sleeve seams and press lightly. Turn the sleeves right side out, and the bodice wrong side out.

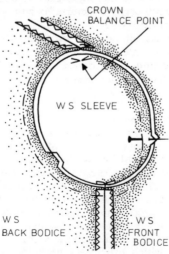

417 *A sleeve brought into position at the armhole. A pin has been correctly inserted at the front balance notches*

Setting sleeves for fitting
Place the right sleeve inside the bodice, bringing the crown to the corresponding right armhole. This will bring together the right sides of sleeve and bodice with the front and back balance notches pairing. The worker should hold the garment so that she is looking down into the inside of the sleeve, and handle the setting throughout with the sleeve uppermost (417).

Pin the sleeve crown to the bodice armhole at the front and back balance notches, and at the crown setting point. The pins setting the crown should be pierced through the sleeve and armhole fitting lines, and brought out at right angles through the turnings. Push the pin heads right up to the sleeve crown fitting line.

Across the underarm line, pin the sleeve and bodice together along their fitting lines between the back and front balance points. They should lie flat here without easing. The bodice and sleeve seams usually meet, and should be arranged to do so if possible. At this lower area of the crown, set the pins in line with the fitting line.

Between the back and front balance points and the crown balance point, it is necessary to ease the sleeve into the armhole so that it will fit comfortably, without straining, over the top of the arm. The amount of ease in the sleeve crown can now be judged, and the method chosen for handling it. There are two ways of doing this:

Method 1   Easing with a gathering thread
Fabric which is firmly woven and cannot be shrunk with damp pressing eg poplin, tricel, etc must be reduced by gathering.

Unpin the sleeve and, using the garment sewing thread, run a gathering thread on the fitting line between the front balance notch and the crown fitting point, and a second gathering thread in the corresponding position at the back. Make the running stitches as fine as possible. If there is much fullness to ease away, a second line of running should be worked on the turning 5 mm outside the fitting line. This gives a better control of the fullness of the turning, and makes it easier to handle when doing the final setting and neatening of the sleeve.

Ease the fabric along the two sets of gathering threads. It will only smooth away evenly if fine running has been used. When the correct sizing has been obtained, secure the gathering threads, but do not fasten off in case any alteration is found to be necessary.

The sleeve is now ready to pin into the armhole as previously directed, but this time continue the pinning all round the crown. Tack the sleeve into the armhole, stitching along the fitting line and using small tacking stitches.

Prepare the left sleeve in the same way.

Method 2   Easing by manipulation
This method is the better choice for fabric which can be reduced by manipulation and damp pressing.

The armhole and crown turnings must be held so that the raw edges come towards the worker with the sleeve edge uppermost. Ease the surplus fabric of the crown into the armhole, pinning about every 12 mm - 15 mm. This distributes the fullness evenly and holds it firmly in place. Tack the crown into the armhole. Keep the eased section moving over the first finger of the left hand as the tacking is done, and use small stitches to hold the fullness as flat as possible along the fitting line.

251

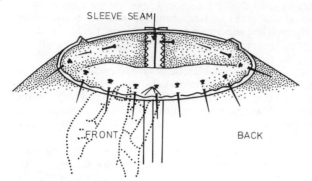

SLEEVE SEAM

FRONT

BACK

418 *A sleeve finally pinned in position. Dotted
lines show position of
thumb and fingers*

Fitting the sleeves
The setting of both sleeves should always be checked before the final
stitching is done.

(a) Fitting the crown
Fasten or pin any bodice opening and adjust the garment smoothly over the
body. Raise your arms to check that essential movement is possible.
Examine the sleeves and note the following points:
1   Length of shoulder seam.
2   Comfortable width at back and at chest line.
3   Sleeve hanging straight with warp down centre line, and weft straight
across width between underarm points, and across crown from back to front.
    If the crown setting is even, the lower part of the sleeve is bound to hang
correctly.
4   The position of the underarm.
One or more of the following alterations may be required:
1   The shoulder line may need either shortening or lengthening.
2   The sleeve crown may need either dropping or lifting.
3   The crown setting point may need moving either backwards or forwards
in order to align the fabric grain.
4   More ease may be required at the back, especially if the figure tends to
be round-shouldered: more ease may be required at the front if the figure is
erect with a prominent bust line.
5   The underarm section may need either raising or lowering to adjust the
hang of the sleeve.
    Check all these points carefully and make any alterations which seem to be
necessary. These must be retacked and refitted to establish a satisfactory
setting for the sleeve.

(b) Fitting the lower sleeve
When the sleeve crown fitting is satisfactory, the lower part of the sleeve must
be checked.
(i) The elbow shaping of a three-quarter or long fitted sleeve:
    If this is darted, there may be either one, two or three darts according to
the pattern arrangement. The fitting must centralise on the elbow point,
which should come in line with one dart, in the centre of the space between
two darts and in line with the middle of three darts.
    If easing has been used, the elbow point should come opposite the centre
of the eased area. Adjust the elbow shaping as required.

252

(ii) The line at the lower edge of the sleeve must be checked to ensure that it is in the right position above the elbow, above the wrist or at the wrist according to style. Mark a new line if necessary.

Making the sleeves
Make sure that any alteration lines have been clearly marked on the sleeves and armholes, and then unpick the sleeves from the bodice. On three-quarter or long, fitted sleeves, unpick the seam tacking. If the crown easing has been done with gathering threads, these should be fastened off securely to the size required.

Make both sleeves at the same time so that they are kept identical.

When making a three-quarter or long, fitted sleeve, the elbow shaping must be stitched and pressed first. Refer to page 77 for making darts and to page 101 for easing.

The sleeve seam should match the underarm seam of the bodice both in type and width. Press the seam on a sleeve board if possible. Failing that, slip a folded pressing cloth inside the sleeve to protect the under layer. Take care not to press creases into the sleeve.

The lower edge of the sleeve should be finished after both the seam and any necessary opening have been made, and before the sleeve is finally set, as it is easier to handle without the bodice attached. Details of sleeve openings and finishes are given later in this sections,

The final setting of the sleeve
(a) Preparing a sleeve crown with gathered ease
Check that the easing is evenly distributed in both sections of each sleeve. Press the eased fabric over a pressing pad to smooth and flatten the turnings. Use a damp pressing cloth if necessary. Do not press beyond the fitting line as this would spoil the carefully acquired shaping of the sleeve crown.

(b) Preparing a sleeve crown with manipulated ease
Check that the fitting line and crown balance point are clearly marked. The pressing and shrinkage are done after the sleeve is set into the armhole in this case.

(c) Stitching the armhole seam
Pin and tack each sleeve into the appropriate armhole. Pair the armhole and sleeve balance notches and work as directed on page 249.

If the ease has been manipulated, place the sleeve crown over a pressing pad, or the end of a sleeve board, and gently press away the surplus fullness. Use a damp cloth if necessary. Also shrink the turnings of the sleeve crown, but do not press beyond the fitting line.

The armhole seam is made by machining together the sleeve and armhole fitting lines with the sleeve uppermost. Begin and finish the machining at the underarm, overlapping the stitching by 25 mm before cutting off the thread ends.

Keep the eased section flat while stitching. This can be done by smoothing the fabric to left and right with the two forefingers just in front of the machine foot. Take trouble to machine a perfectly smooth line or the right side appearance will be spoilt.

While machining, check that the armhole fitting line is kept flat on the underside, and so prevent a fold of the bodice from getting caught into the machine stitching.

(d) Neatening the armhole on the wrong side

The raw edges of the turnings must be strongly finished as they are subjected to friction both in wear and washing. Here are three ways of dealing with the armhhole neatening:

Method 1 Bind the armhole with garment fabric or a suitable thinner fabric. This is the strongest method. There are two ways of applying the binding:

(a) After machining the sleeve in place, trim the turnings to 10 mm - 12 mm and bind over the raw edges (page 119).

(b) On thin fabric the binding may be attached with the setting of the sleeve. Trim down the armhole turnings and make the finished bound turning 5 mm - 6 mm in width.

Whichever method of setting is chosen, stitch the binding onto the bodice side and hem in onto the sleeve side, where the stitches will not have the friction of wear. Make the final join of the binding come over the underarm seam (198).

Method 2 This provides a flat, neat finish on nylon and fabrics of a similar light weight.

Trim the turnings, fold in the two raw edges and overcast the folded edges together (419), making the finished width 5 mm - 10 mm, according to the strength and transparency of the fabric.

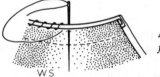

419 *Overcasting the folded edges*

Method 3 Join the turnings together with a second line of machining, stitching 5 mm - 10 mm outside the fitting line according to the weight of the fabric. Trim the surplus turning close to the second line of machining, and zigzag over the raw edges (420).

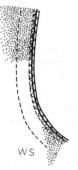

420 *The double mac-hine-stitched finish with zigzagging*

Setting sleeves into a lined yoke

(a) Preparing the garment and setting the sleeve

The yoke and lining shoulder seams must be machined, trimmed and pressed open flat.

The centre back and neck edges of the yoke and lining must be joined and trimmed and then pressed in place right side outside (383c). If there is no collar this method is still used, as the yoke and lining are joined up the back and round the neck line, but without a collar sandwiched between.

The required opening should already be made in the skirt section of the garment if one is necessary. The lower edges of the front and back yoke parts should be set onto the lower part of the garment, following the instructions for making a lapped seam (page 111).

There is now a complete armhole into which the sleeve may be set and stitched according to the previous instructions.

(b) Neatening the armhole on the wrong side
The method of wrong side neatening differs from the previous methods given, as the lining may be used to neaten the edges round the upper part of the armhole.

Snip across the armhole turnings at each side about 5 mm above the yoke line (421). This divides the armhole turnings into two sections: an upper section where the sleeve is set into the yoke of the garment, and a lower section where the sleeve is set into the lower part of the garment. The edges of the lower section of the armhole should be neatened by either method 2 or 3 shown in figures 419 and 420. Loop stitch the short edges of the two snips.

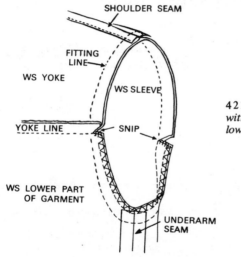

421 *The inset sleeve with snip and neatened lower sections,*

To neaten the upper section, the yoke lining is used in the following way: Tack the yoke and lining together through the centre of their depth, ie parallel with the setting lines and the armhole edges. This holds the lining and prevents it from slipping out of place (422).

Turn under a single turning along the lower edges of the back and front, and then along the armhole edges of the yoke lining, first trimming the turnings to 5 mm - 6 mm. Bring the fitting lines along the folded edges and take care to make the corners neat and square. Pin the folded edges of the lining over the setting lines of the yoke, along the back and front. Fold the upper armhole turnings back onto the yoke and cover them with the yoke lining. The yoke lining can now be tacked and hemmed in place on the wrong side, thus providing a smooth, neat finish along the yoke and upper armhole lines (423).

255

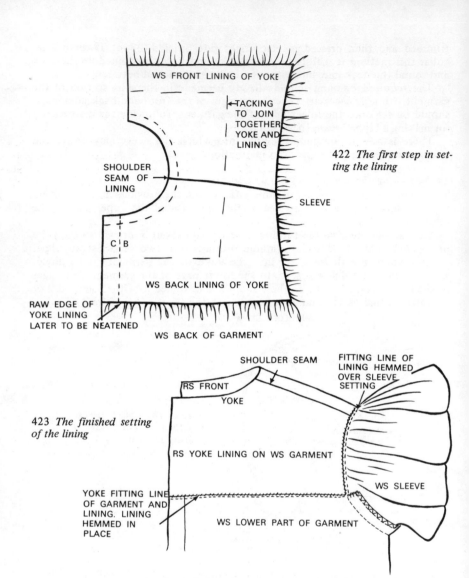

WS FRONT LINING OF YOKE

←TACKING TO JOIN TOGETHER YOKE AND LINING

SHOULDER SEAM OF LINING →

SLEEVE

422 The first step in setting the lining

C | B

WS BACK LINING OF YOKE

RAW EDGE OF YOKE LINING LATER TO BE NEATENED

WS BACK OF GARMENT

SHOULDER SEAM

FITTING LINE OF LINING HEMMED OVER SLEEVE SETTING

RS FRONT

YOKE

423 The finished setting of the lining

RS YOKE LINING ON WS GARMENT

WS SLEEVE

YOKE FITTING LINE OF GARMENT AND LINING. LINING HEMMED IN PLACE

WS LOWER PART OF GARMENT

Handling raglan sleeves
See figure 413 for the finished appearance of a raglan sleeve, and figure 424 for the pattern shape.

Cutting out the sleeves
As the shoulder line is shaped by means of a dart, an alteration to the dart line may be required in fitting. Therefore it is unwise to cut out the dart shaping until the initial fitting has been done (425).

256

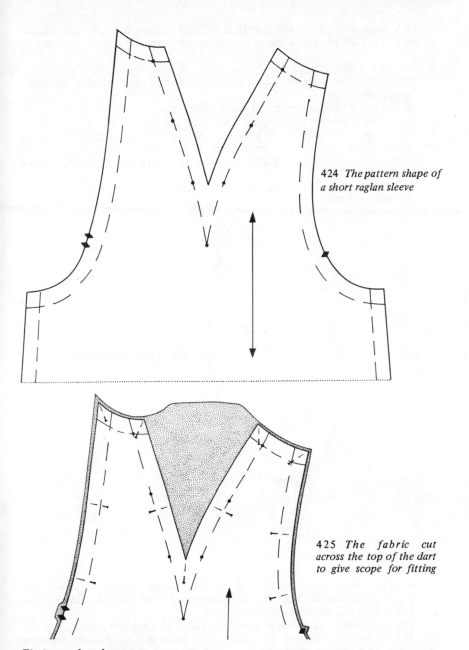

424 *The pattern shape of a short raglan sleeve*

425 *The fabric cut across the top of the dart to give scope for fitting*

Fitting raglan sleeves
(a) Preparation

As the bodice is without shoulder seams, it cannot be fitted without the sleeve in place. Therefore the bodice must be tacked together and any seams running into the armhole should be very lightly pressed open for 50 mm - 70 mm at their top edge.

257

Tack the sleeve dart and deal with the elbow shaping in a long sleeve (refer to page 77). Tack the sleeve seams and press them open lightly at the top.

(b) Setting the sleeve for fitting
Set the pins in line with the sleeve fitting line and pin in the following order:
1   at the underarm,
2   at the front balance notch and front neck point,
3   at the back balance notches and back neck point.
4   Pin in between, setting the pins at right angles to the fitting line where the sleeve needs easing into the bodice. Ease the sleeve according to the directions given for an inset sleeve, choosing the method better suited to the fabric.

Tack the sleeve to the bodice to join the fitting lines together, using short tacking stitches (426).

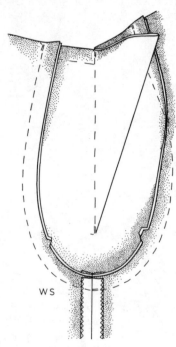

426 *A raglan sleeve tack-ed ready for fitting*

WS

(c) Testing the fit of the sleeve
Fasten and adjust the bodice. Move your arms freely to check for comfortable movement. Examine the sleeves and note the following points:
1   The length and set of the shoulder line,
2   The looseness or tightness at the front and back shoulder lines,
3   The straight hanging of the sleeves, ie with the warp grain dropping vertically from the point of the dart, and the weft grain passing round the arm between the underarm points, and at right angles to the point of the dart.

One or more of the following alterations may be required:
1   If the shoulder bone is pushing into the dart line, let out the dart: If the sleeve stands away from the shoulder, increase the width of the dart.

2   The dart may need shortening or lengthening to provide a smooth shaping over the shoulder and the top of the arm.
3   The front and back seams may require adjustment and also the underarm line. Refer to page 252, points 4 and 5 at the end of the section of fitting the crown of an inset sleeve.

Refer, also, to the directions for fitting the lower sleeve given on page 252.

Making raglan sleeves
Refer to the directions for making an inset sleeve on page 253, but make the dart in the raglan sleeve before making the seam.

To make the dart, stitch on the required line, press the line of stitching and fasten off the thread ends. Trim away the dart 10 mm - 15 mm outside the stitching according to the thickness of the fabric. Press the dart open, flattening the fold over the stitching line at the point (427). Overcast the raw edges to support fraying fabric.

427 *The finished dart in a raglan sleeve. In this case the raw edges have been overcast to protect fraying fabric*

Setting raglan sleeves
Pin and tack the seams as already directed for fitting.

(a) Reinforcing the seam
(i) On loosely woven fabric the seams at the back and front are liable to stretch. In this case tack a length of ribbon seam binding to the bodice side of the seam on both back and front, from the neck point to 15 mm beyond the balance notches, centralising the ribbon over the fitting line.
(ii) On fabric with a tendency to fray, even if firmly woven, it is wise to tack a 40 mm strip of ribbon seam binding across the balance notch area, where the seam has to be snipped later (428).

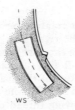

428 *Ribbon seam binding tacked across the front notch area*

WS

259

(b) Machining the seam

Machine the seam into the bodice along the fitting line with the sleeve uppermost. Begin machining the right sleeve from the back neck edge, and the left sleeve from the front neck edge.

Stitch a second row of machining 6 mm - 10 mm outside the fitting line, across the underarm between the balance notches, to join the turnings together.

Snip the seam turnings at right angles to the fitting line at the back and front balance notches, but do not snip the reinforcing tape if it has been used. Trim away the surplus turning outside the second row of machining, and zigzag (or overcast) the underarm area of the seam.

Trim the remaining turnings to 10 mm - 15 mm according to fabric, snipping them at intervals if necessary. Press the turnings open flat (429). Overcast the raw edges if neatening is required.

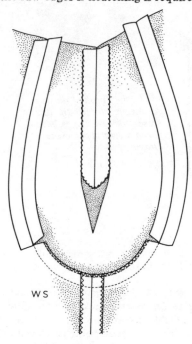

429 *The neatened under-arm turnings with snip-ped, trimmed and pressed upper arm turnings in a raglan sleeve setting*

W S

Raglan sleeves on sheer and semi-sheer fabrics
(a) The dart
This is best made as a narrow french seam dart, refer to page 80, figures 119a and b.

(b) the seam
Ribbon seam binding cannot be used for reinforcing the seam as it is too heavy and would be conspicuous from the right side. It is better to set the sleeve with a narrow french seam to match the dart in width. The double line of stitching, and the enclosed turnings, will give sufficient support. The only problem is the extra length in the sleeve edge of the seam to allow for ease in setting. This can be handled by sewing two lines of fine running stitches along the easing position. Use matching, fine sewing thread and stitch one line on

the fitting line and one just outside on the turning allowance. Ease up the fabric to size and press the area. These running stitches will be covered by machining when making the seam.

Handling kimono sleeves

See figure 414 for a long-sleeved style and figure 430 for the pattern shape of a short kimono sleeve.

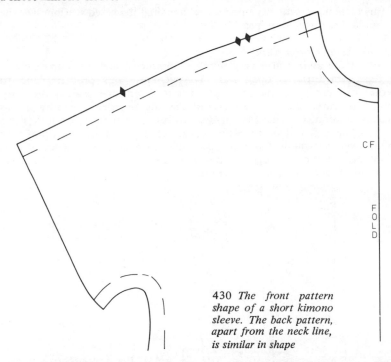

430 *The front pattern shape of a short kimono sleeve. The back pattern, apart from the neck line, is similar in shape*

A Kimono sleeve, cut in one with the bodice, requires no setting, but is given its final shape by two seams. One of these runs from the neck line, along the shoulder, and continues to the lower edge of the sleeve: The other seam is a continuation of the side seam of the bodice, curving to fit the underarm line, and also finishing at the lower edge of the sleeve.

Cut the top, or shoulder, seam with a turning allowance of 25 mm or more for high or square shouldered figures. This will give scope for letting out the seam to accommodate a large shoulder bone.

(a) Tacking for fitting

Tack the shoulder seam on the wrong side. The underarm seam will probably be more easily handled by tacking it right side out to prevent the turnings from dragging.

(b) Fitting the seams

Fit the shoulder seam first and adjust if necessary. A figure with sloping shoulders may need this seam taken in along the shoulder area to a smooth

261

fitting. Let out one or both sides of the seam, as necessary, to fit over a large shoulder.

Examine the position of the fitting line round the underarm and check that the curve fits comfortably. It is better to have a slightly loose fit here, as too high an underarm causes discomfort in wear, and creates diagonal drag lines towards the neck.

(c) Making the top or shoulder seam
Make this seam as an ordinary open seam, handling the eased section over the front shoulder as directed on page 101.

(d) Making the underarm seam
The curve at the underarm is very much pronounced, and it is impossible to press the seam turnings open flat. To overcome this problem, and to strengthen the seam, trim the seam turnings to 5 mm or less along the sharp section of the curve. Neaten the edges of the side and sleeve seams as far as this narrow section, tapering the turnings to run into the 5 mm width. Press the turnings open flat along the whole length of the seam. Lay a strip of tape or ribbon over the trimmed area to cover the raw edges, and machine this to the garment, stitching through to the right side (431). Bias binding may be used instead of tape, but is not as strong.

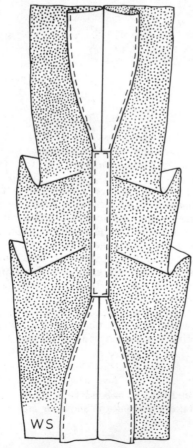

431 *The neatened, reinforced seam at the underarm curve of a kimono sleeve*

An alternative method may be used on Crimplene and similar fabrics which do not fray. The seam turnings can be snipped at intervals, nearly to the fitting line. When pressed apart, the seam turnings will open out, where snipped, and lie flat. Tack the snipped turnings to the bodice (432a). Turn the bodice right side out and machine a very narrow rectangle over the seam to hold the snipped area flat, and to give support to the seam (432b).

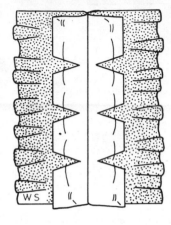

432a *The snipped turn-ings of a kimono under-arm seam, tacked on the wrong side ready for machining*

432b *The rectangle of machine stitching worked on the right side*

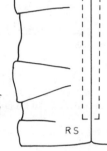

Strengthening a kimono sleeve with a gusset
Greater strength is given to a kimono sleeve underarm by inserting a gusset. This provides extra fabric where the strain comes, and prevents the garment from tearing. If the underarm is squared, the gusset may be set into the seam, but if it is curved the garment must be slashed and the gusset inserted into the slash.

1 Cutting and setting square gussets
The gusset square is cut with a straight grain along each edge. This provides firm edges for setting, and crossway lines on the diagonals to allow for ease of movement in wear. The size of the gusset square varies according to the bust measurement. For bust sizes up to and including 85 cm, cut a square of 115 mm, which makes a finished gusset of 90 mm with turnings of approximately 12 mm. For bust sizes over 80 cm, cut the gusset 140 mm square, making a finished gusset of 115 mm with approximately 12 mm turnings all round.

If the finished fabric frays badly, wider turnings will be necessary than those suggested above.

(a) Preparing a square underarm seam for a gusset
Machine the seam to within 75 mm either side of the corner. Tack the fitting lines round the corner of first the back and then the front bodice. Machine a 'V' at each corner for reinforcement, and slash between the 'V's (433). The corners will now open out and the gusset can be inserted.

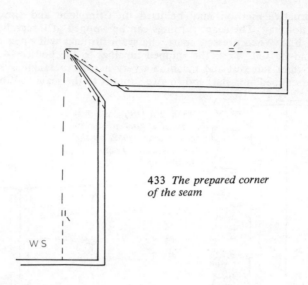

433 *The prepared corner
of the seam*

Inserting the gusset
Machine the gusset and seam fitting lines together on the wrong side, keeping the corners square and strong. Overcast the seam and the gusset edges together. Loop stitch the slashed seam corners on to the gusset turnings.

(b) Preparing a curved underarm seam for a gusset
At right-angles to the curve, and from its centre point, thread mark a line of 65 mm inside the fitting line. Machine a 'V² either side of this line on both back and front bodice. Measuring from the seam fitting line, make the 'V' 5 mm either side of the marked line (434a).

Tack, machine and neaten the underarm seam, stitching the 'V's over each other. Cut through the seam and up the centre of the 'V' on each side (434b).

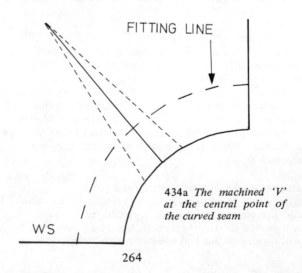

FITTING LINE

434a *The machined 'V'
at the central point of
the curved seam*

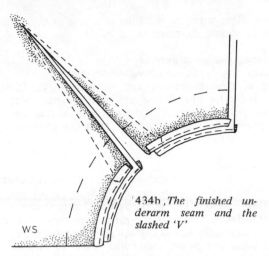

434b, *The finished underarm seam and the slashed 'V'*

WS

After the cuts are made, the seam opens into a square shape at the underarm. Cut the gusset to size as previously directed.

Inserting the gusset
(i) *Preparation*   Prepare the gusset by folding and pressing the turnings to the wrong side along two opposite edges. Fold back each corner diagonally, and press it to rest along the uncreased fitting lines (435a). Fold back the remaining two turnings, thus forming a mitre. Press and then tack round the four prepared sides of the gusset (435b).

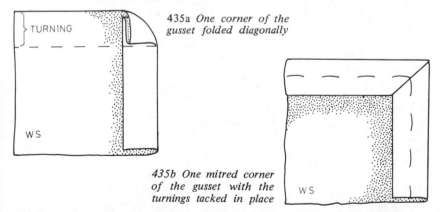

TURNING

WS

435a *One corner of the gusset folded diagonally*

435b *One mitred corner of the gusset with the turnings tacked in place*

WS

(ii) *Setting*   Pin the gusset in place, setting two opposite corners at the underarm seams, and the other two corners over the points of the machined 'V's. Keeping the sides smoothly set, tack the gussets onto the underarm area. Machine it in place, stitching close to the folded edges.

Trim the turnings on the wrong side to 10 mm, and overcast together the raw edges of gusset and underarm.

Alternatively, for a stronger finish, a square of lining fabric may be cut and prepared as for the gusset, making the finished square about 3 mm smaller than the gusset. Hem it to the machine stitching to cover the wrong side of the gusset and to enclose the turnings.

Cutting and setting two-piece gussets
These gussets are usable only on curved underarm lines.

Four triangles of fabric are cut, and one is set at the front and one at the back of each underarm line. These gussets are easier to apply than square gussets, but are not as strong. The underarm seam runs across the centre of the finished gusset, and this is weaker than the stretchable crossway line provided by a square gusset.

(a) Preparing the bodice
Thread mark the gusset guide line at right-angles to the centre point of the seam curve, making it 65 mm long inside the seam fitting line.

Cutting with the straight grains, prepare a 45 mm square of garment fabric, or a suitable thin fabric matching the garment in colour, for a reinforcement.

Crease a line diagonally across the square with right sides together. Set and tack this line along the gusset guide line, with 25 mm extending beyond. Either side of the guide line, mark a fitting line on the bodice, making it 5 mm wide at the seam edge, but curving it round close to the guide line at the top as it passes over the square. Machine the square to the bodice on the fitting line. Cut straight along the full length of the gusset guide line (436a).

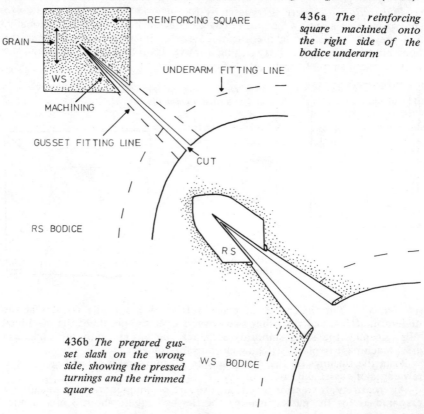

436a *The reinforcing square machined onto the right side of the bodice underarm*

436b *The prepared gusset slash on the wrong side, showing the pressed turnings and the trimmed square*

266

Fold the reinforcing square. through to the wrong side, pulling the machined line slightly inside the edge. Crease the remaining turning of the cut in place, and press the prepared gusset slash. Trim the reinforcing square to leave 15 mm turning round the top of the slash (436b).

(b) The gusset
(i) *The pattern*   Rule a line 75 mm long.
From the centre of this line, rule a line at right angles 65 mm long and mark this for the straight grain.
Rule a triangle joining the three outer points of these two lines.
(ii) *Preparing the gusset*   Cut out four gusset sections with 15 mm turnings on two sides and the usual garment turning allowance on the third side (437). Cut each section on an identical grain line.

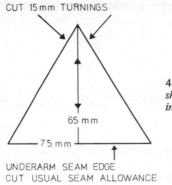

CUT 15mm TURNINGS

65 mm

75 mm

UNDERARM SEAM EDGE
CUT USUAL SEAM ALLOWANCE

437 *The gusset triangle, showing grain line and indicated turning widths*

(iii) *Inserting the gusset*   Place the gusset triangle, right side uppermost, on the table. Lap the prepared slit over the gusset triangle and pin it in place along the fitting line of the triangle. The underarm seam lines of the bodice should run into the fitting line along the base of the triangle. Tack the prepared edge of the slit in place and machine close to the edge on the right side (438).

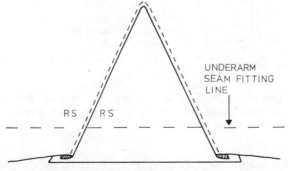

UNDERARM
SEAM FITTING
LINE

RS   RS

438 *The prepared slit machined in place over the gusset on the right side*

Trim the gusset turnings on the wrong side to 10 mm and neaten by overcasting them together.
    Repeat this process in the other three sections of the bodice.
    Pin and tack the underarm seams together, following the underarm curve across the gusset. Machine, neaten and strengthen the seam as previously described.

The finish of sleeve edges without cuffs

(a) Short sleeves

If there are no cuffs, the edges will be finished with either a hem or a facing. Before working the edge finish, the garment should be fitted to test the line of the lower edge of each sleeve. Adjust the line if it is not quite straight, as the edge is sometimes inclined to lift at the centre front.

The seam line of most short sleeves slopes inwards towards the lower edge. In order for the hem to lie flat when set, the turning should be cut to shape, so that when folded back in position on the wrong side, the turning will lie flat (439).

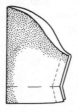

439 *A short sleeve with correctly shaped hem turning*

(i) A hem finish

Tack the hem and slip-hem it in position. As a general rule, sleeve hems should not be machined.

(ii) A faced finish

With a crossway strip   A crossway strip gives the best result on a very short sleeve, as it sets flat over the slightly shaped seam line. Pin the right side of the strip to the right side of the sleeve, arranging the join to come over the sleeve seam. Tack and machine it in place along the fitting line of the lower edge and trim the turning (440).

Fold the facing to the wrong side. Tack and slip-hem it in place, making the finished facing 10 mm - 15 mm wide according to the thickness of the fabric.

440 *The first stage in attaching a crossway facing to a sleeve edge*

With a shaped facing   This is the method most often used on short sleeves. Refer to page 132 in the shaped facing section, where the principles given can be applied to shaped facings for short sleeves.

(b) Long sleeves

A long sleeve which is not finished with a cuff is always fitted to the size and shape of the wrist. It therefore requires an opening and a neat, flat finish at the lower edge.

Leave the seam open for 60 mm - 75 mm above the wrist fitting line, so that the sleeve will pass easily over the hand. The opening is made in a similar way to a wrap and facing opening. The overlap is made by stitching the continuation of the seam turning to form a hem on the back of the sleeve.

The underwrap is formed by snipping across the base of the seam to free the width of the turning, and sewing a crossway facing to this edge so that the hem will close down on it (441a). Any raw edges incurred at the top of the opening must be neatened by loop stitching (441b).

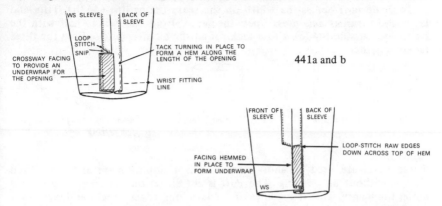

441a and b

The lower edge of the sleeve should be neatened to suit the thickness of the fabric. Make a hem or a narrow facing of the garment fabric or of matching, finer fabric if that would be less bulky. The width of hem or facing should equal the width of the opening finishes. Mitre the corner for added neatness and hem the opening edges along with the lower edge finish. Fasten the opening with small press-studs or with small hooks and worked loops. Strengthen it at the top on the right side with a tailor's bar tack (442).

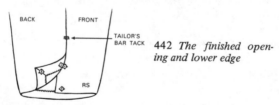

442 *The finished open-ing and lower edge*

Cuffs

The principles of cutting and making cuffs so closely resembles those of collar making, that it is unnecessary to give separate instructions. Most cuffs are interfaced, and the general information about interfacing on page 140, and the directions for making interfaced collars on page 205, can be studied and applied to the interfacing of cuffs.

In the following illustrations, which relate to the handling of cuffs, interfacing has been omitted to prevent overloading with detail. However, a reminder is given at the right stage of construction so that the inclusion of interfacing will not be overlooked.

1   Circular turn-back cuffs
(a) Straight
These cuffs are used on sleeves which have a straight seam and no gathered fullness at the lower edge. Cut the cuff as a rectangle either on the crossway or with the warp grain running longways. The length of the rectangle equals

269

the lower edge measurement of the sleeve: the width equals 2 X the finished width of the cuff. Allow 12 mm - 15 mm turnings on all four edges (443a).

Cut the interfacing to balance the cuff grain and attach it, longways, to half the cuff, following the principles given on pages 206 and 207.

Join the cuff across the width on the seam fitting line (443b). Trim and layer the turnings and press open the seam. Fold the cuff in half with the right side outside (443c). Cross tack round the circular cuff to hold the three layers together.

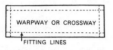

443a *The cuff shape*   443b *The cuff seamed*   443c *The cuff prepared for setting*

(b) Shaped

These cuffs are used on short sleeves with a sloping seam and semi-fitted sleeves without an opening. The cuff is cut either on the cross or warpway along the length. The fitting lines of the two long edges equal the sleeve lower edge measurement: the length through the centre, longways, equals the measurement round the sleeve at the cuff depth above the lower edge. This gives shaped side edges to the cuff which will follow the slope of the sleeve seam when the cuff is made. The width of the pattern equals 2 x the finished width of the cuff. Allow 12 mm - 15 mm turnings on all six edges (444a).

Cut and attach the interfacing as directed for the previous cuff. Join the cuff on the seam line (444b), and finish making it as for the previous cuff (444c).

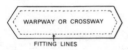

444a *The cuff shape*   444b *The cuff seamed*   444c *The cuff prepared for setting*

2   Open Turn-back cuffs (445c)

These are used for the same sleeve styles as the previous cuffs. In shape the pattern resembles a collar pattern. Cut two cuff shapes as directed on the pattern. Attach the interfacing to the chosen side of the cuff. Place the outer and under cuffs together, wrong side outside, and make up the cuff as for the collar on page 206.

Setting circular and open turn-back cuffs

Pin the underside of the cuff to the right side of the sleeve, matching the fitting lines and arranging the joined edges of an open cuff to balance evenly at the centre front of the sleeve.

When setting a circular cuff, place the cuff seam over the sleeve seam and then proceed in the same way.

Tack the cuff to the sleeve. Prepare a crossway strip 30 mm wide, of garment or lining fabric. Tack it round the fitting line on top of the cuff, planning the crossway join to come over the sleeve seam. Machine round the fitting line, stitching together the sleeve, cuff and crossway strip. Trim and layer the turnings (445a).

Pull the cuff downwards away from the sleeve. Trim the turnings and fold back the crossway strip to form a facing 10 mm - 12 mm wide, according to the thickness of the fabric. This encloses the raw edges. Tack and hem the facing onto the sleeve (445b).

Fold the cuff back to the right side of the sleeve (445c), and press the edge by slipping the toe of the iron just inside the sleeve, thus pressing the wrong side of the setting.

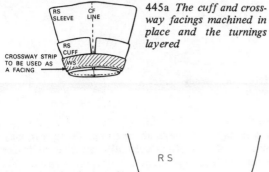

445a *The cuff and cross-way facings machined in place and the turnings layered*

445b *The finished set-ting on the wrong side*

445c *The finished cuff on the right side*

3 Straight band cuffs

These are used on short, three-quarter or long gathered sleeves without an opening. The band is cut as a rectangle with the warp grain along the length. The length of the rectangle equals the slightly easy measurement round the arm at the required level: the width equals 2 x the finished width of the band. Allow 12 mm - 15 mm turnings on all four edges. Cut and apply the interfacing and make the band seam as directed for straight turn-back cuffs on page 269. On the interfaced half, trim the turning allowance to 5 mm - 7 mm. Fold and tack the trimmed turning to the wrong side.

Setting the band

Pin, tack and machine the interfaced half of the band to the gathered sleeve, with right sides together and seam lines meeting. Trim and layer the turnings (446a).

Pull the sleeve through the band to bring it wrong side out. Ease it onto a sleeve board so that the turnings can be pressed downwards onto the band, taking care not to flatten the gathered sleeve.

Fold back the band to the wrong side. Keep seams in line and pin and tack the prepared folded edge along the machine stitching (446b). Hem the band on the wrong side. This hemming must be fine and strong as it is subjected to friction in wear. If the band is wide, a line of tacking should be sewn close to the fold, at the lower edge, before the band is pinned and tacked in place on the wrong side. This keeps the band flat and untwisted for the final setting.

Remove all tacking and press the band lightly on the wrong side. Turn the sleeve right side out (446c).

271

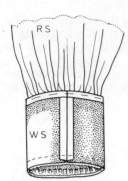

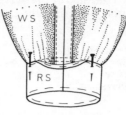

446a *The first stage in setting the band*

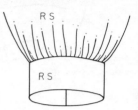

446c *The finished band on the right side.*

446b *The wrong side setting*

4   Buttoned cuffs

These cuffs are used on long sleeves which have an opening. The sleeve may be straight with slight fullness, or wide with much fullness. The cuffs are made to fit the wrists and are set over either gathers or pleats.

(a) Preparing the wrist edges of the sleeve

Try on the garment to test the length of the sleeve, and adjust the wrist fitting line if necessary. Make the opening either in the seam as previously described for a fitted sleeve, or in line with the little finger, using either a continuous straight strip opening (refer page 157) or a wrong side faced opening (refer page 154). The latter opening provides a neat, flat opening and is usually the better choice.

Gather the edge, arranging most of the fullness to provide room for the elbow (447). Alternatively the surplus fabric may be folded into three or four pleats placed to provide room for the elbow (448).

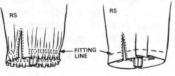

447 and 448 *A gathered and a pleated wrist edge*

(b) Making and setting the cuff
Method A

(i) Making the cuff   Set the interfacing to half the cuff. Machine across the width of the straight edges from the fitting line. Stitch the pointed end along the fitting line from the fitting point, turning the two angles to form the pointed shape of the overlap as far as the fold. Snip the upper turning as shown (449a). Trim and layer the turnings and turn the cuff right side out (449b).

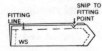

449a *The cuff machined and snipped on the wrong side*

449b *The cuff prepared for setting*

272

(ii) Setting the cuff   Place the right side of the cuff to the right side of the sleeve. Pin and tack along the fitting line, joining the outer cuff to the sleeve. Machine along this line (450a).

Pull the cuff away from the gathers and fold in the turning along the underside of the cuff. Tack and hem it just above the machine stitching on the wrong side of the sleeve. Fasten the cuff with a button and buttonhole (450b).

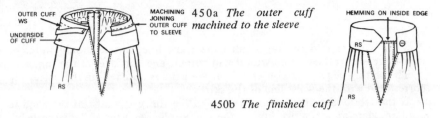

450a *The outer cuff machined to the sleeve*

450b *The finished cuff*

Method B

This method is stronger for fabrics which fray badly as it is not necessary to snip the cuff turning. Set the interfacing to half the cuff. Machine right across the straight width of the cuff from the fold to the raw edge. Machine the pointed end from fold to fitting line (451a). Trim and layer the turnings. On the open edges of the cuff trim the turning allowance to 6 mm. Fold and tack the trimmed turning to the wrong side. Turn the cuff to the right side and tack close to the folded edge to keep the cuff flat.

Set the outer side of the cuff over the gathers, as for an overlaid seam, and machine it on the right side. Tack and hem the underside of the cuff in place on the wrong side as for the previous method. Work a buttonhole and sew on a button (451b).

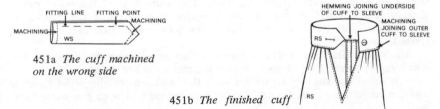

451a *The cuff machined on the wrong side*

451b *The finished cuff*

19 Waist-bands

A waist band should fit snugly into the waist line, but it should never be over-tight and strained, otherwise it will wrinkle and curl over at the top.

The setting edge of the outer half of the band is notched on the pattern to correspond with the waist line of the skirt.

If the fabric is striped or checked, plan the finished width of the band to accommodate an attractive line of the design on the outer half of the band. Otherwise the finished width depends on the style, and figure of the wearer. A narrow waist band, eg 25 mm finished width, is the best choice for a figure with a high hip-line and/or a high waist line, so that this area of the body is not accentuated.

The length of any waist band should equal an easy waist measurement plus at least 30 mm - 40 mm for underwrap plus two turnings of 15 mm each. Cut the waist band with the warp grain running along the length. If a join is necessary, arrange for it to come in line with the right side seam of the skirt if there is a side opening. If the skirt has a back opening, the waist band seam can be lined up with either side seam.

A waist band overlaps to fasten above the zip. At a left-hand side opening, the waist band is set in line with the front edge of the opening, and the underwrap projects from the back. The fastening of the waist band, therefore, laps front over back. At a centre back opening the overlap is planned to fasten left over right. Fasten the waist band with hooks and bars (refer to page 195).

All waist bands need the support of an interfacing to help prevent wrinkling and stretching. A firm, woven interfacing is best to use.

It is usual for the zip to be set into the skirt before the waist band is attached in order to secure the top of the zip tape in with the waist band setting.

The waist edge of the skirt should measure 15 mm - 25 mm more than the finished size of the waist band, so that it can be eased into the waist band. This allows the skirt to set over the hip-bone area, where the body begins to curve outward immediately below the waist line. If this allowance for ease is not provided, the skirt will lift at the top hip line, and ruck across below the waist band.

Check the size of the waist band pattern and alter it if necessary. Compare the checked pattern length with the waist fitting line measurement of the skirt. If necessary, adjust the skirt to comply with the guidance given in the last paragraph.

Before machining the waist band in place, fit the skirt to check the finished size. If a slight adjustment is required, this can be made by lengthening or shortening the underwrap, but an underwrap of at least 25 mm must be left. A large alteration should not be necessary if the waist band has been carefully tested for size before cutting out.

Preparing and setting the interfacing

The interfacing strip is set to the wrong side of the outer half of the waist band. It can be cut and attached in two ways:

Method 1

Cut a length of interfacing equal to the waist band length plus two turnings, and with width equal to the finished width of the waist band plus one turning.

Pin the interfacing to the waist band, tack along the waist and the two side fitting lines, and catch stitch the top edge so that the stitching comes just beyond the centre line of the waist band (452). The interfacing, in this case, is machined in with the making and setting of the waist band, and the turnings are trimmed away close to the machine stitching.

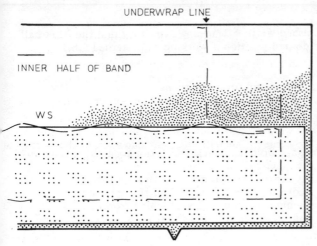

452 *A section of the waist band with the interfacing attached to the wrong side of the outer half of the band*

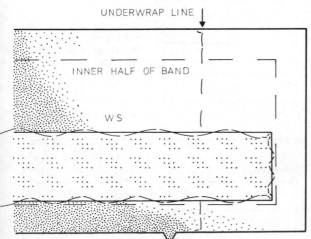

453 *A section of the waist band showing the placing and catch-stitching of the interfacing, see method 2 on page 276*

275

Method 2
This method is suitable for thicker fabric where it is necessary to reduce bulk in the seams.

Cut the length equal to the finished length of the waist band minus 4 mm, and the width equal to the finished width of the waist band. No turnings are required.

Pin and tack the interfacing to the waist band, fitting it just inside the fitting lines, but right up to·the centre line. Catch stitch it on all four sides, stitching into the fitting lines, but just beyond the centre line (453).
A waist band can be made entirely of the skirt fabric, or it can have a backing of lining fabric.

The following methods of making and setting give an adequate range for most skirt making.

Plain setting
Cut the band 2 X the finished width + 2 turnings, checking that the front half of the band is set to the desired position if working on patterned fabric.

Preparing the waist-band
If a join is necessary, make, join and press the seam.

Mark the fitting lines, the underwrap position and any other fitting points provided on the pattern. Apply the interfacing.

Method 1
(a) Making the waist band   Fold and tack the turning on the wrong side along the waist edge of the inner half of the band.

Fold the band along the centre line, wrong side outside bringing the tacked edge just along, but not covering, the fitting line on the opposite edge. Tack the end seams (454a). Machine the end seams, stitching from the fold to the waist fitting line. Trim and layer the turnings (454b). Turn back the band to the right side and press.

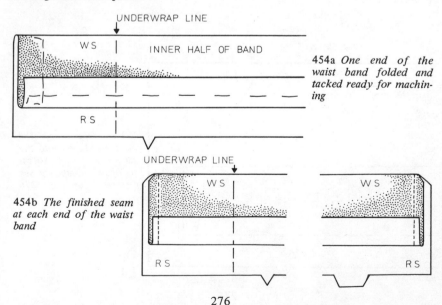

454a *One end of the waist band folded and tacked ready for machining*

454b *The finished seam at each end of the waist band*

(b) Setting the waist band   Pin the interfaced side of the waist band to the skirt, right sides together. Match notches, and set the ends of the waist band accurately in position at the opening. Ease the skirt into the waist band between the setting points, and tack and machine skirt and waist band together along the waist fitting line (455).

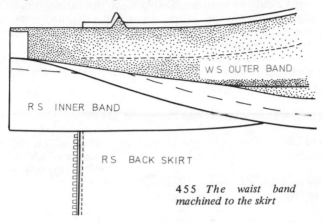

455 *The waist band machined to the skirt*

Cut away the interfacing turning if necessary. Trim and layer the skirt and waist band turnings. Fold the waist band upwards to cover the turnings, creasing it sharply back along the machine stitching. Tack the outer band to the waist turnings to hold the flat setting of the seam, and press lightly. Remove the tacking and press more firmly.

On the wrong side, pin and tack the prepared edge of the inner band along the waist fitting line. Hem it into the machine stitching and slip stitch it across the underwrap.

Press the band and sew on the fasteners (456).

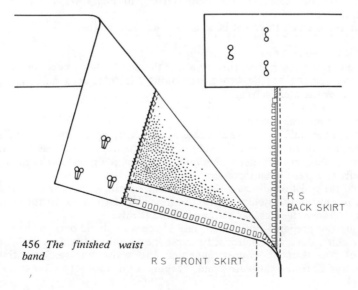

456 *The finished waist band*

277

Method 2
This is a slightly adapted version of method 1, and is useful for thicker fabric, or fabric which is difficult to press. It removes bulk and gives a flatter finish along the waist fitting line. However, it is necessary for the fabric to have a good selvedge.

Before cutting out the waist band, fold back the turning allowance along the waist edge of the pattern (ie the unnotched side), and place the fitting line along the selvedge edge of the fabric. Cut out the waist band with no turning allowance along this edge.

The preparation and setting are the same as for method 1 but, instead of having a folded edge to hem along the waist fitting line, the selvedge is set and hemmed in this position (457).

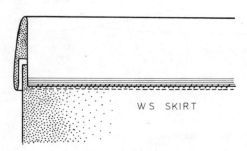

457 *A section of the waist band with a selvedge finish on the wrong side*

W S SKIRT

Top-stitched setting
This is a quick setting which is suitable for sports and casual wear, or for very 'springy' fabric which is difficult to press flat.

This setting resembles the plain setting in many ways, but has some variations.

Cut and prepare the waist band as for the plain setting.

(a) Making the waist band
Trim away the interfacing turning along the waist edge if necessary. Fold and tack the turning to the wrong side along the interfaced half of the waist band as for the plain setting.

(b) Setting the waist band
Pin the inner half of the waist band to the skirt, setting the RIGHT side of the waist band to the WRONG side of the skirt. Continue the setting as far as the machining on the waist fitting line, as for the plain setting. Trim and layer the skirt and waist band turnings.

Fold the waist band upwards to cover the turnings, creasing it back sharply along the machine stitching. Tack the inner band to the waist turnings. Press lightly, remove the tackings and press more firmly.

Bring the prepared, interfaced half of the waist band over to the right side of the skirt. Pin and tack it just to cover the machine stitching. With the right side of the skirt uppermost, machine the waist line, and continue the machining all round the waist band, keeping it not more than 3 mm inside the edge (458).

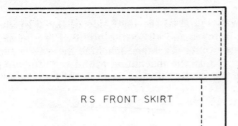

458 *A section of a top-stitched waist band*

RS FRONT SKIRT

A lined waist band

Lining fabric is used to line the wrong side of the waist band. This is useful in two ways: it gives a thinner finish which is helpful for heavy fabric; it prevents stretching, which is useful for fabric which is liable to stretch in wear.

(a) Cutting out

10 mm turnings are adequate on all edges. Cut the waist band with the length as directed on page 274. The width equals the finished width plus two turnings.

Cut the interfacing the exact size of the finished band.

The lining is cut 2 X the finished width minus 4 mm, with the length equal to the waist band length plus two turnings.

(b) Preparation of waist band
(i) The outer waist band

Mark the underwrap line and all the setting points.

Lay the prepared waist band wrong side up on the table. Pin the interfacing in the centre, with all the waist band turnings outstanding. Tack the band through the centre in both directions. On all four sides fold and tack the turnings over the interfacing, mitring the corners. Catch stitch the turnings to the interfacing with widely spaced stitches, except at the corners, which must be held securely (459).

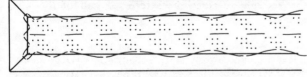

459 *A section of the pre-pared waist band*

(ii) The lining

Fold the turnings to the two short ends, trim and press.

Fold the two long raw edges to meet in the centre of the wrong side. Tack and press (460). The lining is now slightly narrower than the prepared band.

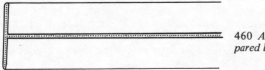

460 *A section of the pre-pared lining*

279

(c) Setting the waist band

Pin the lower edge of the waist band to the right side of the skirt along the waist fitting line, matching notches and all setting points. Ease the skirt into the band between the setting points. Tack and machine the waist band along the waist fitting line, and continue the machining round the remaining three sides (461). Trim and layer the waist turnings, remove all tacking and press the waist band.

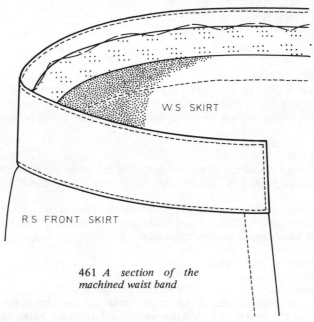

R S FRONT SKIRT

W S SKIRT

461 *A section of the machined waist band*

(d) Setting the lining

Pin the lining over the back of the waist band. If it has been cut and prepared accurately, it will fit just inside the outer edges of the band. Tack and hem it in place (462).

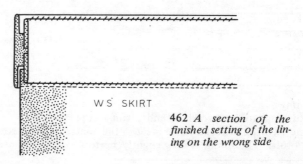

W S SKIRT

462 *A section of the finished setting of the lining on the wrong side*

20 Belts and belt carriers

A belt can add a pleasing finishing touch to a garment, providing it is chosen with some thought. A wide belt draws attention to a waist line and, therefore, emphasises a large waist, so choose the width belt which suits your individual waist measurement. Cut strips of paper of different widths, try out the effect of the suggested belt widths, and choose the width which suits you best.

Measure the length for a belt over the dress, as this is where it will be worn. Remember that an additional 175 mm will be required for the fastening overwrap.

If the belt is to be worn with a one-piece dress, ie one without a waist seam, mark the position for the belt when fitting the dress.

When making a belt from patterned fabric, study the pattern, and cut the belt to bring a suitable pattern line on the outside of the belt.

A bought belt should either match or tone with the dress fabric, unless a suitable contrast is chosen. Check the length of the belt when buying, to make sure it is the right length for you. If a bought belt is too long, it may be possible to shorten it at the buckle end.

Most belts fasten with a buckle. This may be bought, or made from a buckle-making kit. The buckle, or kit, must be bought before cutting out the belt, as the belt width should be 3 mm narrower than the inside measurement of the buckle. This allows the belt to slip through easily. Guidance for fixing the buckle and placing the eyelets is given in figure 464b. The eyelet for the buckle prong must be hand-worked so that it will curve over the buckle bar. The eyelets for fastening can be metal ones if preferred.

Belt carriers are necessary to hold the belt in position, and should be sewn over the waist line at the side seam. When the carriers are sewn to the dress, they should stand away from it slightly, so that the belt will slip in easily. If a belt has been made with a seam along one edge it should be slotted through the belt carriers with the seam downwards.

In the following directions for making various types of belt, some of the figures are out of proportion in length, in order to show both end and central details of construction.

A narrow soft belt

A belt made without stiffening should not be wider than 25 mm, or it will crush in use and present a stringy appearance. Cut the belt to the following directions:

Length — cut warpway = waist measurement + overwrap + 2 turnings of 10 mm eg 660 mm + 175 mm + 20 mm = 855 mm

Width = 2 x finished width + 2 turnings of 10 mm eg, cut a belt of 25 mm finished width, to equal 50 mm + 20 mm = 70 mm

Method A
Fold the belt in half, wrong side outside, and tack it together on the fitting lines, leaving a gap of 60 mm in the centre. At one end, shape the belt to a point. For a narrow belt the size of the point is based on half the belt width. Refer to figure 463, and work to the following directions:

AB = half belt width.

Chalk BC at this width, parallel to the tacking on the fitting line.

BD is half belt width.

DE is half belt width squared from D.

Join BE and EC.

Tack BEC for the point, which is now the fitting line at this end of the belt.

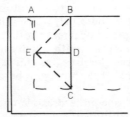

463 *Shaping the point.*
Enlarged for clarity

Machine the shaped belt, leaving the gap. Trim and layer the turnings as shown in figure 464a. Turn the belt right side out, and slip stitch the gap. Press and finish the belt as shown in figure 464b.

CENTRE OF BELT

464a *The prepared belt*

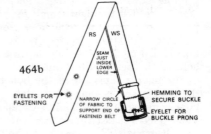

464b

RS   WS

SEAM JUST INSIDE LOWER EDGE

EYELETS FOR FASTENING

NARROW CIRCLE OF FABRIC TO SUPPORT END OF FASTENED BELT

HEMMING TO SECURE BUCKLE

EYELET FOR BUCKLE PRONG

Method B
If the weight of the fabric would give a bulky line along the seam edge of the belt, the seam can be centralised. Machine the full length of the belt, but leave a gap of 60 mm in the centre of the seam. Trim the turnings and press them open, using the point of the iron to prevent pressing the side edges of the belt. Set the seam, and machine the two ends of the belt as shown in figure 465. Trim and layer the end turnings. Turn the belt right side out and slip stitch the gap, taking care not to stitch through to the front of the belt. Press and finish the belt as before.

   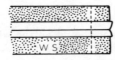

WS   WS

465 *The stitching of the two ends of the belt over the centralised seam*

Stiffened belts.
(a) An interfaced belt
The appearance of any belt is improved if it is supported by interfacing and,

282

in any case, it is essential for a belt which is wider than 25 mm. It gives a firm finish and keeps the belt flat in wear.

Cut the belt to the following directions:

Belt fabric — cut two strips warpway, one for the outer side of the belt, and one to use as a backing strip. If the garment fabric is too thick to use as a backing for the belt, this strip may be cut from lining fabric.

Length — as for a narrow soft belt (page 281).

Width — the finished width + two turnings.

Interfacing — cut one or two strips according to stiffness required, length and width as the finished belt — no turnings required.

(i) Preparation

If two layers of interfacing are to be used, tack them together longways through the centre and also close to each long edge. Press. Shape one end to a point (refer to figure 463).

(ii) Making the belt

Place the prepared interfacing centrally on the wrong side of one belt strip. Pin and tack them together. Trim the belt fabric at the shaped end, leaving a turning allowance of 10 mm outside the interfacing (figure 466a). Mitre the turning on each side of the point, creasing or pressing the folds sharply (figures 466b and c). Tack them close to the fold and trim to 6 mm - 8 mm.

Fold over and pin the turnings on the two long sides of the belt. Tack the turnings with short stitches, stitching into the interfacing only. Press the folded edges and trim. The belt is now ready for backing (466d).

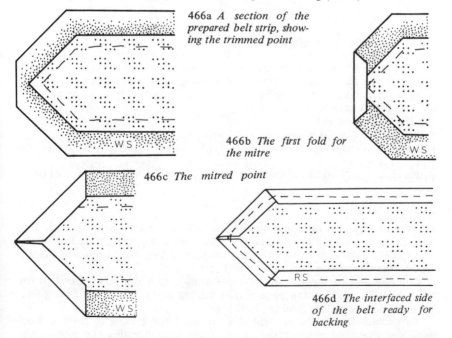

466a *A section of the prepared belt strip, showing the trimmed point*

466b *The first fold for the mitre*

466c *The mitred point*

466d *The interfaced side of the belt ready for backing*

The second belt strip is prepared in a similar way, except that it is not interfaced, and the turnings should be made 2 mm wider than allowed in the first place so that, when prepared, the backing strip is 2 mm narrower all round than the interfaced strip. Trim the backing turnings to 4 mm.

Pin and tack the two prepared strips together, leaving a 2 mm margin all round on the edges of the underside. Trim away the straight end of the backing strip in line with the interfacing (467). Slip stitch the backing strip in place.

Fold back and press the outstanding turning at the straight end of the belt, slightly insetting the side edges. Catch stitch the turning across the width (468). This edge is now ready for attaching the buckle when an eyelet has been made in the correct place (refer to figure 464b).

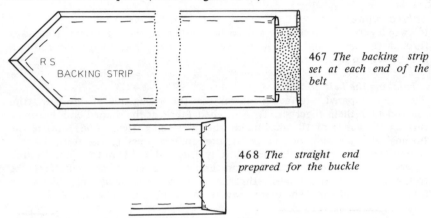

467 *The backing strip set at each end of the belt*

468 *The straight end prepared for the buckle*

(b) A belt made with stiff belting

Stiff belting can be bought by the metre, or in a belt-making kit, and gives a very firm appearance to a belt. Buy belting that is guaranteed for washing and dry-cleaning. When sold in commercial packs, instructions for use are enclosed. The following directions give a straight forward method for its use. Work with a fairly thick needle, eg No. 6 or 7, when sewing through the belting, as it is hard to stitch.

Cut the belt as follows:

Belting length — waist measurement + overwrap

Belt length — cut warpway — length as for belting + 2 turnings of 10 mm - 15 mm

Belt width — 2 X width of belting + 2 mm ease + 2 turnings of 10 mm or 15 mm.

Making the belt

Lay the belt the wrong side uppermost on the table and, with long stitches, tack along the centre line of the belt, and also along the fitting line of the lower edge. Take care to tack straight lines. Fold over the turnings of the top edge to the wrong side, and tack (469a).

Cut one end of the belting to a point and, with the pointed end to the left-hand side, lay the top edge of the belting along the tacked fitting line. Tack the belting to this turning (469b).

Turn the belt over to the right side, bringing the belting to the top. Fold back the lower edge along the centre line, thus bringing the fold of the turning to the tacked fitting line (469c).

Fold over the belting to cover the belt. Ease on a paper clip each side to hold the belting firmly near the pointed end. Machine the pointed shape onto the belt, stitching very close to the belting, but taking care not to catch it with the machine stitching (469d).

Trim the belt at the point, blunting the tip and slightly layering the turnings. Turn the belt right side out, easing the belting into position at the point. Arrange the long folded edge to come just above the lower edge of the belt. Tack and slip hem it in position (469e).

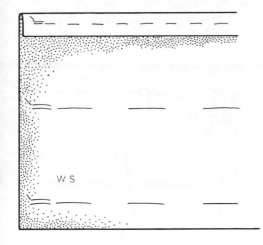

469a ,*A section of the belt showing the tacking preparation*

W S

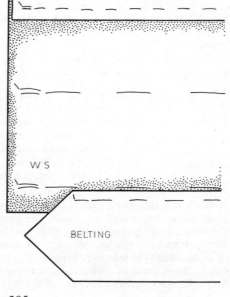

469b *The belting tacked to the belt*

W S

BELTING

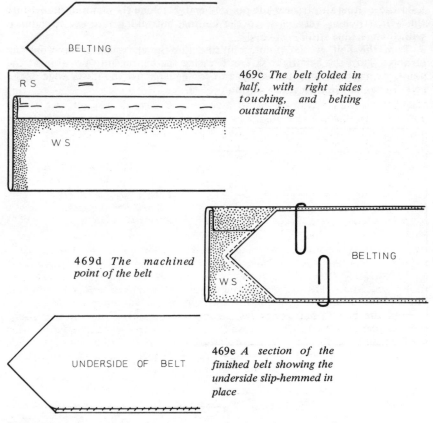

469c *The belt folded in half, with right sides touching, and belting outstanding*

469d *The machined point of the belt*

469e *A section of the finished belt showing the underside slip-hemmed in place*

Finish the belt with a buckle and eyelets as shown in figure 464b.

Tie belts

A tie belt can be made with or without an interfacing in the waist area.
In either case, cut the belt to the following directions:

Length — cut warpways   waist measurement + length required for tie ends. 1 metre ties into a bow with loops of 120 mm (knot to fold) and ends of 260 mm each. These are approximate measurements as the length varies according to the thickness of the fabric and the width of the belt.

Width = 2 X finished width of belt + 2 turnings of 10 mm - 15 mm.
Interfacing, when used, should be cut warpway if woven, with length equal to the waist measurement minus 30 mm (this allows space for tying the knot). The width equals the belt width + one turning.

If an adequate warpway length of fabric cannot be found, the belt can be cut in three sections and joined to bring the seam over the side seams of the dress. Measure across the front of the body, from side seam to side seam, and use this measurement for the central section. Join an equal length strip to either side to make up the length required for the belt. Leave adequate turning allowances for the two seams.

(a) Making a soft tie belt
Fold the fabric in half longways, wrong side out, and tack the open edges together along the fitting lines, leaving a gap of 100 mm in the centre. Machine the belt in two sections, fastening off strongly at each end of the gap. Trim and layer the turnings (470). Turn each half of the belt right side out through the gap. Fold in the turnings evenly across the gap, tack and slip stitch. Press the belt.

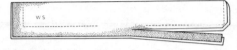

470 *The machined belt with turnings trimmed and layered*

(b) Making an interfaced tie belt
Fold the belt strip in half longways, right side outside, and press the fold. Open out the strip and lay it on the table wrong side uppermost. Pin and tack the interfacing through the centre of the length, with the top edge just below the crease. Catch stitch the interfacing just below the crease with minute, but widely spaced stitches, beginning and finishing 10 mm inside each end (471). The interfaced side will become the inner side of the belt when worn.

Fold the belt in half longways, wrong side outside. Trim the two short ends of the interfacing to a curved shape. Tack and machine as for the previous belt, and cut off the turning of the interfacing close to the machining. This allows the belt to taper into the knot. Trim and layer the belt turnings (472). Finish making the belt as previously described.

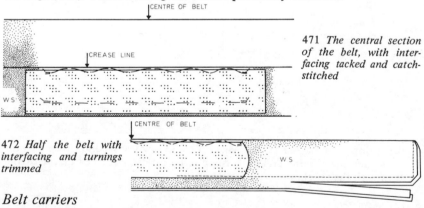

471 *The central section of the belt, with interfacing tacked and catch-stitched*

472 *Half the belt with interfacing and turnings trimmed*

Belt carriers
Fabric carriers
(a) Rouleau carriers for light-weight fabric
Make a length of rouleau (refer to page 192), planning for it to be 3 mm - 5 mm wide when finished. The length of each tube should equal the belt width + 4 mm - 6 mm ease, according to the thickness of the belt, + 2 turnings of 10 mm.

Setting the carriers
Tuck in the raw edges at each end and press the tube flat with the seam along

one edge. Fold over and press the remainder of the turning at each end, making the carrier the length required.

Mark the belt width + 2 mm - 3 mm on the side seams with two pins evenly spaced either side of the waist line. Consult figure 473 for placing, and back stitch the carrier along the crease. Hem the carrier turning very firmly to the dress.

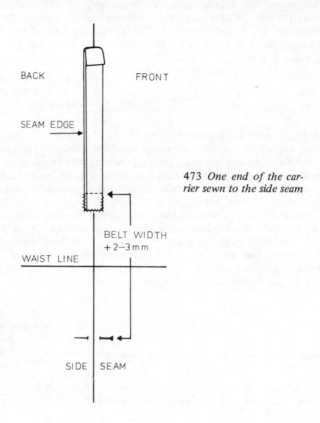

473 *One end of the carrier sewn to the side seam*

Bring down the carrier to the lower pin and sew the second turning to the dress, setting the turning crease to the pin. Be careful not to catch the carrier itself in with the stitching.

Selvedge carriers
These can be made when the fabric has a neat selvedge. Cut a strip of fabric along the selvedge with a width of 15 mm, and with length as directed for the previous carrier.

Making and setting the carrier
Fold the selvedge strip in three longways, right side outside, with the selvedge on top, and slightly inset. Slip stitch the selvedge in position, taking care not to stitch through to the outside. Press the carrier (474). Set as directed for the previous carrier.

474 *A prepared selvedge carrier*

Selvedge carriers for heavy belts

Make the carrier following the previous directions, but with the length 2 X the belt width + 6 mm - 10 mm ease according to the thickness of the belt.

Fold the carrier in half, right side outside, and oversew the raw edges together to join the carrier into a circle. Press the circle flat with the seam in the centre of one side.

Set the carrier with the seam touching the waist line, and pin the underlay of the flattened circle to the side seam, setting the pins as far apart as the width of the belt. Hem this area of the carrier very finely to the dress (475).

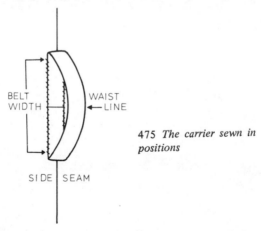

BELT WIDTH

WAIST LINE

SIDE SEAM

475 *The carrier sewn in positions*

Chain loop carriers

These are quick to make and are suitable for belts of light and medium weight. Fancy metal belts are difficult to thread through chain loop carriers. It is essential to use thread which exactly matches the belt in colour. Use buttonhole twist or cotton à broder for preference. Double sewing thread can be used, but is more difficult to handle, as it tends to twist.

Mark the position for the carrier, spacing it evenly either side of the waist line. The distance between the pins should equal the belt width + 3 mm - 4 mm ease.

Fasten on the thread into the side seam turning on the.wrong side, and stab the needle through to the right side. Take a very short stitch over the seam to form a loop. Hold the needle with the right hand. Pass the left thumb and forefinger through the loop, grasp the needle thread and pull it back through the loop. A new loop is now formed which must be secured by pulling the needle thread firmly. Continue in this way until the desired length of chain is made. Slip the needle through the last loop and pull to fasten off. Take a small stitch to secure, stab the needle through to the wrong side, and fasten off into the seam turning.

Alternatively, a fine crochet hook can be used to make the chain on the needle thread.

21 Hems

Plain hems

These are used on underwear, nightwear and household articles. A plain hem is made with a double folding of the fabric, each fold being turned to the same side. There must always be an even width space between the two folds. A hem is usually turned to the wrong side of the fabric; occasionally a hem is folded to the right side as a form of decoration, but this can be done only on plain fabric with no right or wrong side. A well made wrong side hem should be inconspicuous from the right side. This is only achieved if the lower edge is level, the width of the second turning is uniform, the stitching is neat and the hem is well pressed.

A hem marker may be prepared to guide the even folding of the hem. It may be cut from a postcard. A selection of hem markers of various widths is a useful adjunct to a work-box. To make a hem marker, measure the width of hem required along one edge of the card, and cut away a part of the card as shown by the shaded portion in figure 476. The two edges marking the width of hem should fit exactly along the hem turning.

476 *A hem marker*

The amount of fabric required to make a plain hem equals the finished width of the hem plus a first turning allowance. The finished width depends on the position and purpose of the hem. Except for a very narrow hem, the first turning allowance is narrower than the hem width. Outside the fitting line of the hem, trim the fabric to the width required for the hem plus the first turning allowance (477).

477 *The plan of a plain hem*

(a) Hems on straight edges

Fold the first turning to the wrong side, keeping it even in width (478). The following table suggests suitable widths for this turning:

3 mm-6 mm finished hem	first turning 3 mm
12 mm finished hem	first turning 3 mm-5 mm
20 mm-25 mm finished hem	first turning 6 mm
35 mm finished hem	first turning 12 mm

Keep the width of the first turning even by checking it continually with a tapemeasure or a hem marker. If the fabric creases, it may be creased in position; if the fabric is slippery or springy, it must be pinned and tacked.

478 *The first fold of a*
plain hem

The second turning must be kept even in width with the fitting line in a straight, smooth line along the edge. Measure the width frequently. Place the pins at right angles to the edge as this method keeps the turning flatter (479). Tack the hem close to the lower fold. This tacking goes through three thicknesses of fabric, ie the garment, the first turning and the second turning.

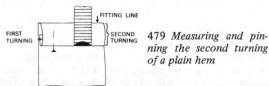

479 *Measuring and pin-*
ning the second turning
of a plain hem

(b) Hems on curved edges

A hem is not usually the best choice of edge finish on a curved edge. A very narrow hem, 3 mm-6 mm wide, is the only type that will set flat. On a concave curve the first turning must be snipped so that it will stretch out and lie flat (480).

When dealing with a convex curve, 'V'-shaped notches must be snipped out of the turning so that the edges can close together, thus making the turning lie flat (481).

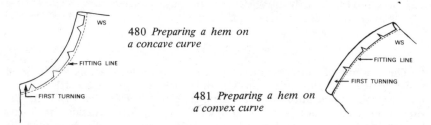

480 *Preparing a hem on*
a concave curve

481 *Preparing a hem on*
a convex curve

(c) The arrangement of hems at corners

Hems which meet at a corner need to be carefully planned so that the corners are neat and strong.

(i) Folded corners

The warp edges should be folded and tacked first, then the weft edges. This makes the corner symmetrical (482). Oversew the edges of the hems, and hem each weft hem across the width of the warp hems. The four hems may then be hand-sewn or machined with a continuous line of stitching. If the fabric is very springy, or frays badly, the warp hems may be stitched between the weft hems stitching lines, before the weft hems are folded. This arrangement applies either when the warp and weft hems are equal in width, or when one pair of hems is wider than the other pair.

482 *The folding plan of*
hems at corners

292

In some fabrics the arrangement suggested for the folding method shown in figure 482 would make the corners too bulky. In this case, crease the two turnings of each hem, marking the position of the lower weft fold with a pin (483a). Cut away part of the second turning of the warp hem (483b). Refold the weft hem back in its original position.

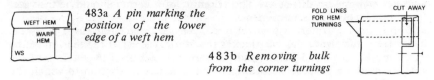

483a *A pin marking the position of the lower edge of a weft hem*

483b *Removing bulk from the corner turnings*

(ii) Mitred corners

Method A   Warp and weft hems of equal width can be mitred at the corners, and this provides a neater, flatter finish than a folded corner. It is wise to practise making a mitred corner if inexperienced.

Work the mitre in the following order:

1 At the corner tack the first turnings in place and crease the lines for the second turnings (484a). Tack out the second turning lines.

2 Fold over the corner to form two right angles, and to bring point 'X' in the centre of the fold (484b). Press the fold and cut off the corner, leaving a turning inside the fold (484b).

3 Open out the turning, fold the corner in half, wrong side outside, and back stitch from X, along the mitre fitting line, to the edge of the hem (484c).

4 Open out the seam and turn the corner to its normal position, setting the seam flat on the inside. The right side of the seam shows as a diagonal line joining the corners of the outer and inner edges of the hem (484d). Press the corner.

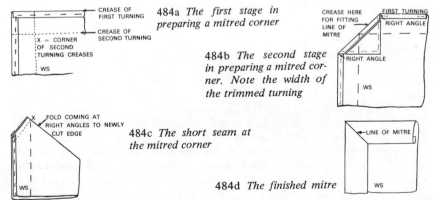

484a *The first stage in preparing a mitred corner*

484b *The second stage in preparing a mitred corner. Note the width of the trimmed turning*

484c *The short seam at the mitred corner*

484d *The finished mitre*

Method B   This does not give quite such a smooth line to the mitre, but is a safer method for springy or badly fraying fabric.

1 Prepare the corner as directed in Method A, point 1 (484a).

2 Fold over the corner to form the two right angles and to bring point 'X' in the centre of the fold (484b). Press the corner and tack the turning in place close to the fold before trimming away the unwanted triangle of fabric.

3 Fold at point 'X', with the wrong side outside, and join the folded edges with fine oversewing.

4 Turn the corner right side outside and press.

(d) Stitching plain hems

Straight machine stitching is rarely used on hems, and is certainly not recommended if a first-class finish is desired.

Sometimes a machine embroidery stitch can be used effectively, but choose one of simple design if a corner is involved, as the fitting of a design to a corner can present difficulty. The stitching of a corner should be tried out first to find a pleasing arrangement.

Slip hemming (refer to page 18) is often the best choice as it is almost invisible on the right side. The thicker the fabric, the easier the tension of the stitch must be to avoid pulling and puckering the fabric. The closeness of the stitches must be adapted according to the amount of friction to which the hem will be subjected in wear, varying from 3 mm-10 mm apart.

(e) Blouse and shirt hems

Before setting any final stitching, check that the centre front edges are equal in length from the neck fitting line. If a blouse has a back opening, check the centre back edges.

(i) A blouse or shirt with a front facing

Fold the facing to the right side of the blouse and machine across the width of the facing on the fitting line of the hem. Cut across the facing 6 mm below the machining and trim away the surplus fabric at the corner of the blouse and facing (485a). Fold the facing back into its final position on the wrong side. The lower edge is neatened and flat. Tack the hem in place near the fitting line. Pin the inner edge in position, placing the facing edge flat across the width of the hem, and hem it in place on to the hem turning. The blouse hem is now ready for the final slip hemming (485b).

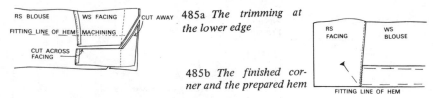

485a *The trimming at the lower edge*

485b *The finished corner and the prepared hem*

(ii) A blouse or shirt with a front panel opening

The hem turnings should be placed and pinned as shown in figures 478 and 479. Tack and slip hem the hem and oversew the open ends.

In some fabrics a hem is too bulky over the thickness of the front panel. In this case, the edge should be finished with a wrong-side facing (refer to page 122).

Dressmaking hems

The hem is the last process to be worked on a garment. All other processes must be completed, and the garment hung for a time to allow the skirt to 'drop'. This is especially necessary for flared or circular skirts, as the skirt usually 'drops' very much at the cross-cut lines. Press the skirt before marking the hem level.

Plan the hem level carefully as this is a fashion feature as well as depending on the age of the wearer and the type of garment. If the dress or skirt will be worn under a coat, check that it will not show below the coat.

(a) Measuring a hem line

A hem should always be levelled upwards from the floor. The best result is obtained by marking the hem line with the garment on the wearer. The smooth, even line of a skirt hem is most important if a smart appearance is to be maintained, and it should be levelled again and corrected later if the fabric of the skirt 'drops' after some wear.

The garment should be put on with all openings closed, and with a fastened belt if one is to be worn with the dress.

Decide on the length required and turn up a few inches of the fabric with pins to ascertain the appearance. If possible wear the shoes belonging to the outfit, as the height of heel is included when measuring the distance of the desired level from the ground. The fitter can work more accurately if the wearer stands on a table so that she has the hem-line at eye-level. The distance from table-top to pinned fold must be measured and the pins removed.

The wearer must stand very still with head erect throughout the levelling process (486). The slightest movement can raise or lower the skirt and give an inaccuracy in the marking. The fitter should move round the table until the line being marked is complete. The hem may be levelled with any patent hem-marker which quickly marks an accurate line round the skirt. Failing this, the line should be marked with pins and measured with a yardstick or a T-square if possible, as this is more easily kept at right angles to the table. Any straight stick will do as a substitute, if the level is clearly marked on it.

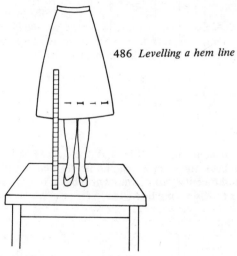

486 *Levelling a hem line*

(b) Marking the hem fitting line

Remove the garment and study the pinned or chalked line. Smooth out any slight irregularities. If the line appears very uneven, it should be re-marked before proceeding to the next stage.

Working on the right side, tack along the marked line to clarify the hem fitting line as a base for setting the hem. When doing this, avoid stitching through any seam turnings, as they will have to be trimmed later.

(c) Preparing the hem turning

The hem for an outer garment is usually made from single fabric, so when this

295

is the case, a top edge turning does not have to be included in the calculation of the turning width. The exceptions are hems on:

(i) light and medium weight washable fabrics, where a top edge turning can be used if desired, and

(ii) circular skirts.

The following suggestions give a guide to suitable finished widths for hems:

Straight hem lines	50 mm-75 mm
Shaped hem lines	35 mm-50 mm
Full, curved hem lines	25 mm

(d) Trimming the seam turnings

To prevent unwanted bulk in the seam areas, part of the seam turnings can be trimmed away from the hem. Snip across half the width of the seam turnings just clear of the hem fitting line, and cut away the freed sections up to the raw edge (487). When the hem turning is folded back in place, the thickness of the seam turning is graduated. Repress the seams if necessary.

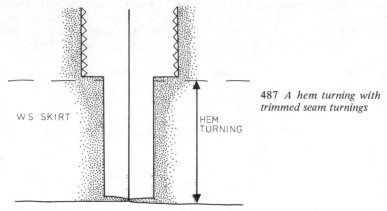

WS SKIRT

HEM TURNING

487 *A hem turning with trimmed seam turnings*

(e) Folding the hem

Work with the garment on a table and the wrong side of the hem edge uppermost. Fold back the hem along the newly marked fitting line, turning and pinning it at the centre front, the centre back and at each seam line first. Pin at right angles to the fitting line (488).

WS SKIRT

RS

SEAM LINE OF TURNING IN LINE WITH SEAM LINE OF SKIRT

HEM FITTING LINE

488 *Aligning the seam of a hem turning*

This initial placing balances both the grain and the seam lines of the hem turning and the skirt. This is important, otherwise the hem will not set smoothly. If the skirt contains gores, pin in the centre of each gore to set the turning flat on the skirt. Any surplus fabric will now become apparent, and will give a fluted appearance to the raw edge of the hem turning. Handle these flutes carefully, keeping them at right angles to the fitting line and pinning the turning flat to the skirt in between the flutes. Tack the hem turning to the skirt about 5 mm-10 mm above the fitting line, according to the thickness of the fabric. Tack firmly to keep the fitting line smooth and even.

When the tacking is finished, remove all the pins. Measure the required width of the hem from the fold, marking the distance with pins through the turning only. Cut away the unwanted fabric, leaving the turning width required (489). For single hems, this equals the finished width of hem. For hems with a top edge turning, 5 mm-10 mm turning allowance must be added to the finished width. For both types of hem, trim diagonally across the top of the seam turnings.

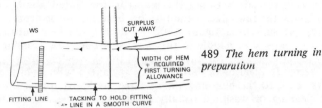

489 *The hem turning in preparation*

The top edge turning, if being used, must be folded under and tacked. Two precautions are necessary: keep the hem equal in width all round and the top edge turning level; handle the top edge carefully so that it is not stretched.

(f) Reducing surplus fabric in a hem turning
(i) In a single hem turning
(a) By shrinkage   Test the fabric first to see if it will shrink. To do this, gather 5 mm below the raw edge of a scrap of garment fabric on the same grain as the hem turning. Draw up the fabric evenly on the gathering thread to shorten it about one third of its length. Steam press the gathered edge gently at first, and then more firmly. This will show whether the fabric responds to this treatment. If the result is satisfactory, the hem can be gathered between the seams, about 5 mm below the raw edge, in the fluted areas. Either hand or machine gathering can be used. Draw up the gathering thread so that the turning lies flat on the skirt (490a). If machine gathering has been used, draw up the thread on the underside of the hem turning. Make a back stitch to hold the threads, but do not cut off the ends in case some adjustment is necessary after pressing.

Fold the turning away from the skirt and steam press the gathered areas (490b). Do not let the iron move onto the skirt, press only the turning area, and keep the iron moving.

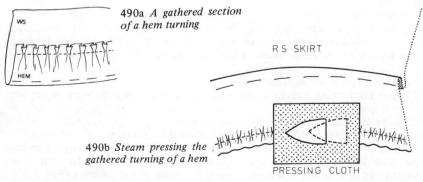

490a *A gathered section of a hem turning*

490b *Steam pressing the gathered turning of a hem*

297

Alternative method for fabric which shrinks easily: Overcast over the raw edge of the fluted areas, making the stitches approximately 2 mm-3 mm deep and 5 mm-6 mm apart. Draw up the overcasting stitches to reduce the edge of the hem turning so that it lies flat on the skirt. Shrink-press the hem turning.

(b) By easing and pressing   If the fabric does not shrink, it may be necessary to reduce the width of the hem by cutting away 5 mm-10 mm from the raw edge. This will remove some of the unwanted fullness, leaving a more manageable turning.

Set gathering threads between the seams in the fluted areas, stitching 4 mm-5 mm below the raw edge of the turning. Ease the fabric evenly along the thread. Press as shown in figure 490b to flatten the hem turning. If the turning if too narrow to handle in this way, slip a strip of pressing cloth or firm, clean paper under the turning to protect the skirt while pressing.

Do not resort to pleating or darting away unwanted fullness in the turning, as this gives bulk to the hem and causes shine marks to appear on the right side after cleaning or washing. Usually small points appear in the hem edge below the pleat, and mar the desirable smoothness of the hem finish.

(ii) In a hem with a top edge turning
This treatment is similar to that already described for a single turning. Test the fabric for shrink-pressing but, in this case, fold under a turning along the raw edge and run a finely stitched gathering thread just below the fold before drawing up the fabric and pressing. If it does not shrink, reduce the width of the hem if possible.

Gather the hem in the fluting areas, ease up the fabric and either shrink-press, or press to flatten the turning.

Finishing the top edge of a hem
(a) *Stitches choice and working*
(i) Slip-hemming. Refer to page 18 figures 16a and b.
(ii) Slip-hemming adapted for use with ribbon seam binding. Refer to page 300 figures 493a, b and c.
(iii) Catch-stitching. Refer to figures 492a, b and c. This is the most satisfactory method of stitching as it is flexible and also invisible except on thin fabrics.   Whichever type of stitch is chosen, it must be worked loosely so that the fabric is not pulled. Invisible stitching must be the aim with every hem, and this is impossible if there is even the slightest tightness in the stitching.

Fasten the threads on and off at the seams, where close, strong stitching can be done without stitching through to the right side. At each seam, whether fastening thread ends or not, stitch strongly into the seam turnings. This gives areas of close stitching and adds extra strength to the hem fixing.

(b) A hem with a top edge turning
Machine the turning 3 mm - 4 mm below the fold in the following cases:
(i) on fraying fabric,
(ii) on springy fabric which is difficult to press,
(iii) when surplus fabric has had to be flattened by pressing.
Tack the turning to the skirt 3 mm - 4 mm below the top edge. Slip-hem the fold to the skirt, spacing the stitches evenly, about 10 mm apart. Remember to hem the fold finely into the turning of each seam (491).

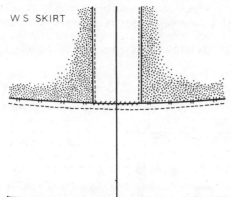

491 *A finished section of a hem. In this case the top edge turning has been machined before working the slip hemming*

(c) Hems with a single turning

(i) For non-fraying and slightly fraying fabrics, the raw edge requires zigzagging or overcasting to give a firm edge. This finish can be used on shaped as well as straight skirts, as either stitch can be worked over the shrunk or flattened edge of a shaped skirt. If the fabric tends to be loosely woven, stitch a line of straight machine stitching just inside the raw edge before zigzagging or overcasting.

When the edge has been stitched, tack the turning to the skirt 10 mm - 15 mm below the top edge (492a). With the left thumb, roll back the neatened edge and catch stitch loosely to join the hem turning to the skirt (492b and c).

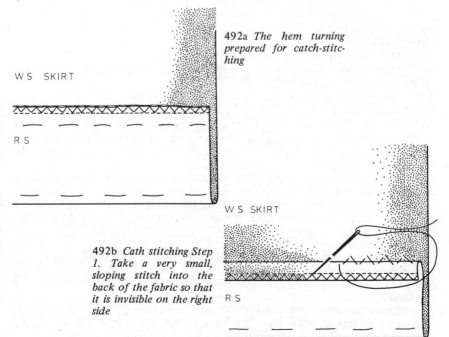

492a *The hem turning prepared for catch-stitching*

492b *Cath stitching Step 1. Take a very small, sloping stitch into the back of the fabric so that it is invisible on the right side*

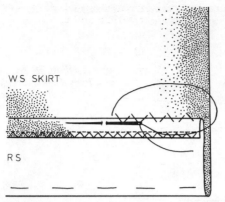

WS SKIRT

R S

492c *Catch stitching Step 2. Move 4 mm - 5 mm forward and stitch into the hem turning*

(ii) Neatening with ribbon seam binding   This finish is useful on medium and heavy weight fabric which frays. It is only satisfactory if the hem line is straight or very slightly curved, as this binding is on the straight grain with two selvedge edges.

Method A For firmly woven fabric

The binding is lapped, for 2/3 of its width, over the top edge of the hem turning, and tacked along its lower edge. Begin and finish the tacking about 50 mm either side of the side seam, leaving an end of binding about 75 mm at the beginning. This gives scope for joining the binding with a narrow, plain seam in line with the skirt seam. Trim and press the seam and finish the tacking. Take care neither to stretch nor to tighten the hem edge.

Machine the ribbon seam binding onto the turning and slip hem it on to the skirt. A slight adaptation is needed in the slip hemming as there is no fold through which to slip the needle. The hem edge is held towards the worker. Take a small stitch through the back of the fabric and through the edge of the binding, at right-angles to the hem (493a). Pull through this stitch. The needle re-enters the binding just beside that stitch and passes under the edge of the binding only for about 6 mm (493b and c).

WS

HEM

THIS EDGE HELD TOWARDS WORKER

493a and b *Stages in working the slip hemming on ribbon seam binding*

WS

HEM

WS

PARIS BINDING

HEM

493c *The finished setting*

Method B For softer fabrics which would pull with slip hemming

Set the binding along the top edge of the hem turning, with the upper selvedge edge in line with the raw edge. Arrange the join as described for Method A.

Machine the lower edge of the binding to the hem turning, and machine zigzag over the top edge. Tack the hem turning to the skirt just below the binding only for about 6 mm (494).

Roll back the zigzagged edge with the left thumb and catch stitch the turning to the skirt, stitching as shown in figures 492b and c.

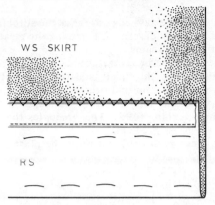

494 *The neatened hem edge tacked to the skirt*

(iii) *Neatening with bias binding or crossway strips of lining fabric*   This finish is useful for fraying fabrics with either straight or shaped hem lines and is a good method to use on any fabric if the hem line is curved.

If using hand-cut crossway strips, prepare an adequate length with an allowance for a final join (refer to page 116). Bias binding must also be cut with a join allowance and must be pressed open flat.

Tack the right side of the binding to the right side of the hem turning, with the raw edges level. Tack 6 mm below the raw edge, arranging the final join to come over a seam. Machine 5 mm below the raw edges (495a). Remove the tacking, press the stitching and then press the binding upwards to cover the machine stitching. Bring the binding over the raw edge and onto the inside of the hem turning. Tack and machine along the seam line on the right side to hold the binding firmly, and to enclose the raw edge (495b). Press the edge and finish by catch stitching along the line of machine stitching.

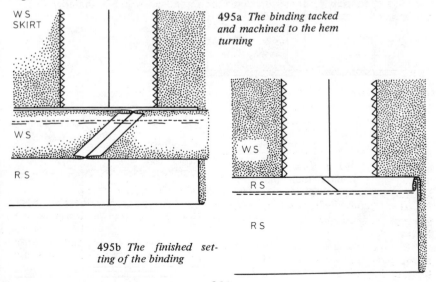

495a *The binding tacked and machined to the hem turning*

495b *The finished setting of the binding*

301

A hem over a pleat with an outstanding seam

This problem occurs when a pleat has a seam on an inside fold (refer page 88).

Press open the pleat seam from the raw edge as far as the stitching line of the hem. Prepare the hem as previously described, trimming the pleat seam up to the hem fitting line as for the other seams.

When the top edge of the hem has been neatened, mark its level on the pleat seam and snip diagonally across the turnings at this point. Round off the corners on the upper edges of the snip and overcast them together. Trim the turnings between the snip and the hem fitting line to make them slightly wider than they are in the hem turning (496). This graduates the thickness when the pleat is finally pressed across the hem.

Stitch the hem line of the pleat as desired and press the pleat in position (497).

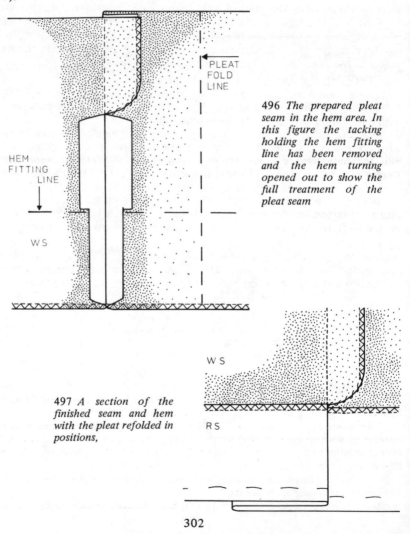

496 *The prepared pleat seam in the hem area. In this figure the tacking holding the hem fitting line has been removed and the hem turning opened out to show the full treatment of the pleat seam*

497 *A section of the finished seam and hem with the pleat refolded in positions,*

Hems for skirt linings

These should be marked 15 mm - 20 mm shorter than the skirt, so that they cannot possibly show below.

Make the hem as directed for a hem with a top edge turning on page 298. If preferred, the hem can be fixed with a simple machine embroidery stitch instead of slip hemming. Straight machine stitching does not give a first-class finish to a lining hem.

Hems for full flare or circular skirts

A very narrow hem is nearly always used as it is impossible to make a flat, well-set hem of any width on such a sharp curve.

When the hem level is being marked, measure it 10 mm nearer the ground than required. This 10 mm provides adequate turning allowance. Trim the skirt carefully along the marked line, taking care to get a very smooth curve.

Fold half the turning allowance to the wrong side, and tack it in place. Machine close to the folded edge (498). Trim the turning close to the machine stitching. Fold the remainder of the turning allowance to the wrong side and tack it in place. This second turning may be machined (499a) or, for a better result, slip-hemmed to the skirt (499b).

498 *The machined first turning*   499a *The second turning finished by machine*   499b *The second turning finished by slip hemming*

Hems on sheer and semi-sheer fabrics

(a) On straight edges
(i) A solid hem

A solid hem is used along a straight edge on transparent fabric. It has the first and second turnings equal in width so that the raw edge comes along the fitting line and does not show through the hem to the right side (500).

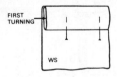

500 *A solid hem*

(ii) A tucked hem

This is an adaptation of a solid hem. It provides a soft, but strong finish to fine fabric which gives extra substance to the hem line.

A tucked hem only sets satisfactorily on a straight edge, unless it is very narrow in width, when it will set on a hem line with a very slight curve. The tuck contains three, and the underlay two layers of fabric, making a depth of five layers where the tuck laps over the underlay (501).

A tucked hem can be used only on plain fabric as printed fabric gives too shadowed an effect.

Any width of tuck and underlay can be arranged, but the widths must be planned in advance so that the requisite turning allowance can be left. The allowance required is 3 x the width of the tuck + the width of the underlay. Try out the folding on paper in the first place.

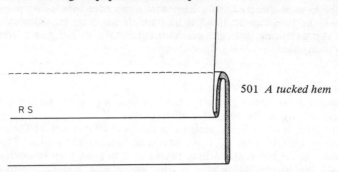

501 *A tucked hem*

Mark the hem fitting line in the usual way, but when tacking it, drop the fitting line for an amount equal to 2 X width of tuck required. Below the new hem fitting line, allow a turning equal to the underlay width + width of tuck, eg for a 20 mm tuck, lying on a 40 mm underlay, drop the fitting line 40 mm, and allow a 60 mm turning below the dropped fitting line.

Fold back the fabric to the wrong side along the dropped fitting line. Fold over again to form a solid hem. Tack the hem in a helpful position to guide the machining which is stitched through three layers of fabric at tuck width above the lower fold of the hem (502).

Fold the fitting line downwards to form the underlay with the tuck lying on it, as shown in figure 501. The skirt is now the required length with the tuck in place, securely holding the raw edge.

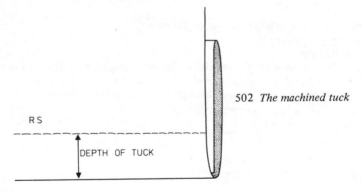

502 *The machined tuck*

DEPTH OF TUCK

(b) On curved edges

A full, curved hem line on sheer fabric can be finished with a very narrow hem as shown on page 303 figures 498 and 499a and b.

In some cases either a double binding (refer to page 119), or a narrow double facing (refer to page 124), gives a more satisfactory result than a hem.

False hems

A false hem may be required for the following reasons:
(a) When lengthening a skirt or dress for a growing child,

(b) when insufficient hem turning has been allowed, or the length of a skirt has been much changed in fitting alterations, or

(c) when the dress fabric of a circular or much curved hem line is difficult to handle for the required narrow hem.

The fabric chosen for the false hem should tone pleasingly or, if possible, match the garment fabric in colour, and it should have identical washability. Lining fabric is often used.

A straight grain strip for a false hem will set only on a straight skirt where there is no deviation from the straight grain in the seam lines, therefore the strip is usually cut on the crossway, so that it will set and lie flat along the curve of the hem. A false hem should be 25 mm - 50 mm in width when finished. Allow a 6 mm turning on each edge of the false hem strip, and a 12 mm turning on the skirt edge. When using a crossway strip for the false hem, make any joins following the instructions given on page 117.

Attach the strip as for a wrong side facing (refer to page 122), but with one exception: when the strip has been machined to the skirt, press open the turnings of skirt and false hem. Fold the false hem to the wrong side 6 mm below the join, ie folding a 6 mm turning of garment fabric to show on the wrong side below the false hem itself. This gives a flatter, smoother fold along the lower edge of the hem.

Fold under the 6 mm turning along the top edge of the false hem, and slip-hem it to the skirt.

Medium and heavy-weight fabric can have a false hem set as a double crossway facing of lining fabric. This gives a firmer hem finish, and provides a smoother line along the top edge of the false hem. Prepare and set the double false hem as for a double facing (refer to page 124), but press open the join and arrange the lower hem edge as previously described.

22 The choosing and care of clothes

When choosing fabrics and colours we are wise to consider personal build and appearance. It is also wise to consider these points when choosing the style of our garments, and to choose lines which suit us best within the trend of fashion. We show a good sense of dress if we recognise current fashion but adapt it to our personal requirements.

Warm colours, eg pinks, some reds and warm browns are kind to pale complexions and colouring as they give warmth to the skin. Remember that there is a great deal of difference between a pale and a fair complexion.

Cold colours, eg blues, greens, greys etc, emphasise the coldness of a pale skin. They are a wise choice for people with a good or even florid colouring, and also for those with red hair.

Take great care when matching colours to the eyes and hair. This will always accentuate their natural colouring, but may not always be the best foil to the complexion, eg a brown outfit worn to accentuate dark brown hair will not be pleasing in appearance if the complexion is swarthy, sallow or very pale. Grey worn to accentuate grey eyes gives a very cold appearance if the complexion is pale. The skilful use of cosmetics can help to overcome the complexion problem however.

Light colours appear to increase and dark colours to decrease size. Stiff and shiny fabrics, eg satin and glazed cotton, have an enlarging effect. Soft and/or dull-surfaced fabrics, eg cotton or courtelle jersey give a more becoming appearance to larger figures as there is no reflection of light. Fabric patterned with large designs usually looks its best on people of average or above average height, with well-proportioned figures. Large designs tend to emphasise very large figures and to overpower small people.

Horizontal lines appear to add width to, and to shorten the figure. They draw the eyes across the body instead of up and down its length. These lines may appear as yokes, bands, decorative belts or, on more elaborate styles, as frilling or added lines of a contrasting colour. Striped fabric is sometimes used to give horizontal lines across the figure.

Vertical lines appear to add height. As the eyes follow any pronounced line on a garment, vertical lines draw them up and down the figure and the width is, therefore, less noticeable. Such lines may be in the fabric, eg stripes introduced lengthways into the garment, or they may be introduced in construction as panel seams or as pleats etc.

Stripes need to be worn with great discrimination. They are most attractive on people of a medium size, although they can be arranged to make short people appear taller and thin people fatter, by using them in either a vertical or a horizontal position. A slight variation in the direction of stripes can look attractive, eg stripes may run across a yoke and downwards in the lower part of the bodice, but avoid too frequent a change of direction. This is displeasing as it gives a restless and unbalanced appearance to the garment.

The care of clothing

Many people associate the word 'grooming' with the care of the hair, skin and hands, but a well-groomed girl also takes care of her clothes, keeping them brushed, cleaned, washed, pressed, mended and carefully stored when not in use. This necessitates regular care and attention, but gives the reward of fresh, attractive clothes which retain their line and smartness throughout their life.

The washing and pressing of modern fabrics is comparatively easy. Washing directions are clearly indicated on care labels, washing powder packets and washing machines. The pressing of garments is dealt with in Section 3 and throughout the information on making clothes. These directions can be applied whenever a garment is pressed.

Darning and patching repairs

We are lucky nowadays as modern fabrics do not require mending as frequently as the fabrics worn in days gone by. However, when a garment shows some sign of wear, it is wise to repair it quickly so that the repair can be as small and inconspicuous as possible.

The method of repair should be chosen according to the type of garment or fabric, and the position of the damage. The two methods used for mending are darning and patching. Darning creates a new piece of fabric within a hole; patching supplies a new piece of fabric over the worn area. Darning should be used in preference to patching whenever possible as it is less obvious and does not require the use of extra fabric. Patching is used when a darn would be too extensive to be practical.

Darning

Darn cotton and light-weight fabrics with a suitable, matching sewing thread and a sharps needle, unless long strands of darning are required, when a darning needle must be used as it is longer than a sharps.

Darn fine, smooth woollen fabric with a thread of fabric drawn from cuttings or a seam turning, if such a thread is adequately strong. A darning needle, or for small darns a cr wel needle, is the best choice as the thread will fit into the long eye. If a fabric thread cannot be used, choose sewing silk of mercerised sewing cotton and a sharps needle. Darn thick woollen fabrics with a suitable ply wool and a darning needle.

Guiding points for darning

(a) Work on the wrong side of the garment

(b) Trim the edges of the hole, keeping it as small as possible

(c) Do not stretch or pull the hole while darning. It is easier to work with the support of a darning mushroom or egg

(d) Make the darn round or oval in shape to suit the shape of the hole. Never darn in a square, as this puts too much strain on straight lines or loops of the fabric

(e) To strengthen the area round the hole, arrange the darn to extend into the surrounding fabric

(f) Darn finely, making the stitches as short as possible where they stitch into the fabric. On medium-weight and thick fabric, stitch into the back of the fabric only. Allow for shrinkage on washing garments by leaving a tiny loop of thread at the end of each line of darning

(g) Strand across the hole, arranging the strands to pass over and under the edges of the hole alternately. When the darn is complete in one direction, turn the work and strand across in the opposite direction to fill in the hole with a solid mend. Keep the same over and under arrangement at the edges of the hole when working the second stranding. The finished area provides a newly woven area within the hole.

Darning a hole in woven fabric
Set the first stranding in a warpwise direction. Figures 503a and b show the arrangement for a darn on woven fabric.

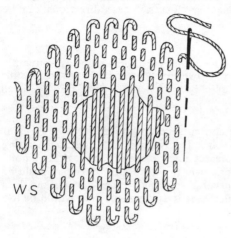

503a *The first stranding for a darn on woven fabric*

503b *The second stranding for a darn on woven fabric, shown in a contrasting colour for clarity*

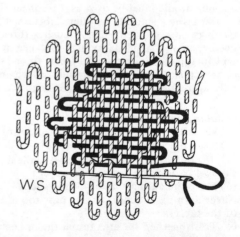

Darning a hole in knitted fabric
When stranding across the hole, each strand should pass through a free loop on one edge of the hole to prevent the loops from running and forming ladders from the hole. Figures 504a and b show how the strands are arranged across the hole. Work the first stranding to correspond with the lengthwise direction of the garment.

308

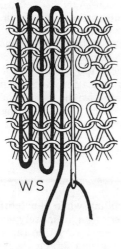

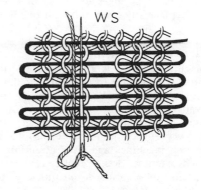

504a *The first stranding for a darn on knitted fabric*

WS

WS

504b *The second stranding for a darn on knitted fabric, shown in a contrasting colour for clarity*

Patching

Guiding points for patching

(a) The size of the patch must be adequate for covering the hole and the worn or damaged part round the hole

(b) A patch is usually square or obling so that it fits to the warp and weft threads of the garment, bringing the grain of patch and garment into alignment

(c) If the fabric is patterned, the patch should match with this also

(d) The patch should extend to, and be set into, a seam or hem if it comes near to one. Unpick the seam or hem and press the turnings. Set the patch on three sides and include the fourth side in the resetting of the seam or hem

(e) When setting a four-sided patch, begin sewing in the middle of one side to prevent the weakness of a join at a corner.

Making a right-side patch

This is the type of patch most generally used on all outer garments except coats, jackets etc made of thick fabric.

Preparation of hole

Outline the area to be patched with tacking stitches or tailor's chalk, marking with the fabric grain.

Preparation of patch

Cut the patch large enough to cover the area to be patched plus 10 mm turnings on all edges. If one edge of the patch is to be set into a seam or hem, allow the seam or hem turning width on this edge. On a square patch, tack the turnings to the wrong side of the patch, first trimming the corners and folding each corner to form a mitre. If the patch is to be set into a seam or hem, two corners and three sides will need this preparation. Press the patch.

309

Setting the patch

Place the patch right side up on the right side of the garment, matching any pattern, and setting the patch straight with the marked outline on the garment. This should bring the grains of patch and garment into alignment.

Pin and tack the patch into position ready for the final stitching. Machine stitching can be used for setting the patch if the appearance is suitable for the garment eg jeans or play clothes. For a less conspicuous setting, fine hemming or felling can be used. Remove the tacking and press the patch.

On the wrong side, trim away the garment allowing 10 mm turnings to match the patch. Overcast or loop-stitch together the raw edges of the turning. These edges are not sewn down onto the patch.

Replace any seam or hem if one has been unpicked.

Mending by machine

Machine darning is a strong, quick method of mending when the fabric is firm. It is unwise to attempt machine darning on very thin, or loosely woven fabric, as the machine stitching is too strong. A special very fine thread is available from the machine shops for machine mending, and should always be used, as ordinary sewing threads give too hard and heavy a result.

Very successful machine darning and patching can be done on modern sewing machines and clear directions are given in the Manual provided with each machine. Some practice is necessary before attempting to work machine darning on a garment, but quick, efficient repairs can be achieved when the skill is mastered.

The care of hem-lines

All hem-lines require watching and adjusting when necessary. A frock hem-line dropping unevenly below a coat looks as slovenly as a slip or lining showing below a frock. This problem is more acute when long, full hem-lines are fashionable, as these need frequent adjustment. Most full-skirted garments are ruined after some wear by untidy hem-lines. However attractive a garment may be, its appearance is ruined if the hem is uneven.

Washing and cleaning

It is essential to keep garments fresh by laundering or dry-cleaning.

The Home Laundering Consultative Council have produced a care labelling scheme which is printed as a chart of eight codes on washing product packets. These labels also appear as a washing guide on ready-made garments. If there is not a care label on anything you buy, make sure to enquire about the fibre content of the fabric, so that you know which washing code to select from the packet chart, or washing machine. Always ascertain the fibre content of fabric bought by the yard for the same reason.

The problem of stain removal has been much eased by the introduction of biological washing powders. These usually deal effectively with most common stains.

Choose the correct iron setting for the fibre content of the fabric. This should be found on the care label. Note whether the fabric should be ironed dry or damp, if damp, continue ironing until the fabric is dry. It will look rough dry if dampness is left in the fabric after ironing. In many cases gloss is imparted to fabric by ironing. If a matt finish is required, iron on the wrong side of the fabric.

Adequate cleaning must be given to shoes, handbags and any other accessories. Neckwear requires frequent washing or cleaning and careful storing to keep it fresh in appearance. Try to do simple repairs at once before the damage is increased. Take shoes to be repaired as soon as they wear thin. They will last longer and keep their original shape if they are not worn in a "run-over" condition.

The care of the wardrobe or clothes cupboard

It is a good plan to keep an anti-moth sachet in the wardrobe, and in the drawer where woollens are stored.

The wardrobe should be kept clean inside and a hanger provided for each garment. Use padded hangers for soft fabrics and special skirt hangers for skirts. All fastenings should be closed when garments are hung up as this is the best way of retaining the original shape. Remove belts and store separately so that they do not pull on the carriers when the garment is hanging. Either roll the belt and keep it in a drawer or thread the buckle over the hanger hook.

When a garment is out of use for any length of time, eg a summer coat, cover it with a polythene clothes-bag as a safeguard against dust and moths.

Index

Armholes, neatening 254-6, 260
  preparation for fitting 64, 249-50
  reshaping after fitting 41
Arrowheads 86

Back-stitch 14, 103, 158
Bands, for sleeves 271-2
  circular 96
Bars, metal 196
  worked 196
Belts: Section 20
  fastening 282
  general information 281
  interfaced 282-4
  narrow, soft 281-2
  stiffened 284-6
  tie 286-7
Belt-carriers, fabric 287-9
  chain-loop 289-90
Binding, angles 120-21
  crossway 118-19
  curves 119-20
  detachable collars 226
  double 119
  hem turning 301
  joining in a circle 121-22
  used to neaten seams 108-9
Blanket stitch 16
Bound slot pockets 234-9
Buttonhole, scissors 10
  stitch 16, 17, 156, 195, 196
Buttonholes, bound 187-9
  hand-worked 181-6
  machine-made 187
Buttons 189-91

Cable-stitching 25
Carbon paper 60
Casing 102-3, 124
Catch-stitch 146, 275, 294-5
Checks 57
Clothing care 307, 311
Collars, detachable 226
  flat 199-200
    interfacing 206
    making 203
    setting 208-13
    setting into lined yoke 225-6
  roll 200-201
    interfacing 204-7
    making 203-4
    setting 213-18
  shirt 202
    making and setting 221-5
  stand 201-2
    making 205-7
    setting 218-20
    setting above a zip 212-13, 219-20
Colour, choice of 306
Cord, looped 197-8
Corners, folded 292-3
  machining 25
  mitring 293
  reinforcing 112-13
Cross tacking 13, 85, 148, 203
Crossway binding, see binding
  cutting 116-17
  facing, see facing
  joining 117-18
Cuffs 269-71, 272-3
Cutting out: Section 7
  notches 59
  scissors 9, 59

Darning, general points 307
    knitted fabric 308-9
    woven fabric 308
Darts, below an opening 159-60
    curved 79
    double-pointed 78
    fish, see double-pointed
    fitting 71
    french, see long
    french seam 80
    long 79-80
    making 76-8
    pressing 80-81
    in raglan sleeves 257-9
    at sleeve crown 80
    tacking for fitting 63
    on transparent fabric 80
    uses 75-6
Double machine-stitched seam 114-15
Dressmaking, necessities for: Section 1

Easing 101, 110-11
Elastic, joining 103
    slots for threading 103
    used to reduce fullness 103
Embroidery, scissors 9
    threads 10
Eyelet holes 197
Eyes 196

Facing, crossway 102, 122-5
    angles 123
    used as casing 124
        to set collars 209-11
            cuffs 270-71
    double 124-5
    used to edge sleeves 268
    shaped: Section 12
        for armholes 127-31
            buttoned openings 133-9
            neck 126-31
            sleeves 132-3
            waist 150-3
False hem 304-5

Fastenings: Section 15
    buttonholes 181
        bound 187-9
        hand-worked 181-6
        machine-made 187
    buttons 189-91
    eyelet holes and lacing 197-8
    hooks 195-6
        with bars 196
        with eyes 196
    press-studs 194-5
    rouleau loops 192-4
    types 167
    worked loops 191-2
    zips 167-80
        concealed setting 173-80
        at dress waist 180
        set in faced opening 168-9
        fixing lining behind 171-2, 175-6
        marking positions for 167-70
        semi-concealed setting 170-2, 180
        with underwrap 178-9
Fabric grain, see Straight grain
Faggoting 14-16, 21
Fishbone stitch 236
Fitting: Section 8
    the bust-line 66
    fullness 71-2
    the hip-line 69
    preparation 62-4, 65, 250-51
    the second fitting 73
    side seams 71
    shoulder seams 65
    skirts 68
    sleeves, inset 252-3
        kimono 261-2
        raglan 257-9
Fitting-lines 31-2
    supporting collar 202
        neck 202
    transfer of new 72, 74
Flat collar, see Collars
French seam 104-5
    dart 80
Frills, calculation of length 98
        turnings 98

width 97
edge finishes 98-9
use of fabric grain 97
folded 100
gathering by hand 99
  machine 99
setting 100,113
Fullness: Section 9
  darts 75-81
  easing 100-1
  elastic 103
  frills 97-100
  gathering 92-6
  pleats 83-92
  ribbon tie-strings 102-3
  shirring 96-7
  tucks 81-3

Gathering 92-6
  fitting 72
  setting to a line 95
    a circular band 96
  spreading 95
  stitching 94
    drawing up and fastening off 94-5
    using machine attachments 94
    planning 93
  tacking for setting 12-13
    for fitting 63
Grain, see Straight grain
Gussets 263-7

Hem-marker 291
Hemming, plain 17-18, 22, 159, 160
  slip 18, 300
Hems: Section 21
  for blouses 294
  care of 310
  corners, folded 292-3
    mitred 293
  on circular skirts 303
  false 304-5
  on flared skirts 303
  marking and preparation 294-8

over pleats 302
plain, curved 292
  stitching 294
  straight 291-2
on sheer fabric, solid 303
  tucked 303-4
on sleeves 268
stitching for dressmaking 298-302
Herring-bone stitch 19
Hooks 195-6, 220, 277

Inset sleeves 248-56
Interfacing: Section 13
  belts 283, 287
  choice 141
  collars 204-7
  cutting 141-2
  joining 142
  pockets 231
  position of 140
  setting 143-153
  types 140-41
  waist-bands 275-6, 279
Iron 26

Kimono sleeves 248, 261-7

Lace, pressing 27
  used to edge frills 99
    with a facing 125
Lacing for eyelets 197-8
Lapped seams 111-13
Laying patterns: Section 6
Loop-stitch 16, 21, 79, 109, 162-3,
  165-6, 191-2, 196-7

Machines, see Sewing machines
Machine fell seam 115
Mandarin collar, see Stand collar
Measuring the body 30
  ease allowance 31
  positions for 30

Mitring, hems 293
  square patch pocket 228-9
Moisture in pressing, use of 29, 297-8

Neck-lines, preparation for fitting 64
  collar making and setting: Section 16
Needles 10
  betweens 10
  crewel 10
  darning 11
  sharps 10
  machine 22
Notches, cutting 59

One-way fabrics 54-6
Openings: Section 14
  continuous straight strip types 157-66
    157-66
    adaptation to wrap and
      facing 161
    above a dart 159-60
    set into seams 161-3, 165-6
    in a slit 157-9
  for long, fitted sleeves 268-9
  setting for fitting 64
  wrap and facing 164-6
  wrong side faced 154-7, 193-4
Open seam 106-9
Overcasting 108, 185, 254
Overlaid seam 111-13
Oversewing 14, 21

Paris binding 109
Patching, guiding points 309
  right-side patch 309-10
Patch pockets 227-34
Patterns, alterations, bodices 40-42
    one-piece dresses 42
    skirts 37-40
    sleeves 42-7
    trousers 47-8
  arrangement on patterned fabric 56-7
  buying 31

dove-tailing 53-4
for kimono gusset 267
  sleeve 261
laying for cutting out: Section 6
pairing sections 57-8
placing to a fold 51-2
  on one-way fabric 54-6
for pockets 237, 243, 244
  raglan sleeves 257
refolding fabric for laying 52-3
for shaped facings 127-8, 137-9
testing for size 32-5
Pins 9
Pin-tuck 82, 97
Plaid 56-7
Plain seam 106-9
Pleats, box 84, 85, 87
  on checked fabric 83
  fabric stay for 86
  fitting 72
    preparation for 63
  hem set across 302
  inverted 84, 85, 87
  knife 84, 85, 87
  making 83-92
  preparation and tacking 84-5
  pressing 92
  reinforcing 86-7
  formed over seams 88-9
  set below a seam 89-92
  stitching 85-6. 87-8
  on striped fabric 83
  thread marking 60
Pockets: Section 17
  bound slot 234-7
    diagonal 237-8
    flap for 238-9
  patch 227
    double 230-31
    with flap 233-4
    lined 231-3
    single 228-30
  side-seam 243-7
  welt 239
    straight 240-42
    diagonal 242-3

Pressing: Section 3
  equipment 26
  darts 80
  final press 28
  general rules 28
  hem turnings 297-8
  use of moisture 29
  marks removal of 29
  pleats 92
  important points 27
  shrinking by 29
  sleeves 253, 259
  tucks 83
Press-studs 194-5

Raglan sleeves 248, 256-60
Ribbon, used for edging frills 99
  setting frills 100
  to reduce fullness 102-3
Ribbon seam binding 227-8, 246, 259,
  300
Roll collar 200-01, 203-7. 213-18
Rouleau loops 192-4
Run and fell seam 115
Running stitch 13

Scallops, machining 25, 103
Scissors 9, 59
Seams: Section 10
  curved 110-11
  double machine-stitched 114-15
    used below an opening 166
      for sleeve setting 115
      on trousers 115
  fitting, preparation for 64
  French 104-5
    used below an opening 162-3, 165
    curved 105
  gussets, inserting into 263-7
  lapped 111
    invisibly machined 113
    reinforcing corners in 112-13
    setting over gathers 111-12
    wrong side finishes for 112

  machine fell 115
  open, see plain
  overlaid, see lapped
  plain 106
    used below an opening 163, 16
    shaping 109
    taping 106
    wrong side finishes for 107-9
  reinforcing, kimono 262-3
    raglan 259
    taping 106
  run and fell 115
  in shaped panels 110-11
Sewing machines 22
  using 23
    for cable stitching 25
    gathering attachments 94, 99
    for gathering 94
      mending 310
  stitch formation 23
  stitching corners 25
    shaped edges 25
  tension 23
Shaped facings, see Facings
Shirring, preparation for fitting 63
  fitting 72
  working 96-7
Shrinking 29, 297-8
Side-seam pockets 243-7
Silk for sewing 10
Sleeves: Section 18
  edge finishes 268-73
  fitting, preparation for 64, 250
  setting into circular band 96
  types 248
    inset 248
      fitting 252-3
      making and setting 253-4
      preparation 248-52
      setting to lined yoke 254-6
    kimono 248
      fitting 261-62
      with gussets 263-7
      preparation 261
      making and setting 262-3
    raglan 248

fitting 257-9
  making and setting 259-60
  preparation 256-7
  on sheer fabric 260-1
Smocking, preparation for fitting 63
Solid hem 303
Stand collar, see Collars
Steam iron 26
Stiletto 197
Stitches: Section 2
  back 14, 103, 158
  blanket 16
  buttonhole 16, 156, 195, 196
  catch 146, 294-5
  cross tacking 13, 85, 148, 203
  faggoting 14, 21
  fastening on and off 20-22
  fishbone 236
  hemming 17, 22, 159, 160
  herringbone 19
  joining threads for 21
  loop 16, 21, 79, 109, 162-3, 165-6,
    191-2, 196-7
  machine stitch 22-25
  overcasting 108, 185, 254
  over sewing 14, 21
  running 13
  slip-hemming 18, 300
  tacking 12, 62
  tailor-tacking 61-2
  thread-marking 60-1
  upright tacking 13, 95
  whipping 18
Straight grain, aligning 50
  on collars 199-202
  arranged for cross cutting 116-18
  use in fitting 65-6
  folding with 52-3
  use on frills 97
    interfacing 141-3
    in pattern alterations 37-48
  lines on patterns 36-51
  plan for pleating 84
  on pockets 228, 233, 235, 238, 243-4
  use on shaped facings 126-9
  warp 49-50

weft 49-50
Striped fabric 57
Style, choice of 306
Synthetic fabrics 27
  threads 10

Tacking, cross 13, 85, 148, 203
  straight 12, 62
  tailor 61, 79
  upright 13, 95
Tailor's bar tack 86, 269
Tailor's chalk 11, 60
Tape measure 9
Thimble 11
Thread marking 60-61
Thread, embroidery 10
  sewing 10
  machine 22
Tucked hem 303-4
Tucks, fitting 63, 72
  guide lines 82
  inverted 82
  making 81-2
  pin 82
  pressing 83
Turning allowance 59, 60

Upright tacking 13, 95

Waist-bands: Section 19
  general information 274
  interfacing 275-6
  setting with lining 279-80
    plain 276-8
    with top-stitching 278-9
    above a zip 152-3, 277
Warp, see Straight grain
Weft, see Straight grain
Welt pockets 239-43
Whipping 18-19

Yoke, gathers at seam 93-5

setting a collar into a lined 225-6
   sleeves 254-6

Zip fasteners 167-80
   setting a collar above 212-13, 219-20
     waist-band above 152-3, 277